Allen R. Lewis

Urban

Open

Spaces

COOPER-HEWITT MUSEUM

THE SMITHSONIAN INSTITUTION'S

NATIONAL MUSEUM OF DESIGN

RIZZOLI

NEW YORK

Editor's Notes

By Lisa Taylor

A city is a museum — with an infinitely large and varied collection of places and people. It is also an accessible and ideal laboratory in which to observe the effect of design on the quality of modern life. As the Smithsonian's National Museum of Design, the Cooper-Hewitt Museum is interested in all areas of design, especially those that have an impact on large numbers of people. Each year, with the help of experts, the Museum explores a different aspect of the urban environment — through outdoor exhibitions of "immovable objects" in real-life settings, and through related educational programs and publications. Our current focus is on URBAN OPEN SPACES.

Since the beginning of cities, open spaces have been regarded as an important public amenity. For equally as long, there have been concerns about congestion, pollution, and vandalism. A great deal has been said about urban deterioration. In recent years, however, there has been a strong and growing movement to revitalize our cities. Essential to such revitalization is the provision for adequate open spaces. Thus, this seems an appropriate moment to analyze such spaces — to show the immense variety available, the problems concerning their management and use, and the possibilities for improving them. For the purposes of this study, we are confining ourselves to public outdoor spaces in large metropolitan centers. Also, as a museum devoted specifically to design, we are limiting ourselves primarily to design-related problems and solutions.

In working on this project, it has become clear to us that, as individuals, we must have a greater understanding of how the ecological system works in order to be able to make intelligent decisions about the environment, and that, as a nation, we must establish a coordinated long-range plan for the preservation and management of our open spaces. Our goals for the use of open space are frequently in conflict. There must be a proper balance between conservation and public use — between preserving nature and providing for urgent recreational needs. Size, for example, is a critical ecological factor: fairly large, undisturbed, contiguous areas are required for certain forms of natural life to exist.

Fortunately, our government has been active in acquiring and preserving land — a staggering third of our total national acreage is publicly owned. While open lands are still abundant in many parts of the country and excellent parks and recreational facilities exist, they are unevenly distributed. Green areas in and around major cities are becoming increasingly scarce. Consequently, we must not only protect those that remain, but search for other spaces that will accommodate the diverse interests of different groups. Our challenge is: to provide accessible and well-balanced facilities to meet the special needs of all segments of the population — infants, youths, adults, the elderly, and the handicapped; and to provide space for various purposes — repose, active play, ceremonial events, and large public assemblies. A number of possibilities are explored in this catalogue.

Ways are suggested for recycling unproductive space; returning abandoned and decayed sites to open land; reclaiming under-utilized and neglected areas —waterfronts, rooftops, reservoirs, alleys, streets, and rights of way. Enjoyable open spaces need not be green or permanent: ideas are given for transforming vacant lots into interim playgrounds or gardens; creating temporary playstreets and strollways; converting pools, markets, and parking lots to full-time use; providing "green screens;" and using mobile recreational units.

Streets are featured as the most plentiful source of open space, and this catalogue shows how little it takes to make them more joyful and attractive: improved street furniture, graphics, and lighting; less dirt and noise; more outdoor art, communal activities, and pedestrian amenities; especially, more living things in contrast to the sterility of asphalt and concrete. Urban beings, it is reaffirmed, need contact with nature and cannot be deprived of it without damaging results. We are encouraged to transform the city into a garden: to plant more trees, shrubs, flowers, and patches of green; to build more fountains and ponds; and to stock them with lilies, turtles, fish, ducks, and birds. We are urged to take an active role in making our cities more humane, beginning with attempts to improve our own neighborhoods.

For urban residents, the preservation and maintenance of open space is vital and must be considered along with other essential services. Although public funds are available, they are inadequate to meet the demands; also, many are earmarked for new projects and do not solve the serious problem of upkeep. The private sector must share the burden. Every means of encouraging support must be explored: tax credits and rebates, zoning and use variances, development rights, easements, land banks, land trusts, incentive loans, maintenance endowments, maybe even token charges for use. As is shown, attempts at some of the above have not been entirely successful. If our expectations cannot be fulfilled through pride, should they be legislated?

Excellent legislation already exists in certain areas, we are told, but it is not always properly enforced. Nor are the sanctions against violators sufficiently harsh. Without an adequate monitoring system, we frequently learn about violations after the fact, when the damage has already been done. Many laws are ambivalent and left to local authorities to interpret. Often there are not enough funds or trained staff to enforce them; sometimes they are deliberately not enforced for economic or political reasons. The law, if strictly administered, will prohibit, but it won't nurture. And *nurturing* is what is needed for our cities to flourish.

It is encouraging that so many public and private groups are working to improve the environment. URBAN OPEN SPACES is dedicated to those who are trying to preserve the natural landscape, natural resources, and energy; to those who are fighting air, noise, water, and visual pollution; and to the many others involved in important related causes. All deserve support. Yet one wonders if more could be accomplished if these efforts were less fragmented. Perhaps this celebration of URBAN OPEN SPACES will help to unify these goals.

Our spirits are closely intertwined with the places in which we live. Despite the faults of cities, few who have ever lived in one and have experienced its energy, stimulation, anonymity, and collective life can be happy anywhere else. It is possible to create functional, healthy, safe, and attractive open spaces even in densely populated urban areas. Certainly it behooves us to try.

Woe unto them that join house to house,
That lay field to field,
Till there be no place that they may be placed
Alone in the midst of the land...

Isaiah 5:8.

Lisa Taylor is the Director of the Cooper-Hewitt Museum.

Originally published in 1979 as a tabloid by the Cooper-Hewitt Museum, the Smithsonian Institution's National Museum of Design. Unless otherwise indicated, all articles were specially commissioned. The opinions expressed are those of the authors, and do not necessarily reflect the position of the Cooper-Hewitt Museum.

Published in the United States of America in 1981 by RIZZOLI INTERNATIONAL PUBLICATIONS, INC. 712 Fifth Avenue, New York, New York 10019

Contents

Cover photo credits, left to right: Globuscope by The Globus Brothers; Boston Redevelopment Authority; Mark Feldstein; Nancy Rudolph; British Tourist Authority; Paul Hosefros, courtesy The New York Times; Ann Stewart; Ekkehart Schwarz, City of New York Transportation Administration; Hubert C. Birnbaum; John Donnels.

The Collective Perception of Cities

We reflect our urban landscapes.

By Lawrence Halprin

Our collective perception of cities depends on the landscape of open spaces. They lace a city with their voids: streets, alleyways, passageways, malls, boulevards, avenues, marketplaces, plazas, underground shopping malls, parking spaces, arcades, leftover triangles, parks, playgrounds, waterfronts, railroad yards, tracks, rooftops, hills, valleys, freeways, bridges, interchanges. In our imagination of cities it is these open spaces, rather than the buildings that surround them, that we remember. They are the places where people congregate to walk and shop and picnic, to play and bicycle and drive. It is these places that we use and in which we encounter each other: where we meet and enjoy and participate in that communal life we call "city."

City is not so much a construction as a landscape of open spaces. It is a choreography of spaces, an ordering of movement through which we move and live our urban lives. The structuring of that open-space system places an indelible and permanent legacy on a city and its inhabitants; grids, diagonals, loops, curvilinear streets — each formation sets a quality on the movement of people within the city; it marks them forever, influencing what they do, establishing a character for their lives.

The city lives within its landscape environment. Each city has grown from the nature of its surrounding landscape— the bedrock from which it has been built — its geology and its natural landscape characteristics. These more than anything have established its original character, the essence of its personality, the quintessence of its usage. Each city lives as an outgrowth of these landscape characteristics — port, riverfront, mountaintop, lakefront, hilltown, desert,

oasis. These imprint forever the quality of life within the city — what it feels like to live there. They impact people's lives for centuries, affecting how they think and feel, their value systems, their images of beauty, what is important to them. The essential nature of their lives for generations is determined by the native landscape into which the city has been inserted—the habitat of their existence. The great city builds with its natural environment, enhancing it, using it as a primary resource for its form and shape and life style.

Each city in its landscape habitat establishes an ecological and cultural environment unique to itself — part natural, part manmade, artifact and archetypal. It develops over the years its own form, its own ambience, its own "feel" — a persona of its own—an understandable profile, a personality. It becomes more than itself, a kind of organic whole that is a synergy of many things: nature, the native landscape, its cultural past, its buildings, the open spaces within it, and the geometry of their formations. Within this organism the vitality and energy of the inhabitants give it life and color and involvement, make it come alive, invest it with themselves. Then it becomes their own; it is their experience, they identify with it, and the city *becomes* them, becomes the people!

The great cities, it seems to me, are those that develop these attributes of self-identification with their people. These cities are not necessarily beautiful in the classically accepted sense of "beauty," but they *are* perceived as beautiful in the same inevitable sense that nature is perceived as beautiful. They emit a sense of rightness, a kind of urban charisma. They develop an almost human personality! Then people relate to

them in a biological sense. The city no longer is only someplace where they live and work. It becomes more; it takes on anthropomorphic attributes. In Jerusalem the people and the city become one; Zion and Israel—city and people—are interchangeable concepts. In the same sense native Americans identify themselves with their holy places, the source —the place and the people are the same.

Some cities develop incredibly profound relationships with the people who live in them. Their native landscapes, the locations of each of these cities, their natural habitats, the choreography of their internal open spaces, the organic qualities of their growth and change within the landscape, their images from afar—seen across the plains or from the air shimmering in the desert — the

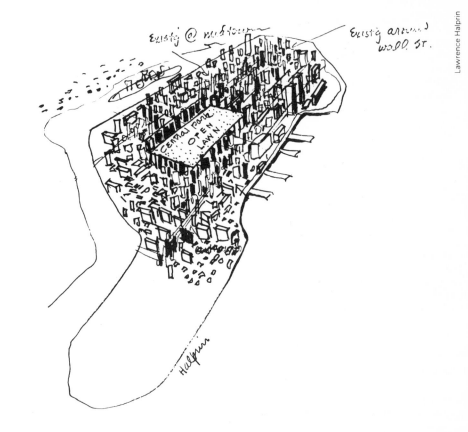

Manhattan

silhouette of their domes, towers, and bridges, their skylines, all these invest our urban lives in these cities with a richness of creativity, and we experience a sense of intimate belonging, a fantasy of self identification. These cities become portraits of ourselves.

People often ask me which cities I have experienced possess these characteristics. There are many, each with its own personality and unique character. Inevitably I think of five: New York, Hong Kong, San Francisco, Venice, and Jerusalem.

New York

When I think of New York I think of Manhattan, of that small, narrow, needle-like island that, for many people, signifies the capital of the world. The rest of New York is hinterland — the "boonies," small town excrescences of drabness on a crystalline core. I remember New York most as a diamond-like jewel lit up at sunset on an early winter evening. I came in — flying by helicopter from Kennedy airport to the Pan Am building—in ten minutes, leaving reality and entering a sparkling, glowing, faceted, colorful, brilliantly lit jewel glittering in the distance. I will never forget the excitement of seeing it from far off and then coming closer and closer and actually penetrating into the skyline, being frightened by its brilliance, and then, finally, entering into the sparkle, like a moth to a flame, into a kind of visual orgasm of color and light.

Down at ground level the lightshow leaned over and became a street to walk on: colorful shops lined the streets, beckoning onward, each one with its display of fantasies, each with its implications of richness for everyone—an invitation to all of the world to own the glitter — a choreography of pedestrians' dreams.

I remember the streets and the small plazas around the nodes of 59th Street and the green residential squares. I think of the rivers, particularly the East River with its echo of Manhattan on Roosevelt Island and the cable tramway suspended on the way across, next to the speeding movement of cars on the Queensboro Bridge—linkages.

And I think, of course, of that great

San Francisco seen from Mt. Tamalpais

green gash through the city, the incredible acreage of Central Park spread like a front lawn in front of the city's house for all to enjoy; for the family's children to play on and the family dog to romp on and father to lounge on and drink his beer. That park, which humanizes the city's hardness and links it to everyday America, links New York to the vast open spaces of our country, symbolizing always our emotional and biological ties with the country out there. Those ties to nature stretch westward from Central Park and New York across 3,000 miles of woodland and prairie and mountain and valley through America.

Hong Kong

Hong Kong is an anomaly. It should be, by any normal planning criteria, a loathsome slum. Its densities are incredibly high. In certain sections of the city they rise to 5,000 persons per acre—as high as anywhere in the world. Zoning is practically nonexistent; buildings rise and fall at will; anything over 20 years old seems old. Traffic is bad; signs festoon the buildings so that they become the architecture; *they* become the city facades. The only large civic space is a race track,

a vestigial organ from the British empire's past. Streets are crowded day and night; people live and sleep in shifts; the proverbial "hot bed" is a ubiquitous reality.

And yet, Hong Kong is a fascinating and beautiful city. What saves it is that it has money to spend, but more than that it is saved by its landscape. Like San Francisco it is a city built on hills around a bay surrounded by seas. Nowhere is anywhere far from the water; the water gentles the density, making it all in some way tolerable. The views are magnificent. The hills clothed by their buildings undulate around the great bays — bays with their ferries and their floating sampan cities and their restaurants festooned by lights. No other city that I know lives as much outdoors at night; the cacophony of street life is continuous around the clock.

My constant image of Hong Kong is that of an architectonic forest. In these woods, skyscrapers grow like trees reaching upward for the sunlight that nourishes them. On the ground, pathways lace the hills where the inhabitants live, like denizens of the forest. The tree-like buildings grow and grow, reach their heights, become old and die, only to be replaced by newer, more healthy and active ones, nourished by the undergrowth and organic compost in the ground. The cycle of life and growth and change and death and rebirth continues seemingly automatically and endlessly. There is a natural order at work here that seems to respond to the inevitability of an architectonic and ecological order with its own logic, its own natural system.

San Francisco

San Francisco is a town of hills with the national system of streets laid out on a grid — as it is everywhere in America — running up over the hills and with a bay instead of a front lawn as its open space. The grid, oddly enough, makes the views accessible — a planning error strangely captures the vistas for everyone. As the grid plummets up and down the hills, the views open out for everyone to enjoy. Contouring the streets would have obscured the vistas.

Across the great open space of the water loom the mountains and hills—

Marin County's Tamalpais to the North, across to Berkeley's hills, and beyond to Mt. Diablo on the other side of Oakland to the East—a ring of green in the winter, golden brown in the summer; ridge lines of open space linked by the great bridges.

San Francisco is a white city. Its Victorian houses climb up and over the hills like the lace fringes of Victorian petticoats gracing the hills, clothing them in a mantle of small scale, livable houses.

When I think of San Francisco I think not so much of the city itself, sparkling in the winter sun, but of its entire region— the entire stretch of it from the offshore Farollone Islands to the Sierra through the foothills of the gold country up to the 14,000 ft. peaks of John Muir's range of light.

San Francisco is Marin and the Peninsula with its greak oak trees and the grape vineyards of the Napa Valley, the incredible coastline stretching, rocky and sculptured, north and south for miles—inhabited by its seals, migrating gray whales, and the romantic abalone. San Francisco is the streams and waterfalls of the Redwood canyons plummeting to the ocean, the brilliant surf pounding the Franciscan matrix rock into coves and weatherbeaten beaches and casting up enormous driftwood

View of Hong Kong

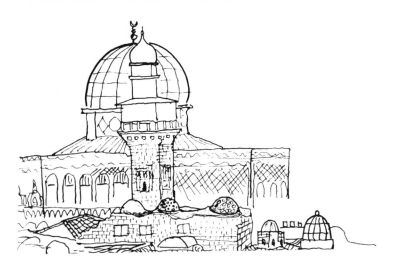

Temple Mount, Jerusalem

piles against the cliffs. San Francisco is a reflection of its landscape.

Venice

I remember with great clarity the greatest urban experience I have ever had. It was in Venice in winter. In front of the church of San Marco, the great square, which Napoleon called the most beautiful drawing room in Europe, was empty. It was cold and foggy, and the top of the Campanile barely showed, sunlit above the low hanging sea mist. The tide was in and the black and white stones of the intricately laid pavement were covered with a thin film of water. There was no sound—no automobile exhausts, no buses. Absolute quiet in the very heart of a great city. In the distance I could hear, faintly, some young people singing. All of a sudden the air became dark with birds, the square filled with the beating of thousands of wings, the noise increased and increased until it was deafening, and the deserted square became absolutely filled with pigeons. The noise was incredible — even frightening. They had come to feed, and when they had finished, they left just as quickly, and the great beautiful square was empty and quiet again.

Jerusalem

I think of Jerusalem as its history — as what has happened there — of the long struggle up from primitive pre-history, as the place where Abraham was willing to sacrifice Isaac and then, just as he raised his knife, received the ultimate reprieve from God, staying his hand at the last

moment, symbolizing in effect our own rejection of human sacrifice. I think of David coming to the Mountain of Ophel, finding a spring where he camped, and building his capital (Yerushalayim) as a resting place for the Ark and the word of God — the symbol of our shift from nomadism to settled urbanism.

I think of Solomon moving up from the Valley of Kidron, where David's spring was, and building his temple on the Temple Mount — made possible by technology and the then new engineering knowledge of how to move water by aqueducts. I think of his ability to marshall the settlement into an organization capable of building the city walls — the labor of felling trees in the hills of Lebanon. I think of Jerusalem as a city of walls—of their building and destruction, of their invasion and rebuilding century after century, conqueror after conqueror. Unlike other cities Jerusalem has no intrinsic "value." It is on no trade route—no caravan passed logically here —no river, no port, no natural resources, no reason to be there! All that is in Jerusalem comes from the investment of people, their spirit, their identification of their city with God.

The air is luminous, the hills clothed in their pines — beautiful; the black sheep cascade down the hillsides in the

words of The Song of Songs like "the black curls of my love's hair." What Jerusalem is is a golden dome on a spot holy for centuries on a modest plateau surrounded by hills in an amphitheater of the spirit dedicated to the universal idea of love.

There it sits in its stony landscape— built from the pink stones of its foundations, glowing in the orange sunset on the knife edge between the harsh aridity of the desert to the East and the soft green fertility of the Mediterranean to the West. Jerusalem and its people are one and the same. There is no separation. The city has always represented a portrait of its inhabitants—perhaps of all of us.

"If I forget thee, oh Jerusalem, let my right hand forget its cunning."

City watching and walking and experiencing has been a hobby as well as a professional passion for me all my life. I have spent days tramping through cities all over the world enthralled by their people, their diversity, their culture, and their physical makeup. I have perceived cities as great works of art, as exciting and adventurous dramas and theater events, which possess that ultimate creativity of allowing participation, involvement, and the act of being inside the work of art itself.

My hope is that my descriptions of my favorite cities will activate you to discover your own. Perhaps my ultimate hope is that it will encourage you to examine your own neighborhood and the city in which you live. Examine it closely for those qualities that make it a creative environment for living, that allow you to see yourself reflected in the mirror of your own city. And, if you don't like the reflection, I encourage you to change it and in the process yourself, to what you would like it to be.

Landscape architect and planner **Lawrence Halprin** is the author of Cities; The RSVP Cycles; Freeways; New York New York; Taking Part; and Notebooks of Lawrence Halprin. Recently as consultant to the Mayor of Jerusalem, he started redesigning the downtown area and restructuring the old city.

Piazza San Marco, Venice

The Historical Development of Urban Open Space

What kinds of spaces define our cities?

By Dora Polk Crouch

In the beginning urban open space was used for community meetings, whether religious, commercial, or governmental. There was little interest in setting aside one space for one activity. Rather, the same space did triple duty. In the Middle Eastern cities of 4000 years ago, however, we already find that the temple square and the market square were separated physically as well as functionally. The difference in the quality of these spaces was indicated by the fact that, while the temple square was walled off from the city, the market plaza had no such rigid boundary, but rather melted into the urban fabric along the busy commercial streets that penetrated every quarter of the city.

If we think of the pre-historic urban gathering space, which had many uses, as a prototype that still survives in simple communities everywhere, then we can begin to acknowledge how great an act of invention the walling-off of a temple square was. The separation tells us, as it told the residents of Babylon, "Here something special is going on." As if exhausted by this leap into complication, the people in this region remained satisfied with a two-part division of urban open space.

Meanwhile the Greeks, for example, were evolving not only a multiplicity of building types but also sophisticated systems for laying them out. Besides that, the Greeks intermingled functions by putting the city treasury into the chief temple and by having shrines and altars in the midst of government buildings like the council chamber. Because of this mingling, their urban open spaces reflected a view of man's place in reality that was much more complicated than the view revealed by Mesopotamian cities. We know that the Greeks despised the Persians as "barbarians." This at-

Stage, Teatro Olimpico, Vicenza, 18th century engraving

titude was based partly on the observable differences between the cities of the two peoples. Mesopotamian culture was strongly hierarchical whereas the Greeks flourished in a milieu of dynamic tension. In the Greek city, it was possible to be more richly human and to engage in a far greater variety of human activities. The ideology of the culture promoted this. Also, the pattern of urban arrangements — the diversity of urban open spaces and proximity of such spaces to the working and living quarters of the people — made a richer common life possible.

Three new possibilities for urban open space were emphasized by the Romans. The first was the concept of an outdoor but fully enclosed room. In the last two centuries before Christ, the Hellenistic Greeks had increasingly regularized their agoras (downtowns) by edging them with horizontal office buildings called stoas. The Romans carried this idea to its logical conclusion by deliberately laying out rectangular spaces that were completely surrounded by long rows of columns. Behind the columns were offices, markets, temples, or other buildings—all subordinated to the

open space upon which they focused. Such subordination reflected the Roman sense of hierarchical order. Even the streets intercepted the open space through the colonnades, and so were visually subordinated. The Romans also experimented with other shapes than rectangular. Some, like the Forum Boarium, where meat was sold in Rome, were irregular in shape. Squares, circles, and ellipses were also tried, such as the Oval Plaza at Gerasa. Choice of shape was sometimes dictated by geography. For instance, the Forum of Constantine at Constantinople was rounded to fit about the summit of the hill on which the emperor had once camped. Often, shape seems to have been an aesthetic decision.

The second new idea was to make something special of the streets themselves. This was done by continuous rows of columns along important streets. The streets were widened. Sidewalks were laid between the colonnades and the walls of shops. Intersections and terminations of streets were emphasized with a new kind of furniture — the triumphal arch. These streets functioned as exciting and active kinds of urban open space. The mild climate promoted all-year outdoor activity. Street-corner fountains, many little cafes, and the common mixture of rich houses, poor houses, apartments, and shops on nearly every block contributed to a lively scene of urban life in these newly monumentalized streets.

Thirdly, the Romans developed to a fine art the notion of common recreational open space. Owing to their great success in conquering the Mediterranean world, the Romans could afford a more leisured life than had ever been possible before. In Rome itself there were 180 holidays a year. To use up all

this free time, theaters, stadiums, amphitheaters, and baths were built generously throughout the city and the empire. Each of these functioned as public open space. Some, like the baths and smaller theaters, were enclosed. Most had plazas or gardens connected with them. Emperors and other rich persons vied with one another to build such recreational structures for the people. They also endowed them to cover operating costs, so that attendance could be free or nominal.

Christian sentiments after the 5th century put an end to theaters and amphitheaters. Economic and military necessity put an end to the chariot and horse races of the stadium. But the baths persisted on a reduced neighborhood scale until the 14th century, when the Black Death made all social gatherings impossible for a while. Even so, changed into the "Turkish" bath, one recreational open space of the ancients has persisted in recognizable form to our own day. Our sports stadia, race tracks, and theater auditoriums owe their original forms also to that ancient need to fill up leisure time.

After the collapse of the Roman Empire in the West, social life gradually reconstituted itself. Mediterranean towns retained some Roman features, such as the urban open space at the center where the two main roads crossed. Northern European settlements, on the other hand, were largely rural for several hundred years. Urban life began to revive in the North after 1100. There we can see the tensions between, and mutual adjustments of, religion, market, and government playing themselves out in control and use of the main urban open space, the cathedral square. At Chartres in France, for example, certain goods were sold at each great doorway of the church, by license from the administrators. Wine was even sold in the basement of the church, to avoid taxes that would otherwise have been levied on it by the local nobility. Workmen for specific trades could be hired in various parts of the church, and visiting pilgrims could sleep there. The interior of the building was as much urban open space as the square outside. In fact, not only did the town depend largely on pilgrimage for its economic well-being, but when the church was finished in 1225, most of the town residents could fit inside at once—a real correspondence between users and space. This open space does not seem to have been designed as consciously as Roman or Greek; the order here is functional rather than visual.

The next steps in the history of open space in cities were the regularization (again!) of plazas in the Renaissance and the dramatization of the city during the Baroque period. For example, although

too clever to utilize mere rectangles, the Venetians definitely regularized the Plaza at Saint Mark's. They began with the erection of the Library in the 16th century, to balance the late medieval Doge's Palace opposite. Over the next two centuries, the edges of the Piazza and the Piazzetta were formalized with stoa-like buildings that combined shops below and elegant residences above. Static perfection of this kind, however, did not long remain the ideal.

In more normal cities, wheeled traffic combined with the idea of powerful national sovereignty to stimulate the development of dramatic and dynamic urban open space. Growing from ideas of Sixtus V about streets as agents of urban formation in late 16th century Rome, the new urban open space corresponded to new theories and practices of conscious and extensive planning. Parts of cities were considered "works of art." These parts were not only the private palaces of the rich, but also the

After Winslow Homer. "The Boston Common," 1858, wood engraving

open spaces and streets provided for the use of all. The open spaces of the city became again a "theater" for newly vivid urban life.

Not surprisingly, these Renaissance and Baroque ideas were brought to the New World as part of the intellectual baggage of the colonists. Spanish city settlements, from the largest to the smallest, were organized around the plaza prescribed by the Laws of the Indies. After the work of the day was done, the community would gather at the plaza. In addition, the town was required to set aside a "commons" for the grazing of animals, and to hold title to unassigned lots so that latecomers could be provided for. The old Mediterranean feature of colonnaded streets persists in these New World towns also, notably in Santa Fe, New Mexico.

On the East coast, residential squares like then-new ones in London were laid out in Philadelphia and Savannah. An older tradition was mirrored nostalgically in the village green of New England and the North Central states. This tradition was composed partly of remembrances of English country towns and partly of a vision of the Heavenly Jerusalem as described in the Bible. Whatever the source, these greens preserved some open space at the heart of the settlement.

This gentle and idealistic agrarian urbanism was almost obliterated by the onset of the Industrial Revolution. In the decades before and after 1800, there was a quantum jump in the area of cities and the density of population. For a while, urban open space was treated as a frivol-

ity that people could get along without. As early as the 1830s however, a reform movement that coupled urban parks and rural cemeteries began to counteract the effects of agglomeration. One may note that it was cities like Troy, New York, which called itself the birthplace of the Industrial Revolution in America, that led the reform movement in favor of urban open space. This movement culminated in the creation of great urban parks all over America in the second half of the 19th century. Central Park in New York City, Golden Gate Park in San Francisco, the necklace of parks around Boston, and the Kansas City park system, were designed by Frederick Law Olmsted. (In the case of Kansas City, the creation of parks was used to increase property values. Taxes on the increased values paid for the parks.) For the first time, the city dweller was cut off from pedestrian access to the country by the sheer size of the city. Olmsted brought to the city dweller some of this lost country. He envisioned his parks as the "lungs of the city." In addition, he was able to envision how to accomplish these goals economically. We have much trouble emulating and even maintaining these 19th century parks, though we think of ourselves as so much richer than our predecessors.

Urban open space, even when well designed and well executed, does not express the actual order of society, as sociologist Sylvia L. Thrupp would have us believe in her essay "The City as the Idea of Social Order." Probably it never did. Rather, such urban open space is an art form expressing potential order and helping to bring it to actuality. Density, compactness, and traffic define the streets as backdrop for urban life. Relative calm in plazas and parks and in enclosed urban space, such as arenas and theaters, plays against that multiplicity in the streets. Together these two sorts of urban open space define the city.

Dora Polk Crouch teaches architectural and urban history at Rensselaer Polytechnic Institute. She is Editor of the newsletter of the Society of Architectural Historians and founder of that organization's Urban History Committee.

By René Dubos Reprinted by permission of Charles Scribner's Sons from *So Human An Animal* by René Dubos. Copyright © 1968 René Dubos.

From great estate to municipal park, from slow-paced country road to multilane parkway, from city playground to national recreation area, from village to city, from suburb to satellite community, and from one-room schools to complex educational systems, the environment endlessly evolves in response to changing human needs and dreams. The concept of an optimum environment is unrealistic because it implies a static human life. Planning for the future demands an ecological attitude based on the assumption that man will continuously bring about evolutionary changes through the creative potentialities inherent in his biological nature.

The constant feedback between man and environment inevitably implies a continuous alteration of both. However, the various aspects of biological and social nature constitute such a highly integrated system that they can be altered only within a certain range. Neither physicochemical concepts of the body machine nor hopes for technological breakthroughs are of use in defining the ideal man or the proper environment unless they take into consideration the elements of the past that have become progressively incarnated in human nature and in human societies, and that determine the limitations and the potentialities of human life.

The past is not dead history; it is the living material out of which man makes himself and builds the future.

National Concerns for the Urban Environment

The boundaries of land conservation are being enlarged.

By Cecil D. Andrus

Over 70 percent of America's people live within the urban environment. Those who live in cities are a part of the urban landscape, influenced by city surroundings as much as by the grandeur of a mountain or the calm of a forest. In the city the "luxuries" of open space, water, and outdoor light become necessities.

The sheer density of the city, with its static, large-scale structures, reduces our association with nature's regenerative powers. E. B. White's lyrical observation

about the urban experience is apt: "The city is the place for people who like life in tablet form, concentrated: a forest resolved into a single tree, a lake distilled into a fountain, and all the birds of the air embodied in one transient thrush in a small garden."

Those of us concerned about the quality of urban life must look critically at the dominant institutions of urban society, including those within the federal government, and measure their skills as

architects of this environment. Historically, the United States Department of the Interior has not been one of the primary influences in American urban development. Until recent years, the Department's focus has been largely on the countryside and its resources, mainly in the West and Alaska.

Thirty years ago the great American conservationist Aldo Leopold called for a land ethic that "enlarges the boundaries of the community to include soils, waters,

plants, and animals," an ethic that affirms the value of life apart from the commerce of man. In a time of rapidly intensifying pressure on our natural assets, a large measure of the Department's work has been, and in the foreseeable future will continue to be, concerned with the preservation of wilderness.

The living environment does not stop at the boundaries of a national park or wildlife refuge, however, or at the city line. The urban environment is a com-

San Francisco from Marin Headlands,
Golden Gate National Recreation Area

Historic Ships at Aquatic Park,
Golden Gate National Recreation Area

Playground for All Children, New York City

munity of human assets and humanly created resources; it is as vulnerable to exhaustion as the resources of any wilderness community. Cities and towns are a primary feature of the American landscape and home to most of us. They must be embraced in our national conservation standard.

In 1966 Congress passed the National Historic Preservation Act. The Act gave the Interior Department a central role in urban conservation and gave an urban society the means to identify and protect its significant cultural resources. Currently more than one-half of our Historic Preservation Fund grants are applied to the preservation of irreplaceable properties in urban areas. In addition to providing a stimulus for the economically sensible re-use of handsome downtown buildings, these matching funds have generated substantial state, local, and private redevelopment investments in neighborhoods from Los Angeles to Hartford. Measuring the cost of energy and materials, and the intangible cultural values associated with early building design, such historic and architectural preservation activities have proven to be a far less expensive way to revive urban neighborhoods than conventional clear-and-rebuild methods.

Almost all of the city dweller's time is spent in buildings and in built settings. This places enormous importance not only on the scale and design of city structures, but also on the availability of open spaces.

In 1977, at the direction of a Congress concerned about the adequacy of recreational opportunity in the nation's urban areas, the Interior Department conducted a nationwide evaluation of open space and recreation needs, problems, and potentials in the country's most populous regions.

The National Urban Recreation Study, as it is known, found that there is substantially more urban open space land with the potential for scenic, cultural, or recreational development than is generally supposed. Many of these open spaces are surplus military properties, abandoned, derelict, or underused lands, or special landscapes such as urban waterfronts. In such cities as Seattle, New York, Cincinnati, and Detroit, waterfront or other underused land spaces have been reclaimed for public recreation purposes, thus offsetting the annual loss of millions of acres of open space to commercial development and prohibitively high land values. As a creative and cost-effective redevelopment strategy, reclamation of these areas is one of the most promising revitalization tools available to the urban conservationist.

The study also found urban recreation systems in a state of crisis in most of the cities surveyed. In the communities sampled, 77 percent of the residents reported dissatisfaction with available recreation opportunities. In low income neighborhoods, dissatisfaction approached 100 percent.

Almost without exception, participants in the study declared that their greatest need is for recreational open space, programs, and facilities close to home. But, observed the study report, "neighborhood park and recreation areas are often deteriorated, inadequate, or entirely absent, despite their importance as community focal points."

Recently Congress passed the Urban Park and Recreation Recovery Act (Title X of P.L. 95-625). Proposed by President Carter and the Department as an element of the Administration's 1978 Urban Policy, the Act established authority for a five-year, $730 million Urban Park and Recreation Recovery Program.

The program, administered by Interior's Heritage Conservation and Recreation Service, provides matching grants directly to local governments to rehabilitate deteriorating urban recreation systems. One of the primary aims of the program is to stimulate local efforts to restore existing park and recreation facilities that have fallen into disuse or disrepair, and thereby to improve the physical environment of the city and conserve resources in which investments have already been made. Other segments of the program seek to retrieve disappearing neighborhood park and recreation opportunities through strengthened recreation planning, programming, and management.

Also, as President Carter directed in his Urban Policy Message a year ago, the Interior Department and all federal agencies are rigorously examining all of their activities to identify those that could effectively serve the urban environment.

The National Park Service has expanded its programs to encompass the park and open space interests of metropolitan communities. Of 294 diverse sites administered by the Service in the United States, more than one-third are surrounded by or adjacent to urban centers. These include Gateway National Recreation Area in New York Harbor, Golden Gate National Recreation Area in and around San Francisco Bay, and Cuyahoga National Recreation Area between Cleveland and Akron, Ohio. At Boston National Historical Park, the Department is cooperating with Boston University to provide the several hundred children participating in the park's Historic and Urban Environment Study program the occasion to learn simultaneously about their environment and the history of their city.

In the spring of 1978 the Department announced ten "Rails-to-Trails" projects to demonstrate the effective conversion of abandoned rail and trolley rights-of-way to public trails for bicycling, wheelchair use, jogging, and hiking in the city.

With assistance from Interior's Land and Water Conservation Fund, a 2.6-acre plot of existing parkland in the New York City borough of Queens will be developed into a Playground for All Children, a park for handicapped and able-bodied children between the ages of 3 and 11. The Fund has also provided grants to assist in the purchase of 13 acres of ocean property, including 1000 feet of beach frontage, to be put to use for public recreation purposes in the heavily populated San Francisco Bay area. The Lowell Heritage State Park, a 118-acre park located within the city of Lowell, Massachusetts, will be developed with Land and Water Conservation Fund assistance. Fund monies have been provided to rehabilitate, or adapt for use by the handicapped, existing park and recreation areas in 15 major metropolitan centers across the United States. In Denver, four sites surrounded by development on the South Platte River floodplain are undergoing redevelopment as parkland, with Land and Water Conservation Fund assistance. Funds have also been granted to transform 15 rubble-strewn vacant lots into recreation areas in New York City's South Bronx.

To help make federal programming more coherent in urban areas, the Interior Department has also examined its relationships with other federal agencies working to restore the urban environment.

The Department has signed a memorandum of agreement with the Environmental Protection Agency to encourage open space and recreational development at wastewater treatment facilities. Interior is at work with the Department of Housing and Urban Development on metropolitan and regional planning strategies to insure that open space is maintained and that recreation facilities are developed along with any major new HUD rehabilitation project. Interior also participates in a cooperative management program with the Defense Department and other federal agencies that own or administer lands with open space or recreation potential.

When Aldo Leopold asserted the sanctity of wildlife, soil, water, and forests, he recognized that, for some, the adoption of his land ethic would require a radical shift of values. In his words, "perhaps such a shift can be achieved by reappraising things unnatural, tame, and confined in terms of things natural, wild, and free."

As the nation's principal land conservation agency, the United States Department of the Interior has appraised the unnatural constrictions of city life in terms of its own traditional commitment to "things natural, wild, and free." As a result, it has enlarged the boundaries of Leopold's community of protection to encompass the resources of man. Conservation of the urban environment is crucial to the physical and psychological fitness of our people — human resources on which the future of the American city utterly depends.

Cecil D. Andrus is Secretary of the Interior.

Warning:

The Surgeon General has determined that Open Space...

By Peter Blake

Living, as I now do, in Boston, a city located less than a foot or two south of the polar icecap, I look at "open spaces" somewhat askance. To most of us up here, open space is something to avoid, roughly twelve months out of the year. What we need *more* of, in Boston and environs, is *less* urban open space. We need *closed* space.

Yet the city of Boston, in recent years, has gained more urban open space, per capita, than any place outside the South Bronx. We have been endowed with so many piazzas, piazzettas, parks, promenades, pedestrian malls, and other blessings of the urban designer's art that we now look, on paper, like Savannah, Georgia — *on paper*, but hardly in fact: we are, in reality, under 10 feet of snow most of the time.

Our City Hall Plaza is, admittedly, a dozen-acre pedestrian oasis of considerable beauty. I have enjoyed it, together with tens of thousands of others, on a summer night, listening to rock music and sniffing great wafts of pot drifting

City Hall Plaza, Boston

Government Center, Chandigarh

down from Beacon Hill. I even enjoyed it last New Year's Eve (again with tens of thousands of others — all watching the fireworks), when, surprisingly, the polar icecap suddenly seemed to melt, and the weather turned semi-beneficent.

But, let's face it, these were isolated occasions, with much grimness in between. Most of the time, our urban open spaces are of little use to anyone, except photographers. And I'd like to get into that just a little more deeply.

A number of years ago, Philip Johnson told me that the Seagram Building, on which he had worked with Mies van der Rohe, was the only really *visible* skyscraper in Manhattan, because it had a large plaza in front of it so that you could step back far enough to see the tower itself. I thought that was a very revealing remark: because it suddenly became clear to me that many of the great urban open spaces being planned today were designed not for you or me, but for wide-angle photography! If it were not for the Boston City Hall Plaza, you could never photograph the Boston City Hall; if it were not for the Boston Christian Science Center Plaza, you could never photograph the Mother Church; and if it were not for the Lincoln Center Plaza in Manhattan, you could never take a snap

of the Metropolitan Opera House — in the unlikely event that you should ever want to do so. By the same token, the reason the Shah Mosque, in Isfahan, is relatively unknown, is that it is boxed in on all sides by buildings that block the photographer's lens. Only the domes and minarets are visible above the surrounding congestion.

In short, most of our urban open spaces seem to be designed largely for the convenience of architectural photographers. The vast public plaza at the Le Corbusier-designed government center at Chandigarh, the capital of the Punjab, in the foothills of the Himalayas, is a good case in point. Except, possibly, during the months of December and January, when human beings have a fighting chance to survive outdoors in India, this impressive urban open space is a death trap. To attempt to cross it is to invite sunstroke and the instant suspension of all vital signs. I know — I have tried (I mean, to cross, not to suspend). I have not been in Brasilia, a similar photographer's delight; but I gather that the vast urban open spaces, with which Le Corbusier's disciples blessed us there, are equally useless to anyone not wedded to a Linhof camera.

On the other hand, very large urban open spaces seem to be not very good for demonstrations or riots (both of which seem like desirable civic endeavors, to be

East River Drive, New York City

encouraged in any democracy); such spaces appear to be much better for parades and for "spontaneous" rallies in the manner of the Nürnberg spectaculars, staged in part to be filmed by Leni Riefenstahl. Very large open spaces permit riotees to shoot down the rioters, and filmmakers to record the event; or to record endless columns of spontaneously marching loyalists. Very interesting. The medium — photography, film, TV — determines the message, and designs the space.

I am, of course, in favor of certain kinds of urban open space. I love waterfronts, and I now live on one. I will forgive Robert Moses a great many things, and even give him credit for *some* things; but I will never forgive him for having cut New Yorkers off from much of the 550 miles of waterfrontage available in the five boroughs, by building superhighways there because no voters lived there. I love parks, and I live next to our nice "waterfront park." And I love pedestrian enclaves, like the one created in the center of Munich.

But there are limits. The Albany Mall — an architectural grotesquerie unlike any built since Mussolini — has to be one of the nation's worst open spaces for any mammal that cannot function very well at below 32° Fahrenheit. I haven't been there during the winter — but I have been on another Albany extravaganza — the campus of New York State University — and it wasn't exactly cozy. I was, in fact, frostbitten.

Well, what are the alternatives?

The first alternative, quite clearly, is to enclose open space. In London, Brussels, Milan, Cleveland, Moscow, and elsewhere, the most successful public open spaces have long been glass-covered arcades. A lot of people have learned that simple lesson recently: the architect Gyo Obata, for example, made his "Galleria" in Houston a skylit mall that contains a skating rink, restaurants, shops, and much more. Others have learned the same kind of thing—there are now enclosed or at least covered public spaces in almost every city in the Western or Eastern World. Those enclosed "open" urban spaces are enormously successful. They don't necessarily have to be heated or airconditioned (which would make them prohibitively expensive to build); they just need to be decently ventilated.

The second way of making open urban space more inhabitable is to put it through some wind tunnel tests. I am serious. Over the past few years, the science of testing buildings and urban complexes in wind tunnels has become very sophisticated: you can build a very detailed scale model of a plaza or a street, and set it into a wind tunnel and have the wind tunnel blast off with a roar, at which point little sensors placed throughout the scale model will pick up air currents and vibrations. Smoke introduced into the wind tunnel can then be filmed—and all of this interesting information will then tell you if the plaza or the street is likely to sweep you off your feet, whenever it blows, or whether it will be a pleasant place in which to co-exist with the man-made environment.

And the third alternative is to take the whole business of designing open urban space away from the architects, and hand

Main Street, Disneyland, U.S.A.

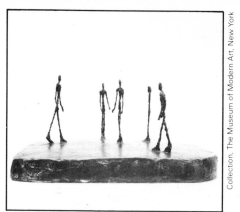
Alberto Giacometti, "City Square" (La Place), 1948; bronze, 8½" X 25⅜" X 17¼"

it to Walt Disney Enterprises. (As Clemenceau said, this whole business is "too serious a matter to leave to the generals.")

To all of us who have looked at modern open spaces over the past few years, it has become clear that the only really successful ones built in the United States since World War II, are those to be found in Disneyland and Walt Disney World. (The Disneyland streets and squares, being somewhat tighter than those in Orlando, seem to work a little better.)

These streets and squares are not merely cozy and picturesque and full of fun. They are also extraordinarily well-calculated exercises in urban design. Not long ago, in the Walt Disney studios in Burbank, California, I talked to some of those who helped design Walt Disney World, south of Orlando. "We really had to get rid of all those architects," one of them said. "They didn't know anything about how people walk down a street. We went back to our own people—and they laid out all the successions of images, of colors, of graphics, and so on that finally make a street. Disney World is really made up of a lot of images like that—all moving you on."

Well, that may be the third alternative, and not a bad one. I am not sure that you can ever design instant charm, but I *am* sure that you can design yourself—and your city—into an instant wasteland. Alberto Giacometti's sculpture, "City

Square," in the collection of The Museum of Modern Art, New York, is a devastating commentary on that kind of wasteland: a vacant panorama, inhabited by lonely souls blindly traversing its paved vastness, without hope, utterly disoriented. Giacometti's terrifying vision came to life in Chandigarh, and in Brasilia.

All the classic "open" urban spaces that all of us admire are really "closed" urban spaces. Even the great piazzas, in places like Vigevano, or Isfahan, or Venice, are ringed by arcades that shelter you in inclement weather. I have been in Venice in January, when there are no tourists around, and that is not a very terrific time to be in the Piazza San Marco; but the arcades save you every time. And I have been in Radiant Cities, full of sun, space, and greenery, and I am fortunate to be here to tell the tale.

As this is written, the City of Boston is experiencing 50 mph gales. I am in my

modern apartment, on the 30th floor of an award-winning building that meets many standards, magnificently, inside, and meets almost none once you emerge into the urban, open space created around it. In fact, the windswept plaza that surrounds what I like to call my "home" looks, at this moment, like one of those chilling scenes from Eisenstein's "Alexander Nevsky"—not very cozy at all.

If you get to read this text, you will know that the good guys won, and that God lost. If you don't get to read this, just remember that I tried to warn you. In any event, stay away from urban open space. The Surgeon General Has Determined That Urban Open Space Is Dangerous To Your Health.

Peter Blake is an architect and architecture critic. He is Chairman of the Boston Architectural Center.

The Galleria, a covered street in Milan

Galleria, Houston, Texas

Utopia Wasn't Yesterday

Things aren't what they were—and they never have been.

By Russell Lynes

Sleighing accident in Jersey City, 1868

"Broadway is too narrow for the immense travel, business, and locomotion of various kinds, of which it is the constant scene," Asa Green, a physician turned novelist, wrote in 1837. "The attempt at crossing is almost as much as your life is worth. To perform the feat with any degree of safety, you must button your coat tight about you, see that your shoes are secure at the heels, set your hat firmly on your head, look up street and down street, at the self-same moment, to see what carts are upon you, and then run for your life."

City folk had been running for their lives long before that (the Romans did) and have been ever since. We are inclined, however, to measure the plights of life in our cities today by what we somewhat romantically regard as the delights of life there yesterday. Much of our memory of the past comes, if we are architecturally inclined, from restoration of old buildings or reconstructions of old towns such as Williamsburg or the restored sections of cities like Savannah or New Orleans. If we are museum-goers,

we judge the past by the art it made—in America in the last century by expansive landscapes unblemished by commercial buildings under skies free of factory smoke, by family scenes in cozy homes by friendly fires, by the noble toil of noble farmers who go whistling about their chores as though they were perpetual fun. Painters have bathed immaculate cities such as Venice and Paris and Dresden and New York in clear light, and novelists have filled the air of cities with the fetching cries of street vendors. But if the artists and novelists of the past often prettied up the lives of their times, the cosmeticians of the movies and Disneyland give the past an even more sentimental and romantic gloss.

What is missing? Above all the foul smells of sweat and open sewers and coal smoke, the polluted ponds in the parks and the beaches and rivers stinking with refuse and carcasses, the inescapable heat in summer and the nearly inescapable cold in winter, the steaming manure and rotting garbage, the scavenging rats and swine in the streets, and the scarcely illuminated dark at night when the muggers did their work as they still do, the rude jolting of carriages and coaches on cobblestones, the clouds of horseflies in the dining room and the restaurant, the infernal buzz of midnight mosquitoes in the bedroom. (We forget that the window screen did not exist until the 1870s, and its invention did more to preserve men's sanity and comfort than air conditioning ever has.)

Was life less hurried a century ago in

our cities, less crowded, less competitive, less dangerous, less likely to man-made and nature-made violence? Was it quieter? Were carriage accidents less frequent and less lethal than car accidents? Did drunken drivers race their carriages in city streets less than they do their hotrods today? Was it any better to be run down by a horse-drawn street car or cable car than by a yellow cab, or any less frequent? Was the chasm between the life of the rich and the poor any less than it is now, the slums less desperate, the mansions less extravagant than penthouses? Obviously not. And open spaces in the cities? To be sure the country was nearer to the most concentrated parts of cities, but it took a great deal longer to get to it by carriage or riverboat or even by trains that started their journeys on tracks down the

A slippery day in New York City, 1868

center of city streets and poured their smoke and cinders into the windows of tenements and boardinghouses and what we now call "luxury apartments" and they called "French flats."

Essentially cities are not dwellings and pavings and parks, offices, warehouses, markets and manufactories; they are concentrations of people who insist on congregating, partly for company, partly for protection (many cities were fortresses before they were cities, Detroit for one), partly for work, partly for amusement, and partly for anonymity. Traditionally they have been looked upon by rural Americans as centers of sin, as though sin was geographical, of sharp dealing, of oppression, temptation, and trumpery. And, of course, they were right —or at least as right as they were wrong.

Most American cities started in a hurry and grew at a headlong pace. Geography said where they should be: where there were protected harbors, confluences of rivers, sources of minerals and food, and later junctions of railroads.

The lake port of Chicago in 1833, when a New York journalist stopped there on his way west, was "two or three frame buildings and a few miserable huts." (It was so cold indoors that the ink froze while he was writing his report.) When he came back 18 months later, he was surprised to find "five hundred houses, four hundred of which have been erected this year, and 2,200 inhabitants." San Francisco boomed even before the Gold Rush of 1849. In July 1846 it was "a ragged-looking trading village" with a population of about 200; 18 months later its population was 1,000 and boasted 200 buildings, and by 1855 it found it expedient to hire a planner to draw a plan for the emerging city on whose main streets there were already imposing business buildings, hotels, and horse-drawn street cars. In 1849 the population exploded from 2,000 to nearly 25,000. Chicago and San Francisco may have been unique, but so was every other American city. When the English novelist Captain Frederick Marryat arrived in Buffalo in 1837, he wrote in his

The seven smells of New York, 1880

diary, "It is hardly credited that such a beautiful city could have risen in the wilderness in so short a period." Twenty-four years earlier it had been burned completely by British soldiers.

It would be pleasant but false to say that for every land speculator, quick-buck artist, and venal politician whose only concern in the growth of cities was what they could get out of them to line their own pockets, there was a dedicated citizen ready to fight for the amenities of city life. Far from it. It would be equally false to say there were none. Indeed there were a good many and still are. New York, for example, had its poet-editor William Cullen Bryant, a country boy who came to the big city in the 1820s, loved the city for its intellectual excitement but loved to walk by streams and among trees. It was he whose crusade for open spaces in the city led in the 1850s to the creation of Central Park by Frederick Law Olmsted, who spread his genius across the country. Chicago had its Daniel H. Burnham, the inspiring genius of the Columbian Exposition of 1893 —"The White City,"

which gave that metropolis a new vision of its future. He went on to make plans for the beautification of Washington, plans for Baltimore, Duluth, and San Francisco. Behind such plans there was always a scrappy group of public-minded citizens eager to fight for them.

If yesterday was not the utopia, the "good old days" our mistaken nostalgia would like to make it, neither was it blind to its shortcomings. The growth of cities is an unending battle between expediency and the toadies of Mammon on the one hand and enlightened self-interest and disinterested progress on the other. But Asa Green's advice on how to survive in the city is still sound and is likely always to be: "See that your shoes are secure at the heels...look up street and down street...and then run for your life."

Russell Lynes is the author of *The Tastemakers* and *The Art-Makers of 19th Century America*. He is currently working on a book about the Cooper-Hewitt Museum.

A scene on Broadway, New York City, late 19th century

The Psychology of City Space

Culturally defined values may be stronger than innate needs.

By William Kornblum

There is not one psychology of parks, there are many. The most important psychological research on parks and open spaces today seeks to understand the variety of human behavior in outdoor settings. Studies of human ethology—of how we behave as territorial creatures — studies of how we use and abuse the resources of the natural environment, and studies of how we resolve conflicts over the allocation of scarce resources of land, water, and leisure time fall into this school of environmental psychology. But discussion of these aspects of park psychology requires consideration of the role parks have played in the psychology of American aesthetics and urban design. It is out of this "consciousness of the value of nature" and of play that parks as we now enjoy them emerged.

Parks and open natural spaces within reach of urban people have always been justified in psychological terms. Pioneering social workers and psychologists of the Gilded Age — men and women like Jane Addams, Jacob Riis, and W. I. Thomas — argued that outdoor recreation areas were a critical need in crowded industrial cities of the 1890s. "Recreation is stronger than vice," Jane Addams wrote, "and recreation alone can stifle the lust for vice." The earlier founders of the American park and conservation movements were less certain about the psychological benefits of natural open spaces. Inspired by Thoreau and Whitman, park planners and conservationists like Olmsted and Marsh did argue that the role of parks was to refresh the mind and soothe the nerves of city people. But as they struggled to convince urban leaders to set aside valuable city property for the public, their greater purpose was to give nature its rightful place in the urban envi-

ronment. Theirs was not so much a psychology of social hygiene as it was a movement to heighten public consciousness of the need to stop the destruction of natural environments, to heal the scars of industrialization, and to cultivate the earth and its people.

Few social scientists today would claim that humans have an innate need to experience open spaces or that recreation can conquer "vice." Developmental psychologists have proven that humans seek out new environments and that we have a need for diverse stimuli in our early development. Clearly parks and open spaces can and do fill this need for many of us whose daily lives tend to be spent in "built" environments. But it is also certain that our needs for energy, shelter, social relationships, and security are primary. They are undeniable requisites to physical and psychological health. In the search to satisfy these needs in the urban world, parks and open space are often a backdrop or a setting.

Yet if a psychology of parks is grounded in culturally defined values and behaviors rather than in innate psychological needs, this does not diminish its importance. Access to natural open spaces is a central value in modern society. The desirability of living near attractive land or seascapes at the same time that one is close to other people is a feature of the modern, urban temper. It is a value duality that goes quite far in explaining the ecology of modern metropolitan growth. Given the material means, some people would choose a dwelling with an expansive view of the city or of nature, others would choose to live along the water, or in a somewhat secluded grove of trees, or within sight of an open landscape. And since scarcities of time and space do not permit

everyone to live in such surroundings, the mass of people invariably lists access to public parks as a primary value in defining the quality of their lives. Attitude polls that seek to determine the cultural preferences of the American public invariably find that parks and

open spaces are assigned a high value regardless of class and status differences. And the behavior is consistent with attitudes: more than 250 million yearly visits are made to the national parks. How many more billions of annual visits are made to all the parks,

Coney Island, New York City

Les Jardins de Trocadero, Paris

beaches, picnic grounds, and playgrounds of America?

Crime and vandalism

If parks and open spaces play a central role in the value system of urban people, why is it that these same places are so often viewed as dangerous or threatening? Why are they so often the target of vandals and the gathering place for social outcasts and human predators? Psychologists and other social scientists have devoted a great deal of attention to these and related questions. The answers they give are often found in studies of human territoriality and of behavior in public places. Part of the answer lies in what social psychologist Erving Goffman has termed the "looseness" of condoned behavior in parks. In contrast to the "tight" rein we must maintain over our behavior in many social settings, our parks, plazas, beaches, and other public places were designed to allow some degree of "letting loose." We can lose ourselves in behavior with little regard for the outside world. We can quarrel, make love (within limits that vary greatly throughout the society), stare into space, massage an aching muscle, shout to a friend, or concentrate on kicking a ball with little concern for side involvements and "keeping up a front." But there are also some negative consequences of this normative looseness, as Goffman observes in *Behavior in Public Places:*

In general, then, when we find that places such as parks can become the scene of robbery, refuse dumping, sexual solicitations, loitering (on the part of drunks, bums, and ambulatory psychotics), we must understand this collapse of public order not merely in terms of the fact that it may be possible to avoid the police in these places; we must understand that the involvement structure institutionalized in very loosely defined behavioral settings reduces appreciably the degree to which these nefarious acts are improper. A park may be the place that maximizes the acceptability of these acts and hence minimizes the price of being caught performing them.

Goffman should not be interpreted as suggesting that parks are the inevitable or legitimate gathering place for anti-social individuals. An implication of his observations is that the control of these negative behaviors is a responsibility we all share. It is not something that can be merely delegated to the police or other official agents of social control. But of course the problem of danger and threat in public places goes far beyond this aspect of normative looseness. The role that parks play in defining the physical and psychological boundaries of neighborhoods and communities also has a great deal of bearing on issues of public behavior and public safety.

Territoriality

Psychologists and sociologists often note how patterns of social cleavage and territoriality that exist in urban neighborhoods are extended into nearby parks and open spaces. Patterns of segregation in nearby communities are often reproduced on a more fleeting temporary basis in nearby parks. Sociologist Gerald Suttles shows this to be the case for parks and open plazas in the contemporary life of the Chicago community where Jane Addams created Hull House at the turn of the century. A small park and playground bordered on one side by a Chicano neighborhood, on another by a black neighborhood, and on another by an Italian neighborhood is the scene of a marvelously complex system of territorial claims by youth and adult friendship groups. This use pattern varies by time of day and week and constitutes one way of establishing a moral order among people who are only beginning to learn to trust each other. One can cite many other examples of this type of territoriality just as one can think of examples where spatial and temporal segregation of groups and uses is not the rule. Indeed, the patterns of segregation and sharing a park or open space can be a valuable barometer for learning about the climate of social relations in adjacent communities.

There are many other park psychologies that have not been touched in this brief review. There is a field of psychology that studies littering behavior and another that measures changes in public attitudes toward the natural environment. Another group of psychologists studies the impact of crowding on human aggression, while still others study how conflicts over natural resources of space and water are best resolved. The reader who wishes more information about these psychological schools might well look at the journal *Environment and Behavior* (published at the C. U. N. Y. Graduate School) or the *Journal of Leisure Research* (the scientific journal of the National Parks and Recreation Association). For our purposes it may be most appropriate to close with a note on the relationship between the psychology of parks and the broader psychology of city space.

Modern studies of how people perceive their cities show that we develop mental maps that guide our circulation in urban regions. Psychologists such as Stanley Milgram and psychologically informed planners like Kevin Lynch have pioneered in this research. Their research shows that few urban physical features are as important in defining how we perceive our surroundings as are parks, open plazas, and the green boundaries of boulevards and riverbanks. Earlier generations of social scientists and planners sometimes thought that the central business districts of our commercial cities were the primary beacons in urban perception. Their theories lent some credence to the attitudes of urban boosters who were wont to make statements like, "You can't eat Mount Rainier," or "When you've seen one sequoia you've seen 'em all." Modern urban psychology allows us to say that "the urban core is thrilling but you can't find your way through it without parks and natural grass. The modern office building is imposing but you can't make love under it."

William Kornblum is an Associate Professor of Sociology at the City University of New York Graduate School. He has been a member of various National Park Service planning teams.

Roller Coaster, Coney Island, New York City

Open Space: Freedom and Control

Use is an indicator of social growth and change.

By Stephen Carr and Kevin Lynch

Open space, like an open society, must be free and yet controlled. Freedom of action in public spaces is defined and redefined in each shift of power and custom.

In those small, interdependent communities, in which we have lived for most of our human history, the use of the shared space was an integral part of the social order, like the obligations of kinship. Sanctions that enforced these rules were immediate and unwavering, for maintaining spatial order was essential to the social order. Conflicts occurred, if at all, at the territorial boundaries, where one group faced another.

As larger towns developed, residents at first maintained these settled ways. In the medieval Islamic city, for example, the residential quarters were walled enclaves. Those within were closely related, and the use of the common space was regulated as in the village. Even the main streets, as they passed through these enclaves, were closed off at night by pairs of gates. The market spaces were likewise shut off, divided between the separate merchant guilds. Paths between quarters, other spaces, and the ground outside the city walls were no-man's-lands, places for inter-group battles, the territory of misfits and criminals, that growing underclass caught between village, guild, and army. Here also flourished the storytellers and other entertainers. In other cities, some of this space was shaped to accommodate the rituals of institutionalized religion or government: those processions, executions, and displays of armed men necessary to uphold the temple and the throne. In St. Petersburg, Tsar Alexander built a gigantic chain of squares, one kilometer long, through which his human machines might march. Along with such places, however, there also came the possibility of mass protest and riot.

Like the anti-matter of physics, open space has been the opposing complement of the committed uses of any settlement, and, like anti-matter, it may have explosive consequences. It is the common ground for movement and communication, and likewise the place for deviance and crime. What is felt to be threatening in public differs from place to place, and time to time. The line constantly shifts between freedom and riot, and the struggle for control has sharpened as cities have grown larger and more diverse.

Battersea Park, in London, was built to provide "wholesome recreation" in place of the rowdy joys of the Battersea

Sproul Plaza, University of California, Berkeley

Fields, once described by *The City Mission* magazine, in September, 1870, as if it were a program for downtown revitalization today: "Surely if ever there was a place out of hell that surpassed Sodom and Gomorrah in ungodliness and abomination, this was it ... horses and donkeys racing, footracing, walking matches, flying boats, flying horses, roundabouts, theaters, comic actors, shameless dancers, conjurers, fortune tellers, gamblers of every description, drinking booths, stalls, hawkers, and vendors of all kinds of articles...."

Sproul Plaza in Berkeley, California, was a decorative, rather empty entrance to the university when first built. Now, after the tumults of the 60s, it is vibrant with activity. Yet a regulation of this diversity is also evident. Rallies on those famous steps are now confined to certain hours and to certain decibel levels. The tables promoting various activities are lined up in a decorous row. The food vendors and the "street people" in their bizarre clothes are held, as if by an invisible barrier, to that end where the plaza meets the street. The freedom of use is greater than it once was, and it has been established through a process of testing, riot, repression, and, finally, more subtle and differentiated controls.

A humane mix of freedom and control may flow directly from the ways of a dominant culture. The English parks are known for their tolerance of eccentric or "private" behavior, but they are ruled by an unspoken agreement as to proprieties that are never to be violated. In more pluralistic cultures, public space becomes a battleground over appropriate behavior. It was feared that the opening of New York's Central Park would attract crowds of dangerous ruffians. Olmsted thought that his success in creating a park police, trained to correct public manners unobtrusively, was more important than the design of the park itself. Today, some street improvers worry that their outdoor comforts will attract unseemly vagrants, and so they contrive water sprays, spikes, hard surfaces, backless benches, and seats too short to sleep on.

Popular revolutions have always shown their strength in the central open

Mardi Gras, New Orleans

spaces of great cities and have there been suppressed. The wool workers and small craftsmen of Florence rallied in the Piazza Signoria in the summer of 1378 to protest their exploitation by the great guilds. There, in control of the center, they created the first democracy of Europe. There, too, some months later, they were put to flight. The *place* before the Hôtel de Ville in Paris has been the focus of action each time the people arose: 1789, 1830, 1848, 1871, 1944, 1968. The tumultuous events in Tehran demonstrate once more the power of an aroused populace unleashed in the streets and open spaces of a city.

More often, we are threatened by the muggings, rapes, and knife assaults that have become so common in U.S. cities. In the memories of the urban middle class, reaching no further back than the 20s or 30s, this is a marked deterioration of public conduct. Yet, it is only a partial return to earlier behavior. The streets of 18th century London, for example, were far more dangerous for unarmed pedestrians. In medieval Florence, anyone caught on the streets at night without a special written pass was a proven criminal.

The free use of open space may offend us, endanger us, or even threaten the seat of power. Yet that freedom is one of our essential values. We prize the right to speak and act as we wish. When others act more freely, we learn about them, and thus about ourselves. The pleasure of an urban space freely used is the spectacle of those peculiar ways, and the chance of interesting encounter. It is an opportunity for the expression of self and group, unfettered by routine constraints of workplace and family. Watch the joy of both spectators and performers at Mardi Gras in New Orleans.

Except in final, violent confrontations, politics is waged with symbols. It is a struggle for minds and must be allowed full play. The citizens of 16th century Rome attacked their papal government in "pasquinades" or satiric verses attached to "talking" statues. The murals and wall posters of Lisbon and Peking are well known. Speakers mount soap boxes in the streets — never in public places indoors. Open spaces should allow for communication, peaceful protest, and demonstration in ways that will not disrupt the ongoing function of the city. There must be locations where a demonstration will be visible and have symbolic weight, where access is easy and panic or entrapment unlikely. The crowd must be able to sense itself and its leaders, have ample room and yet not be dwarfed. It needs skillful management to keep the expression of one group from inhibiting that of others.

Far more frequent contradictions occur when individuals are threatened or offended by some free behavior. Most of us agree on suppressing assault, theft, and damage to property, but what will be judged offensive will vary. The necessary management is accordingly complicated: to distinguish the harmful from the harmless, controlling the one without constraining the latter; to increase the general tolerance toward free use, while stabilizing a broad consensus of what is permissible; to separate—in time and in space—the activities of groups that have a low tolerance for each other; to provide

marginal places where extremely free behavior can go on with little damage. Freedoms flourish as the system of regulation becomes more differentiated and the regulators more skilled in their art.

In open space design, we seek a balance between openness and the articulations that allow mixed occupancy and use. We want spaces that reflect the complexities of our social life. This challenges our ingenuity, since the subdivisions and supports that smaller-scale activities require are in conflict with the use by crowds. Present central squares have gone to one extreme or the other. The new City Hall Plaza in Boston, designed with Siena in mind, functions well for occasional Stanley Cup rejoicings. At other times, activity clings precariously to its windswept edges. More often, central squares are designed like parks, filled with trees and fountains that prevent effective use as a stage for great public events.

The Streets

Streets provide us with the essential freedom of movement on which city life depends. They make and reveal the city. But in the rush to connect, we have ignored their other functions. Should we not re-invent the street to reflect the reality of its mixed use? The range of freedom can be enlarged by greater control, as when we liberate city zones by bringing the car to heel or encourage a freer use of the streets by making the police visible. On some residential streets in Holland, the tables are now turned. The pedestrian holds the right-of-way over the entire pavement; the driver is a tolerated intruder, legally liable in case of any accident. The whole street space may then be used for play and for other activities.

In the parks and playgrounds, the tension between control and freedom becomes poignant. Intended as a common ground where all people might act openly and come together peacefully, they are the scenes of a growing conflict over turf. Frequently enough, they are "captured" by some single group. Indeed, at the smaller scale, one solution is to give over such a space to those who live around it, creating a one-to-one territorial identity that ensures its stable

control and defense. Another way is to "harden" the space, making it impervious to violent freedoms. But that will limit other uses, and, by implying that violence is expected, encourage what it seeks to control.

In larger parks, the solution is again one of partitioning in time and space, and, above all, one of sensitive management. Design and management go hand in hand. Negotiating acceptable divisions of ground, providing the subtle markers that allow groups to find their places, teaching tolerance to those who operate the space, and controlling unobtrusively are keys to free use.

Wastelands

Freer than parks, the wastelands are places on the margins. They are eddies in the city stream, out of sight and out of mind: the vacant lots, back alleys, dumps, and abandoned rights-of-way, the province of the young and the derelict. Here children have a chance for risk and adventure, in the company of their peers and away from adult supervision. Here they can dig a cave, throw up a fortress, hoist sticks to build a high nest. Yet even these wastelands are not rule free. Games have their own rules; repeated use builds territory and tradition; and society is anxious over bodily harm.

In remodeling any open space, one begins with the rule system. What is legal and customary here? Does that fit with the ideas of those who use the space, or is it imposed on them? Who safeguards the system? What will be the repercussions if the place is liberated, and how may those repercussions be contained? Who manages and enforces the system? What are their own feelings toward their work, and toward those whom they control?

Opening a place to new activities can extend the realm of freedom too. Allowing cyclists and joggers to use the drives of Central Park, or people to walk on Memorial Drive, along the Charles River in Cambridge, is an entering wedge for other free uses. Importing entertainers and seasonal celebrations into shopping streets changes those atmospheres. As the streets become warmer, more relaxed, and greater fun to be in, the sense of public

life is refreshed. Again, this takes careful management, since these changes can easily be seen as out of place or threatening. Boston's inventive "First Night," a public New Year's Eve festival staged in the central streets and public places, was clumsily damped down this year, due to a few bottle-throwing incidents that occurred on its first run.

The use of open space is an indicator of social growth and change. Here one first senses some shift in social relations, or an evolution of dress and manners. Here is the public place for free commentary and artistic expression. To design open space well, one must understand how the social order is developing — no small task. Not only must one know the people one is designing for—they should themselves be involved in the design, along with those who will manage and maintain the place. This involvement leads to a better place, but also to that investment that makes more likely its future care.

Each using group should find some reflection of itself there, be able to lay partial claim to some territory. Management should include users, to keep management open to shifting values. The controls and shapes that make space free are difficult to achieve and precarious to maintain. Spatial freedom is sufficiently precious to make that effort worthwhile.

Concert, Central Park, New York City

Stephen Carr and **Kevin Lynch**, urban designers, are principals in the Cambridge, Massachusetts, firm of Carr, Lynch Associates. Mr. Lynch was for many years Professor of City Design at MIT and is the author of *The Image of the City* and *What Time is this Place?*

The Management of Open Spaces

Who runs them, and with what aim?

By August Heckscher

View of Central Park, New York City, from West 72nd Street

The problem of park commissioners is that they are almost invariably at the bottom of the budgetary totem pole. When the crunch comes—and these days it not only comes but seems to remain as a permanent fact of life — parks departments are the first to be cut. While mayors hesitate to make slashes in the police force or the sanitation workers, they see parks as the place where the ax can fall with least immediate harm to the public.

In vain the parks commissioner pleads with his chief, telling him that a few extra dollars spent on parks will bring a large return in the pleasures of civic life, and will also improve his political image. Against the harsh realities of budget-cutting, the case for amenities rarely prevails.

The mayor's rejoinder is to do more with less—to increase the productivity of park workers and to introduce more efficient systems of management. Up to a point, this works. In most city parks de-partments, manpower is rather waste-fully deployed. The workers tend to think of themselves as following the life-style of farmers rather than of production workers: they key their labor to the season and to the changing weather. Yet in this apparent wastefulness there is much that gives to a park system its capacity to answer the city's needs.

In New York we discovered it was more "efficient" to move clean-up crews about the city, from park to park, than to have a single man stationed at a regular post. Yet how often the worker who ap-peared to be idle much of the day had in fact been lending a presence to the park that moderated disorder and gave a touch of humanity to a neighborhood lacking in social services. Other attempts at efficiency can also be self-defeating. To maintain buildings by substituting as-phalt shingles for slate damages the ar-chitectural qualities that are important to the park environment. Black-top in place of cobblestone walks, chain-link fence in place of wrought iron, can be signs of good management but of poor policy in the long run.

A natural tendency is to cut down commitments so as to more nearly match resources. But you cannot run a parks department the way a skilled manager runs a chain of supermarkets — eliminat-ing those that do not attract a sufficient clientele. Park lands are acquired with dif-ficulty and, once disposed of, are usually impossible to replace. The press recently reported that golf courses in the New York City parks domain had become non-profitable; therefore the golf courses should be sold off to corporations seek-ing large open spaces for their headquar-ters. But if golf should no longer pay its way, the fees should be substantially raised; the courses should be rented out as concessions, or, perhaps, simply planted in fast-growing trees.

When neighborhoods change, a small park often is abandoned or mis-used. Nevertheless it is less than prudent management to dispose of the land. The life of a city is continually changing; small open spaces can be a focal point for a neighborhood's rehabilitation, or the cen-tral feature of one that recovers a lost charm.

With city budgets so hard-pressed, the transfer of open spaces to a larger government entity may appear attractive. In cities where county and state share park responsibilities with the urban gov-ernment, the city's share of the green spaces is nearly always the dirtiest and most unkempt. The county does better, and the state can appear a model park-keeper. Something is lost, nevertheless, when the management of a local park is not in the hands of the locality itself. The city may be poor, but it is apt to be health-ily responsive to community groups and pressures.

Some federally administered parks exist within U.S. cities—the waterfront in St. Louis, for example. They are well kept but invariably somewhat removed from

Thomas Worth. "Central Park—the dangers that threaten it." 1879

the life of the city. Central Park in New York is frequently talked about as ripe for federal take-over. This historic open space unquestionably is more than a local Manhattan park; it belongs to the whole city, and in some sense it belongs to the nation. But to make it a national park would subject it to a form of management and control detrimental to its basic character. The genius of Central Park (like its sister, Prospect Park in Brooklyn) is in the individuality of its various parts, the oddities and idiosyncracies of its design and landscaping. Until miracles come to pass, the National Park Service—keyed to the management of large naturalistic spaces, remote and impersonal in its rule—will not be able to deal effectively with a green setting that is the very heart and soul of New York.

However pleasant it might be to have sylvan retreats in the midst of the crowded city, places of calm set apart and characterized by perfect cleanliness and order, the modern city is not made that way. It is alive with tensions, and when controversies rage or large social issues are at stake, the open spaces will be filled with clamor. To set limits to those uses of the parks that permanently damage them is an essential element in their administration. But it must be done

with an understanding of the city's true nature, and not merely with managerial officiousness.

This is not to say that federal funds for maintenance, in this and other parks, are not highly desirable. The traditional readiness of the federal government to provide money for capital expenses, while rejecting support for maintenance, remains one of the anomalies of our park system. Legislation providing a certain amount of upkeep is now before the Congress, and its passage is earnestly to be wished. Provision for a hundred extra men in Central Park alone—a force that would not only be available for clean-up and repairs but as a safeguard against recurrent small vandalism—could make all the difference in the safety and the outward aspect of Central Park. Frederick Law Olmsted instituted what he called "path-masters," a uniformed group to aid, inform, and subtly control the public. How satisfying if that could be achieved through federal support today!

The private sector must also be looked to. In cities like Dallas and Atlanta, businessmen have gone to great expense to create open spaces in dense downtown areas. In New York, Paley Park and Greenacre Park are models of

what an urban amenity should be. If so much is given to create a park from scratch, and then to maintain it, should not private business be responsive to suggestions that it assume a role in the maintenance of parks that already exist, often at their very doorsteps? A study is now on foot to determine whether Madison Square park in Manhattan cannot be restored to an agreeable and lively open space through the input of the insurance companies and other businesses surrounding it.

To the extent that the private sector may help in the maintenance of designated open spaces, one hopes it will cooperate closely with city officials charged with ultimate responsibility. In particular, private interests must resist the temptation to exclude certain portions of the public. Parks belong to all the people, and should be accessible to all except those that are plainly disruptive.

It would require a highly developed social consciousness on the part of a pri-

Jay Keppler. "The only way to have the exhibition in Central Park—have it on stilts." 1880

vate business to remain hospitable to the kind of messy but harmless activities that Hippies formerly engaged in. It would be an unusual corporation that, in reconstructing a park, left a little space for the bums and "winos" that had established an almost natural right to sit there. The city can do such things. Could the private sector be expected to do them?

In most downtowns today the open spaces created by business and institutional complexes rival in importance those squares and plazas owned by the public. The development of these areas is encouraging, but the disadvantages begin to appear. Encouraged by zoning laws that allow extra height and bulk in return for amenities at the ground level, the skyscraper has devoured a disproportionate amount of sky. The resulting open space, moreover, has too often proved sterile and windy, its overall design seeming calculated to prevent the public from making too intimate or enthusiastic use of it. But the level of maintenance in these private open spaces is admittedly high. They are clean and orderly, while the small city parks show signs of decay.

In the end the city cannot escape the task of managing its own open spaces. It can get help from other agencies, public and private, but the tone, the atmosphere, and the quality of its common life are in no small part dependent upon the way its parks and squares are administered. The ultimate choices are political, not managerial; they are philosophical in the most exact sense. Do we want the modern city to be open, humane, tolerant, adaptable to changing causes and fashions? Do we want it to reflect the diversity and innovativeness of urban men and women at their best? The park is an extension of the street; and the street has always been the place where mankind mixes and mingles, and gossips and makes deals—in short where they are most thoroughly urbane.

August Heckscher is a former Parks Commissioner and Administrator for the City of New York. He is author of *Open Spaces—The Life of American Cities.*

Open Space Legislation

Innovative concepts create public amenities.

By Donald Elliott

Urban open space legislation is a peculiarly local phenomenon. There are no federal or even state-wide statutes that affect the amount or kind of open space to be provided in a particular locality. Until fairly recently, not very sophisticated attention was paid to open space beyond concern in local zoning ordinances over "light and air" and requirements for front, rear, and side yards around buildings. In most cities there has been little effective concern over usable open space in the densely developed commercial downtown districts. But increasingly it has become a greater priority, and several cities such as San Francisco and Detroit have been implementing innovative concepts. New York City has long been in the forefront of concern over land-use regulation and in 1961 rewrote its zoning ordinance to give high priority to open space. Since then a number of changes have been made to improve the quality of urban open space and, therefore, this discussion deals exclusively with the experience of New York City.

McGraw-Hill Park, New York City

When you walk behind the new McGraw-Hill building on Sixth Avenue in Rockefeller Center in New York City you pass under a waterfall and can sit next to a small fountain and have a cup of coffee and a danish pastry; the pleasant sound of rushing water drowns out the noise of the city and you may think: "Wasn't it nice of Rockefeller Center to do this?" You might be surprised to know that the laws governing development and the desire of the city government had more to do with creating this space than did the owners of the land.

Much of the open space in the densely developed office districts of New York is there because the public required it before granting permits for the highly profitable, very dense office towers that it complements. Buildings set back on plazas like the Seagram and Chase Manhattan Bank headquarters, and parks like the one across from the Merrill Lynch building on lower Broadway, or open pedestrian ways and enclosed pedestrian spaces through the middle of the block all result in large part from requirements and incentives of the municipal law.

Urban open space used to be primarily of three sorts: streets and sidewalks conceived essentially in terms of access; vacant land not yet developed, but used informally by the public; and parks and playgrounds built and maintained with public tax dollars. In recent years sophisticated regulation of development has become a major additional generator of other kinds of useful open space.

In the office building district, where land prices often exceed $10 million an acre, public monies are not available to create sufficient open space to ameliorate the density. So we have long recognized that regulating the use, the density, and to some extent the design of development is in the public interest. New York City in 1916 enacted the first zoning ordinance. It was, in part, a reaction to the "canyons of Wall Street" created by buildings going to the building line and using their entire lots. This early law required setbacks permitting the intrusion of light and air. In 1961, overall density was lowered and major zoning innovations were added. A building could get a "plaza bonus," by which a developer could add up to 20 percent more floor space to his building if he provided a "plaza" open to the sky. The amendment also requires buildings to be set back above a certain level on a sloping line called a "sky exposure plan," unless the tower takes up only 40 percent of the site.

The results of the 1961 changes were largely helpful, but the generality of the statute did not achieve a uniformly beneficial result. Open space should do more than let some light and air reach the ground. Legally, a plaza has to have certain minimum dimensions, but it doesn't have to be a space the public can use. It can end up leading to a blank wall or be a dismal space behind a building used only for exhaust fans and illegal parking. A particularly distressing example is behind 300 Park Avenue next to the Waldorf Astoria Hotel. Or it can be the great space in front of the Seagram Building. The law doesn't differentiate.

The plaza bonus provision was a general law designed to treat everyone equally and also eliminate discretion by public officials, which might lead to corruption. But ironically, such general laws encourage development of minimal quality, since a building that meets minimum standards receives a maximum bonus. If a builder creates a higher quality and more useful space such as a small park with trees, places to sit, and even a waterfall, the basic plaza bonus is the same.

Open space that is useful for circulation, alive with activity, and adequately designed is the goal of modern land-use regulations. Such design is often more expensive than minimum general standards. In the past 13 years, numerous ways have been found to encourage developers to build and maintain useful space. Arcades, pedestrian malls, covered plazas, pedestrian connections, esplanades, pedestrian decks, loggia, enclosed pedestrian spaces, have all been added to the vocabulary of the land-use regulation. Performance requirements as well as architectural dimensions are increasingly being specified. The results are not always perfect, but in sum they have improved the quality of urban life.

The trend has been to design, with some particularity, various unique areas of the city and to codify those design decisions into special zoning districts, in order to control private development.

Rockefeller Center Skating Rink, New York City

Seagram Building, New York City

Already, 25 districts have been created, giving considerable discretion to New York City officials to encourage high quality design and amenities. Pedestrian convenience and usable open space have been primary goals of many of the special districts, which include Lincoln Center, Greenwich Street, South Street Seaport, and Fifth Avenue.

Seven buildings illustrate the trend to greater concern over space associated with a particular building. Five are already completed: McGraw-Hill, Olympic Tower, the New York Telephone Company, the Galleria, and Citicorp Center; and two are under construction— the IBM and AT&T headquarters buildings.

Through the late 1950s and 1960s there was an enormous amount of con-

Galleria, New York City

struction on Sixth Avenue north of 42nd Street. Starting in 1968, the Planning Commission tried to encourage a series of open spaces through the middle of the blocks to achieve a new north-south pedestrian street. One of the most successful is the connection behind the McGraw-Hill Building.

Rockefeller Center, which has stood since its construction in the early 1930s as a monument to sensitive open space design and integration of different buildings

Citicorp atrium, New York City

in a single complex, was being expanded by the addition of three buildings. The management of the Center and the prospective major tenants in these buildings did not want them integrated into Rockefeller Center, but wanted them to stand independently as individual monuments. It took determined work by the Planning Commission and finally a meeting between Mayor Lindsay and the chief executives of the companies involved to achieve the mid-block connection behind them.

The throughblock in Olympic Towers results from the Fifth Avenue Special District Zoning. It should be a special public space with an interior waterfall and a place to sit and eat. Unfortunately, it has never been finished and it is more often the subject of criticism than acclaim. Still, when the waterfall is running, it is a dramatic place to sit and ponder the questions of life.

The Galleria has an adventuresome connection through the block in an extremely complicated multi-use building. Some of the ideas have failed. The public space is downstairs, through closed doors, and the shop space has not rented, largely because the building went bankrupt early before the apartments were tenanted.

The New York Telephone Company built a major building housing switching equipment and offices on the border of Bryant Park at 42nd Street and Sixth Avenue. As part of the construction, the entrance to the subway was set back under the building and dramatically opened up and improved; also a delightful open space was created behind the building.

Citicorp Center is a widely ac-

claimed and highly successful merger of retail uses, open and enclosed public spaces, and dramatic architecture. It is the result of a complex series of public and private acts, including the demolition and rebuilding of a church on the site and the construction of an open air entrance to two subway lines. It has become a standard against which subsequent buildings will be measured.

Almost the entire base of Philip Johnson's AT&T building, now under construction on Madison Avenue and 56th Street, will be a covered pedestrian area 60 to 100 feet high, open to the public, filled with chairs and tables, and lighted in the rear by a curved skylight. Food will be available and programs for visitors will be professionally organized. This building is certain to become one of the centers of attraction in the city. Next to it is Edward Barnes' IBM building— another high quality building where the architect has paid special attention to the generous enclosed public spaces. In each of these seven buildings, cooperation between the private developer and the city has led to particular city actions that encouraged these open spaces, primarily by trading them for more profitable buildings.

One of the most spectacular and dramatic open spaces of 6 acres is in lower Manhattan stretching west from the Chase Manhattan Bank to the World Trade Center. It results from decisions by public and private developers, the requirements of zoning law, and special actions of the city. It ties together and makes more human the densest concentration of office buildings in the world. As Ada Louise Huxtable has described it:

This small segment of New York compares in effect and elegance with any celebrated Renaissance plaza or Baroque vista. The scale of the buildings, the use of open space, the views revealed or suggested, the contrasts of architectural style and material, of sculptured stone against satin-smooth metal and glass, the visible change and continuity of New York's remarkable skyscraper history, the brilliant accent of the poised Noguchi cube—color, size, style, mass, space, light, dark, solids, voids, highs, and lows—are

all just right. These few blocks provide (why equivocate?) one of the most magnificent examples of twentieth-century urbanism anywhere in the world.

A fascinating footnote illustrates some small part of the complexity that was overcome in creating this space.

Marine Midland Plaza

One of the blocks that was to become a park was improved by a 21-story office building. The right to develop this land was transferred to the block to the north and became part of the Merrill Lynch Building. However, a Chock Full O' Nuts lease in the old building could not be acquired. So the 21-story building above Chock Full O' Nuts was demolished, leaving the store, which must be demolished when its lease is up.

Residential Open Space

In residential areas the zoning ordinance requires a certain minimum amount of open space on each lot. Particularly in developments for lower and middle income people, public open space most often results directly from public acquisition and ownership of the land. Urban renewal projects where existing deteriorated buildings have been demolished and superblocks have been created with towers set among substantial landscaped areas are a common sight in most major cities. Sometimes careful thought is given to such spaces, such as the Astor Foundation's redesign of the open space in Jacob Riis Houses, a public housing project on the lower east side of Manhattan or in Bedford Stuyvesant in Brooklyn, where the space is part of low-rise public housing built by the Model Cities

South Street Seaport Museum, New York City

program. Sometimes, however, in typical public housing, the open spaces are poorly designed, then neglected and allowed to become more of a liability than an asset.

If the residential development is on a large plot, then regulation of land use and placement of buildings can achieve usable public open space. In a cluster development, common open space is required by law and is owned in common and maintained by a charge on all the residents.

Such developments have at least as many houses to the acre as traditional suburban lot development but, by grouping them, at least 20 percent of the site becomes usable by the whole community as common open space. This technique was taken even further in the Borough of Queens, where a 100-acre golf course has been forever saved as open space by regulations permitting three large apartment buildings to use up all of the available development rights from a 108-acre site, and by convenants running with the land guaranteeing that no development will take place.

Basic to land-use regulation is the concept that a developer may build a certain limited amount of floor space on a given amount of land. Increasingly, the possibility of transferring that development from one piece of land to another in order to create open space is being recognized. In a free enterprise economy this is potentially the most powerful tool available for the creation of open space or for the preservation of old low-density buildings in high-value areas.

The South Street Seaport, located on the east side of Manhattan just south of the Brooklyn Bridge, is a historically important group of low-rise buildings and open spaces that is an important amenity for lower Manhattan. Existing zoning would allow 2 million square feet to be built on the Seaport land, whereas the current buildings comprise only 250,000 square feet. Mortgages of $14 million had been made in expectation of development.

By creating a special zoning district, however, the right to build on South Street Seaport Museum land has been made transferable to six other lots more appropriate for development. The holders of the mortgages agreed to attach their liens to the air (the development rights) instead of the land, and the Seaport was saved. The first of the receiving lots is about to be developed by the Continental Insurance Company for its national headquarters. A most felicitous result.

Unfortunately, some attempts to create such open space have failed. The courts have struck down a requirement that the development that is now allowed on the park land in Manhattan's Tudor City apartment complex had to be transferred to more appropriate locations; the grounds were that requiring such transfer eliminated the value of the land. Unfortunately, the court did not permit evidence on this question to be introduced. In my opinion, the decision is not only wrong legally, but destructive of the public interest.

In sum, the creation of humanizing usable urban open space requires the creative cooperation of the public and of private builders and developers. It is not easy and is often controversial, but the results justify increased attention in the future.

View of South Street, New York City

Donald Elliott is an attorney who was Chairman of the New York City Planning Commission from 1966 to 1973.

Wishful Thinking Legislation

What urban open space legislation would you most like to see enacted?

Roy M. Goodman
Senator
State of New York

I strongly favor a law that would give localities the power to preserve outstanding urban open spaces by detaching the unused development rights from the specific site and permitting the owner either to transfer them elsewhere or sell them to the locality for resale from a municipal "development rights bank."

The purpose of the "development rights bank" would be to provide an orderly market place for the purchase, sale, or trade of development rights that have been detached from sites being preserved as open, and also provide a depository where the owner of detached development rights could profitably "store" the rights until it became desirable for those rights to be used in connection with the development of another site.

James F. Lynch
Research Biologist (Ecologist)
Chesapeake Bay Center for
Environmental Studies

High priority ought to be given to the acquisition by municipalities of the largest possible tracts of land for parks and preserves. Given the realities of real estate values and the strictly limited acreage of land available within city limits in most areas, these land purchases would necessarily be in flanking areas, but within easy commuting distance of urban population centers. Perhaps the magnificent regional parks system that exists in the Berkeley-Oakland area is the best model. These parks are managed as a system, rather than as individual entities, and as a result the sometimes conflicting needs for recreational use, open

space, watershed protection, and wildlife conservation are all addressed in a rational fashion.

Daniel Patrick Moynihan
United States Senator
New York

In the last Congress there was a welcome attention paid to the recreational and aesthetic needs of urban residents, and numerous worthy bills were passed. Among these were laws that provided for federal-state-local joint management of areas that, if not precisely suited for the more narrowly defined status of national parks, were nevertheless recognized as areas of national significance. These new bills went far in creating innovative management arrangements and protection schemes that would allow preservation of a given area while at the same time maintaining the rights and desires of local residents.

I would like to see greater emphasis on this new direction in land use and preservation: it offers models for protection of some of those urban landscapes now in such deteriorated condition. If we can expand the definition of significance such that more of our urban areas will qualify for consideration, while at the same time becoming more flexible in incentives and directives we will use for preservation, we will have come a long way toward beginning to meet this important goal.

Chris Therral Delaporte
Director, Heritage Conservation and
Recreation Service
Washington, D.C.

Some of our most wishful thinking might include new authority for direct federal action to save critical urban spaces. However, in this era of increasing

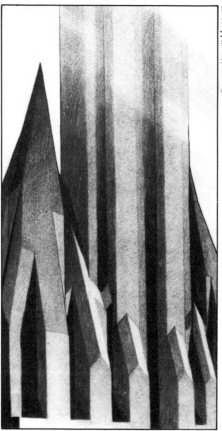

Hugh Ferriss. Illustration of the Maximum Mass Permitted by the 1916 New York Zoning Law

demands on the taxpayer's dollar, our wishes have been focusing on more practical opportunities to build state and local capabilities and establish systematic approaches to protecting urban open spaces.

A new alternative could be provided by legislation authorizing federal assistance for state and local action to protect open spaces. Such legislation would

establish a partnership, relying heavily on state and local police powers to achieve open space goals. Emphasis would be placed on building state and local capacity to develop and implement a plan with various traditional and innovative open space protection techniques such as zoning, mandatory dedication for subdivision approvals, property tax incentives, and easements. The primary federal function would be to provide technical and financial assistance and to insure consistency of all government programs affecting the area. The private sector would be encouraged to manage its land in accordance with the approved plan and provide recreation facilities that are revenue producing.

Some elements of this type of partnership approach are found in the legislation establishing the Lowell National Historical Park and the Pinelands National Reserve. However, new legislation would be required to establish a generic program of federal financial assistance for state and local open space protection efforts relying primarily on alternative to direct acquisition. This type of arrangement has frequently been discussed as a method of protecting open space on the metropolitan fringe as "greenline parks" or "areas of national concern." The same principles also might be applied to help protect the few remaining open spaces in already developed areas.

A broad legislative program to address urban open space needs could include some provisions to encourage better planning for existing spaces and special attention to the potential of urban waterfronts.

Tom Bradley
Mayor, City of Los Angeles

Last summer I was pleased to see one of my long standing hopes for open space preservation enacted into the Santa Monica Mountains National Recreation Area. A major impediment to its implementation, however, is the lack of adequate appropriations from the federal government to acquire needed parcels for park sites. For a "wishful thinking" list, funding is an important consideration.

In California, as a result of Proposition 13, we will be compelled to re-think our approach to providing open space. A larger role may have to be considered for the private sector, particularly non-profit groups like the Trust for Public land, who can accept land donations and accept less-than-fee acquisitions.

Carefully drafted new legislation can encourage the private sector to provide open space or "dedicate it" as a condition of development not only for subdivisions, as is required in the City of Los Angeles, but also in commercial and industrial projects for use by employees as well as in redevelopment projects.

In Los Angeles, no final subdivision map can be approved until land has been dedicated for park purposes or a fee has been paid. The area of land within a subdivision required for dedication is determined by directly relating net density to open space; that is, the higher the number of dwelling units per acre, the greater the percentage of gross subdivision area required to be dedicated.

The Department of the Interior's National Urban Recreation Study, which surveyed open space and recreation needs throughout the country, also recommended legislation to authorize local governments to require mandatory dedication of park land, or payments to a recreation fund, by developers.

Robert F. Wagner, Jr.
Chairman, City Planning Commission
New York City

Presently the New York City Zoning Resolution contains several provisions for the protection of scenic views, rare natural features, and the creation of new types of urban plazas and open spaces, including pedestrian malls, waterfront esplanades, and vest-pocket parks.

We hope to achieve legislation enabling us to create green belts and a network connecting these various open spaces, with particular emphasis on the waterfront.

One of the problems we face with such legislation pertains to a more mundane and realistic problem, i.e., how to acquire property or development rights to achieve our objectives with minimal impact on the city treasury. In this connection we will be exploring various zoning and non-zoning techniques such as:

- The use of scene and conservation easements;

- The adaptation of transfer of development rights (TDR) mechanisms from wetlands and estuaries to developable areas; and

- The creation of a public tax policy adapted to open space preservation (e.g. tax exemption, preferential assessment).

Peter Wolf
Institute for Architecture and Urban Studies
New York

A law should be passed that freezes development of any existing urban open space, including space on streets and space now created by empty lots, including on-grade parking lots everywhere in New York City. Owners of such lots should be compensated at present market value from an Open Space Bond Issue. The lots should then become a park land bank, incrementally converted to public use.

In addition all empty space in the public domain along, adjacent to, and above existing highways should be treated in the same manner. (This would put an end to the Westway controversy, among other things, and stop development out into the rivers.)

Robin Chandler Duke
Population Crisis Committee
Draper Fund

It is my hope that we try to retrieve as

Hugh Ferriss

much green area as possible. Where open spaces become available, it seems to me wise not to rebuild but to go to trees and park areas as often as possible.

The new landfill at Battery Park in New York City would be a great asset if it were a park area. Bearing in mind that our financial problems will become far more critical in the next months, we must balance our ecological and financial responsibilities. It may develop that revenue-producing sites are going to take huge priority over the need for urban open space.

Robert S. Cook, Jr.
Vice President
Institute for Environmental Action, Inc.
New York

Zoning legislation, which controls land use, can only channel market forces. Furthermore, zoning arouses deep-seated passions because it involves land, to which people have emotional attachments, and because it puts limits on the operation of the free market. Given these caveats, I would like to see cities have the power to zone beyond their boundaries in order to curtail suburban shopping mall development.

Curtailment of suburban malls would put a brake on the centrifugal forces of sprawl that are siphoning people away from city centers, to the detriment of their public spaces. People give urban open space the activity, color, and diversity that are the essence of urbanity. Give them good reasons to go downtown by eliminating the reasons for going elsewhere.

Some cities already have this power, but because of political and economic forces do not exercise it effectively. A change of attitudes is urgently needed.

William Donald Schaefer
Mayor
City of Baltimore

My wish list for new legislation (especially at the federal level) would include:

1. Greater emphasis on developing recreation and park facilities closer to our large population centers rather than developing National Parks, Forests and Wildlife areas in relatively remote areas of the country. That is, priorities should be people-oriented rather than resource-oriented. A good beginning was made by the Department of the Interior in the development of the Urban National Parks. However, many other areas would benefit by an extension of this program, for example, our proposed Middle Branch Park plan.

2. The present economic distress, which affects many older American cities, has made it extremely difficult to continue funding operations and maintenance of parks and recreation facilities at previous acceptable levels.

If we are to deliver high quality park and recreation services to our urban populations, operations and maintenance funding assistance must be forthcoming from the federal government. This remains one of the few areas of intergovernmental relations where capital funding is available, but program assistance is not.

President Carter's Urban Park and Recreation Recovery Program begins to address this need in a very limited manner. I believe a broadening in scope is necessary.

Kevin H. White
Mayor
City of Boston

We feel it is particularly important that federal open space funding programs be modified to:

1. Pay acquisition and development costs up front rather than reimbursing cities for money spent after the fact. The high cost of municipal bonds, and the legal limits to bonding authority make this change imperative, especially for the older large cities where the great majority of this country's population is located.

2. Recognize that open space in densely populated areas costs more and serves more people, and thus deserves greater support than projects in less densely developed sites. We recommend a flexible matching formula that would increase the federal share for high cost — high utilization sites such as center city parks.

3. Encourage non-traditional uses for urban open spaces. Boston's innovative "Urban Wilds" program demonstrated that even an older, developed city can offer a wide variety of natural experiences to residents and visitors if sufficient funds are available to locate, protect, and mark attractive sites. Open space programs should not be limited to athletics, but should include passive sitting areas, natural sites, vistas, historic locations, etc.

4. Finally, the grant should allow for the creation of a modest maintenance and upgrading endowment fund, designated for that particular project, that will insure the continued usefulness of the site and the maximum benefits from the original investment.

Dennis J. Kucinich
Mayor
City of Cleveland

We would like to see a substantial increase in the funding level of the Urban Park and Recreation Recovery Grants Program authorized as part of the National Parks and Recreation Act of 1978. An annual appropriation of only $150 million for the entire country hardly addresses the open space needs of its cities.

In terms of new legislation, we would like to be able to initiate a program of land banking for future open space funded under the NPR Act. Unfortunately, that thought truly does fall into the category of "wishful thinking."

Kenneth A. Gibson
Mayor
Newark, New Jersey

I would like to see legislation requiring substantial federal and state funding (e.g. 90 percent of the project) for municipalities that create and upgrade urban parks and park-like areas. Inasmuch as the municipalities lose tax ratables when they create park areas, especially in central business districts, they should be encouraged to pursue open spaces by dint of federal or state funding.

Elinor Guggenheimer
Trustee, National Recreation
& Parks Association
New York

I would like to see a heavy fine imposed on anyone who owns an open lot on which refuse has been allowed to accumulate. I believe that owners of lots should be required to keep their property in the same condition that the street is kept (or hopefully better!).

Most of all I would like to see a law passed that would require open space to be put to simple use as a sitting area or for some similar public purpose if it has been vacant for more than six months.

Harold Lewis Malt
Professor and Director, Urban
& Regional Planning Program
University of Miami, Florida

I keep "wishing" communities would use their *existing* laws, ordinances, or open space plans to better advantage. I think most of the things we would like to do are permissible. Much of the legislation is in place at the local, state, or federal levels. The deficiencies are lack of ideas, incentive, money. The bottleneck is in implementation, not planning.

Edward H. Able, Jr.
Executive Director
American Society of
Landscape Architects

There are two recently enacted laws for which the federal government is currently seeking funding for fiscal year 1980. These new programs are the "Livable Cities Act of 1978" and the "Urban Park and Recreation Recovery Act of 1978." Funding of $15 million has been requested by HUD for the Livable Cities program and $151 million by the Heritage Conservation and Recreation Service for fiscal years 1978 through 1982 for the Urban Park and Recovery program. Strong support will be needed to achieve successful funding to implement these programs. Admittedly, these are existing laws, but the achievement through the initial appropriation is important.

We have thought of a proposal that, from our personal knowledge, is needed. The proposal would require an amendment of existing legislation.

We suggest that the current Land and Water Conservation Fund program under the direction of the Heritage Conservation and Recreation Service be amended to provide some flexibility of funding for certain urban open space projects:

Amend the basic act to provide total federal funding for certain qualifying urban open space projects. The funding would include land acquisition, planning and design monies, and development costs, if any. Under the present law, states and municipalities must match the federal dollars on a 50-50 or in some cases 70-30 basis. One of the major problems of urban open space programs is that once the projects are acquired and developed; there is little or no funding for management, operation, or maintenance of the area. This is a state and local responsibility. Hence, in short time the open space has deteriorated and may be an *urban liability*. If the present laws were amended to allow the states and/or cities to make an agreement that they would guarantee the funding and the proper management and maintenance of the open space, then this would consitute the state and local contributions to the Land and Water Conservation Fund projects and they would not have to match the federal monies.

Many states and local jurisdictions utilize most of their funds to match the federal grant and, consequently, have little or no funds left to operate and maintain the open space.

John C. Mitkus
Executive Director,
Philadelphia City Planning Commission

First, the conversion of large, old properties to other uses: zoning laws should be passed allowing conversion of mansions, institutions, and historic structures, with provision for donation of open space easements to maintain the basic character of an existing open space.

Second, federal participation in projects involving more than one municipality to create regional facilities: with regard to regional recreation facilities, Philadelphia has been making efforts on a regional basis to preserve those open spaces that are most important from an environmental point of view. Often those spaces straddle municipal boundaries, and often there is a great disparity between the ability of adjacent communities to effect certain open space improvements. Therefore, it would be highly desirable if federal laws were changed to allow for a higher percentage of federal matching grants in situations where more than one municipality was involved. In this way, it would be possible to extend watersheds and other major open space amenities across municipal boundaries.

Thirdly, legislation that would allow a higher percentage of federal aid where

educational facilities are included as part of an open space experience: with regard to educational functions within open spaces and parks, at present there is no federal operating subsidy nor sufficient capital dollars to support educational facilities within special environmental areas. We have examples of working farms, wildlife preserves, and nature centers, which are either privately-owned or owned by the City, that are also valuable educational resources. It would be highly desirable to have federal operating funds for these specialized facilities in that they provide a program that is as much educational as it is recreational.

S. William Green
U.S. House of Representatives
New York

The highest priority for such legislation goes to an appropriation to fund the 1978 Urban Parks law, which provides funding to local governments to develop and implement a municipal "action plan" for parks. The law authorizes a $150 million appropriation for fiscal year 1980 but no appropriation was passed by the 95th Congress.

It had been anticipated that the Administration would request a supplemental appropriation for this program. However, the Administration's budget goals make it unclear in what amount — or indeed whether — such a request will be made.

Thomas Kapsalis
Commissioner, Department of Planning,
City and Community Development
City of Chicago

On our wish list of open space legislation would be some incentive tax credits for private interests that maintain and operate recreational facilities and open space for the public on a non-profit basis. Some tax credits may also be appropriate for installing and maintaining good outdoor design in keeping with the design district idea.

Another idea might be federal grant monies made available to public recreational facilities and parks in proportion to their use: the higher the use, the

greater the grant. Another possibility might be the funding of operations as well as the rehabilitation of relatively unique areas and facilities such as the historic parks designed by the pioneer landscape architects.

M. Paul Friedberg
Landscape architect and urban designer
New York

I would like to see a revolving fund established—similar to the highway fund —based on a tax placed on off-track betting and/or liquor and/or luxury-class restaurants. Money collected from these taxes shall be placed in a pool to be used for the acquisition and maintenance of both additional green areas and all seasonal recreational facilities within the city.

The objective of the improvements from this tax is to enhance the physical environment and, subsequently, the lifestyle of those who live within the cities.

Raquel Ramati
Director, Urban Design Group
New York City

All buildings opposite existing parks should be limited to such a height as to minimize the shadows cast by them.

Urban open space legislation should include mandatory provisions to landscape rooftops and setbacks of buildings. Landscaped roofs will serve as tenant recreation spaces and replace the bare concrete appearance visible from higher floors with attractive landscaped green areas.

Jacqueline Kennedy Onassis
Editor, Doubleday & Co.
New York

Create a promenade around the waterfront so that it will be possible for people to enjoy it.

Banish to Devil's Island anyone who builds a mid-block skyscraper blocking out the sun and destroying the small-scale human quality of the side streets.

John Diele

Harold M. Proshansky
President
The Graduate School and
University Center
The City University of New York

Two laws I would like to see passed are: *One* requires that for every given amount of commercial and private space used for business, homes, or what have you, there must be an open space available for recreation, communication, and other social interaction, free from any and all commercial enterprise. By this I mean no automobiles, vendors, stores, or anything else allowed. The *second* is related to the first and would be a set of requirements that involve open spaces being evaluated, changed, and kept diverse by means of a variety of recreational and cultural activities supported by public funds.

Henry Geldzahler
Commissioner
Department of Cultural Affairs
New York City

First is a "1 percent for the arts" bill, to be enacted at both the city and state levels, which would incorporate the arts into public architecture by mandating that at least 1 percent of the cost of governmental capital projects would be expended on works of art. Major public works can all too easily intrude upon and traumatize their surroundings. However, by including in their design such features as murals, mosaics, and sculptures, the public spaces in and around public buildings can become dramatic and humanizing elements that would highlight art in the environment and thereby enhance the daily interaction of all New Yorkers with our cultural traditions.

Second would be the creation of a comprehensive Urban Cultural Park System by the New York State Legislature. The urban cultural experience is not to be confined to interiors and museums alone. Rather, the fabric of our urban cultural heritage weaves through the City's neighborhoods such as Harlem, Little Italy, Chinatown, and Greenwich Village; it extends to its shore at Snug Harbor and the South Street Seaport; and it is elegantly draped along Fifth Avenue, Lincoln Center, and Broadway. An urban cultural park system would designate historic areas of special significance to serve as focal points for the coordination of preservation, education, recreation, and economic development activities. We are learning, hopefully not too late, that our cultural resources and their roots are scarce commodities that must be nurtured and preserved wherever they are found. An urban cultural park system would be a major step to that end.

Cedric Price
Architect
London

FIVE LAWS TO PROVIDE URBAN LUNGS RATHER THAN CIVIC TRAPS:

●No Open Urban Space should have more than one-twentieth of the area covered with anything higher than a seat unless it grows.

●No O.U.S. should dictate pedestrian movement by its layout.

●No O.U.S. should cost more initially, in capital costs including design fees, than twice its annual maintenance costs.

●No O.U.S. should be used to disguise the horrors that surround it.

NO OPEN URBAN SPACE SHOULD REMAIN THE SAME FOR MORE THAN FIVE YEARS.

Theo Crosby
Architect,
London

By the time I got to rule 13, I remembered that they are all in Camillo Sitte anyway. In our own time there are only two precepts to be added:
1. Ban all motor traffic.
2. Provide an enormous, grandiose, and preferably unnecessary monument of the highest complexity in the middle.

Richard M. Rosan
Director, City Office of Development
New York City

I would like to see a law passed requiring trees to spring full grown with well-behaved root systems, mindful of foundations, pipes, wires, and constant urban change, wherever I'd like those trees to spring; and I'd like to see a law requiring grass to be hardy enough to stand up to repeated tramplings, the weight of urban traffic; and I'd like to see a law that forbade welfare for urban open space and required it to work to support itself; and I'd like to see a law requiring the spontaneous generation of new land and new space wherever urban man might feel a momentary need for space or land (or building). But then legislative bodies are known for their humility and the courts would claim no precedent.

Laws, I fear, are not the answer. There are already too many laws. As is the case with most urban problems, what is needed is a sensitive and caring community. There must be a personal, public, and corporate desire and respect for open space; an awareness that urban open space is a luxury and as such expensive; and the realization that most American cities in 1979 are pressed with basic service delivery issues concentrating on the care of their needy more than the shearing of their shrubbery. It is unlikely that these governments, strained to supply essential services, will expand their supplies or upkeep of open space. However, more could be done for less if the citizenry extended a proper concern and respect for the upkeep of such space.

Marietta Tree
Partner, Llewelyn-Davies Associates
New York

Legislation that could turn over selected streets to pedestrian use—for regular events or holidays — could set the stage for a variety of related design and development actions by the public and private sectors and allow them to take advantage of such new temporary open space. Available on a predetermined schedule, it would supplement both existing city parks, as well as proposed permanent malls. It would expand the present open space system and could periodically connect current isolated parks with pedestrian malls and traffic-free shopping streets.

The intent of this enabling legislation would be to establish the temporary closing of selected streets on a permanent schedule of weekends or holidays. Implementation of such a plan could result in public sector actions including street landscaping and improvements or additions to existing adjacent open space: amphitheaters, open-air exhibit spaces, quiet parks, active playgrounds. It could also result in reciprocal private actions, including outdoor cafes and restaurants or building-facade revitalizations.

Established precedents for such legislation exists. What remains is to formalize a permanent schedule, which will ensure the regular and ongoing creation of such pedestrian activity malls.

Robert M. Makla
Founder, Friends of Central Park
New York

If only some of our municipal parks could be as well maintained and as intelligently enjoyed as the national parks in our country are. Is federalization the way of the future for these parks?

Short of federalization, no new law is needed—only intelligence at the top. Here are some easy and inexpensive first steps:

●Promote parks with an intelligent public relations program for their scenic and natural values.

●Upgrade current concessionaire policies.

●Staff parks with capable, well motivated personnel.

●Train all park employees to heighten their skills as gardeners, horticulturalists, and arborists.

●Develop a program for using parks as an educational resource.

S. Dillon Ripley
Secretary, Smithsonian Institution
Washington, D.C.

One of the most useful new laws that could be passed could be one that would encourage the growth of environmental educational programs using existing urban open space.

Environmental education programs can be conducted to greater or lesser degrees at most urban open spaces regardless of size or character and could utilize the total range of spaces from lawns to forests. There is an extraordinary amount to be learned from an open space as small and simple as a patch of lawn. Indeed, studies have shown lawns to be a very successful environmental teaching tool for children and adults alike.

Legislation to promote environmental education related to urban open spaces would provide increasing opportunities for urban residents to learn and enjoy their environment and would serve to create an informed public on environmental issues yet to come.

Gordon J. Davis
Commissioner
Department of Parks and Recreation
New York City

There is much talk these days of legislation enabling the federal government to take over major urban parks such as Central Park in Manhattan and Prospect Park in Brooklyn. It is an idea whose time has clearly not come. It is no more thinkable or practical than a federal takeover of the Brooklyn Bridge or the Metropolitan Museum.

The unique quality of our great parks springs precisely from the intimate and historic relationship with New York and New Yorkers. Like mirrors they reflect all that is glorious and valued in our city: its diversity and heterogeneity, its sophisticated liberty and relentless creativity, its grace and style, and perhaps above all else, its resistance and democratic openness. These qualities of urban civilization are in many ways intangible and, indeed, fragile. They are well understood by those of us who live, work, and take our leisure here. They are qualities often dimly perceived by those who do not.

It is, of course, also true that our parks reflect our city's present fiscal plight and its seemingly intractable social ills.

The answer, at least in part, is not to federalize our urban parks, but rather to federalize portions of our parks' budget.

In many ways that is precisely what Robert Moses achieved during The Depression, when great portions of the city's park system were first built or restored with federal assistance. And I believe it is possible to do so again.

John Dobkin
Director, National Academy of Design
New York City

Legislation about disposable vs. nondisposable objects, garbage, and dog litter, although not the most esoteric subjects, are nonetheless important to the basic comforts of the metropolis.

Oregon has traditionally been in the vanguard in protecting the quality of life of its inhabitants. Oregon has outlawed the disposable bottle, and other states and municipalities have followed, despite a disinclination for such legislation on the part of container companies and the unions. Such legislation would help greatly to reduce the volume of garbage and to reduce the use of natural resources in the manufacture of containers. The phenomenon of the non-returnable bottle is a recent one—dating to the early 1960s. Disposable lighters and, more recently, razors are the wasteful progeny. I believe very strongly that the trend should be reversed by legislation, imposing definite limits on the manufacturer as to what may be disposed of and what must be reused.

UP TOWN.

THE GARBAGE FLEET.

DOWN TOWN

DUMPING GROUND

W.P. Snyder. "How the streets of New York are cleaned," 1877

Kübler Collection, Cooper-Hewitt Museum Library

The collection of garbage has been a problem facing cities since their beginning. In Austria, where I spend the summer, we must separate all garbage into material that will burn, that will decompose, and that will do neither one nor the other. Items in the third category—and these are very few—are collected. The remainder are burned or buried. The control of garbage in the city presents a problem of much greater magnitude. It depends on a cooperative population and on efficient collection techniques. The population must be educated and systems of collection improved. Obviously one reinforces another.

The third item, dog litter, is an example of corrective action taken by an unwilling city government after many years of pressure. The legislation, instituted in the summer when many dogs and dog lovers were having a fling in the country, and enforced on the unsuspecting in the autumn when they returned to a relatively litter-free city, was a wise and well-choreographed measure. It has improved the quality of life in the city, a fine example of corrective legislation.

John Morris Dixon
Editor
Progressive Architecture

Our most pressing need is for legislation to protect what we've got against the tax-supported vandalism of municipal parks departments. In many years of living on Prospect Park, Brooklyn, I watched structures decay for lack of the simplest upkeep measures and I saw irreplaceable trees undermined by unchecked erosion. That could be blamed on shortages of funds and high labor costs if it weren't for the obvious expenditure of funds for destructive "improvements." Onto Olmsted's subtly differentiated landscape, the parks people would superimpose random sprinklings of saplings, distributed as if to meet some numerical quota; the broad meadows and intimate clearings of the original plan were, of course, the obvious target areas for these invasions. The result, in the long run, would be to eradicate all of the designer's intentions in a featureless smudge of greenery, beneath which the rotting bridges, benches, and pavilions would be less noticeable.

This threat is by no means limited to New York. In fact, landmarks legislation and other controls may already be operating there to discourage this official vandalism. The threat in some parks, instead of mindless tree-planting, may be the all-too-common process of turning every square yard of open space into a

graded, marked, and (presumably) drained playing field or court.

Perhaps respect for beautiful open spaces cannot be legislated. But most of the nation's public spaces need the protection of some basic master *design* plan and some review board — to save them from the well-intentioned ravages of petty bureaucrats.

Edmund N. Bacon
City Planner
Philadelphia

I would like to see a law that nobody anywhere could build or occupy a house, including mobile homes, without public sewer and water systems being available and hooked up unless the lot is ten acres or more.

This would stop the despoiling of the countryside, it would prevent the ghastly public waste of providing public sewers to septic tank subdivisions, which become sewage-logged, and it

would mean that a rational sewage and water system on a stream-valley basis would determine the direction and density of urban extension.

And it wouldn't abrogate any valid property rights.

Ivan Chermayeff
Designer
New York

With the feeling that Mies' "less is more" holds truer and truer as it is attacked by its own offspring:

• Less signs, even to the point of no signs.

• The law: no sign may be larger than that which conveys absolutely necessary information to the interested pedestrian.

With the thought that urban space is only of value when it is populated:

• The law: no building can face upon urban space that does not remain accessible to the general public a minimum of 18 hours per day.

Hans Hollein
Architect
Vienna

I would like the law defined in such a way that space planners and not traffic planners or sewage system designers determine the nature of our spaces.

Paige Rense
Editor-in-Chief and Vice President
Architectural Digest
Los Angeles

I wish there were a law requiring that the person who invented concrete pedestrian plazas (or malls) get his head examined. Walking across those expanses of hot, glaring concrete is one of the most alienating things imaginable. They have all the charm of a shopping center without

the shops, and actually are more uncomfortable on nice sunny days. The shadeless, sickly trees are particularly depressing, sticking up through the pavement. But I do feel a certain comradeship with them as fellow living things: I greet them across the plaza as though they had arrived in the land of concrete on the same space-ship with me.

RA

Everyone should have the right to enjoy sunshine. It should be against the law to build a structure that deprives anyone of sunlight.

Paul Franzeny. "Street sweepers' roll-call," 1868

The Urban Park as a Work of Art

Classical values are being rediscovered.

By Henry Hope Reed, in memory of the late Christopher Tunnard

Frederick Law Olmsted often declared that New York City's Central Park was a work of art. For him that fact was the strongest argument to prevent encroachments. This concept he owed to his associate, Calvert Vaux. From the start the latter had a clear insight on what they had undertaken by winning the competition for the design of Central Park in 1858. For Vaux it was only natural that he should look on the future park as a work of art. He had executed the small oil sketches that had accompanied the winning plans.

In the 1860s when Olmsted, for reasons of health, had abandoned New York for California, Vaux sustained his interest in the park as a work of art by defending the use of the then novel title, landscape architect. For he saw in it a noble responsibility, a sense of mission, that of building beautiful parks in the city. One immediate result was that Olmsted came back to New York, and together the two men designed Brooklyn's Prospect Park.

What followed was not only an extraordinary career for Olmsted but also the implanting of the picturesque or "natural" as the style for the urban park in America. Even today a dehydrated version of the picturesque style continues for the urban and suburban park, although the result is too often a caricature of the Olmsted-Vaux ideal.

Their ideal landscape was a mixture of meadow, single trees, clumps of trees, thickly wooded sections, still water, flowing water, cascades, and, in the case of Central Park, rock outcrops. Their word for it was "pastoral," because of the importance given to sloping and undulating lawns such as the Sheep Meadow in Central Park and the Long

Bow Bridge and The Ramble, Central Park, New York City, 1861

The Terrace, Central Park, New York City, 1864

Brewer Fountain, Boston

Bethesda Fountain, Central Park, New York City

Meadow in Prospect Park. Buildings and structures such as bridges were to be kept at a minimum, and if they had to be there they were, if possible, concealed. And in some ways the chief distinction of their parks was the insistence on variety in planting. In fact, this variety is the chief element that distinguishes the two great New York parks from the picturesque ones of London and Paris. Olmsted and Vaux underlined the concept even by prescribing plants that eventually proved nuisances. Such a one was Japanese knotweed, *Polygonum cuspidatum*, which was introduced into Central Park in the 1860s and spread from there throughout the Northeast and, no doubt, elsewhere in the country.

With the arrival of the 1890s the picturesque had a rival in the formal treatment of the landscape. Magnificent private gardens were built on classical lines, especially in the Northeast and California, on a scale never seen before

or since in this country. Outside of Boston, New York, Philadelphia, Wilmington, Chicago, Santa Barbara, and San Francisco rose terraces, fountains, orangeries, conservatories, canals, allées, and extensive flowerbeds. A few have survived and are now open to the public, such as Longwood Gardens outside Wilmington, Old Westbury Gardens

on Long Island, and, not to be overlooked, Villa Vizcaya in Miami.

If the private garden, like the house of the period, became classical — a formal style — park design remained informal. Only in Washington was there a change. I refer to the small park that once filled the Mall in front of the Smithsonian Institution's main building, "The Castle," with scattered trees and shrubs and winding paths. Andrew Jackson Downing, aided by Vaux, laid it out in 1851. With the Macmillan Plan of 1901, a reaffirmation of Major L'Enfant's plan for the city, the Downing park was wiped out to clear the vista from the Capitol to the Washington Monument.

To be sure, there were some other signs of the classical in city parks. In New York City, Bryant Park, behind the New York Public Library, was transformed by being given terraces, balustrades, trees planted on line, a fountain, and flowerbeds. In Chicago, the architect Edward Herbert Bennett created the classical Grant Park by the use of pylons, balustrades, and fountains on what had been mud flats along Lake Michigan. Martin Luther King, Jr., Park (formerly Meridian Hill Park) in Washington obtained a high terrace divided by two long flights of steps and a cascade with fountains at the base.

Nor should the Brooklyn Botanic Garden be overlooked. Its original plan in the picturesque manner was made by Olmsted Brothers but the latter firm was replaced by Harold Ap Rhys Caparn, who was to furnish formal lawns, lines of Japanese cherry trees, and terraces with pools. The result is splendid in its marriage of the formal and informal.

Scott Fountain, Detroit

Brooklyn Botanic Garden, New York

One interesting by-product of the American Renaissance was the introduction of classical structures into picturesque settings. Whereas buildings were barely seen in the Prospect Park of Olmsted and Vaux, they appeared triumphantly in the form of a Palladian tennis house and a boat house — part Pal-

ladio and part Sansovino — bringing a fresh note, being beautiful in themselves, and fitting wonderfully into the landscape. Where the devices of the informal were confined to the unbroken lawn, sloping or rising and falling, and to the plants of trees and shrubs to achieve a "natural" effect, the formal landscape called for an architectural treatment in the form of flights of steps, statues, obelisks, terraces, fountains, cascades, ornamental sculpture, and columned buildings.

In the matter of fountains as park decoration it is impossible not to mention the Scott Fountain on Belle Isle in Detroit. Set at the southwest tip of the island, in the middle of the Detroit River, it was given a pyramidal form by its designer, Cass Gilbert, to compensate for a flat site. It is made of a series of richly decorated basins, joined by cascades, which rise to a large flat bowl. Abundant sculpture takes the form of lions, lion masks, boys riding dolphins, grotesque masks, swans, horses, and reliefs. Spouts

are everywhere. Without question it is the nation's most beautiful fountain, as much a lesson in park embellishment as the Bethesda Fountain on the Terrace in Central Park or the fountain to be found on the Boston Common at the corner of Park and Tremont Streets.

When writing of urban parks it is essential to point to university campuses, especially if one wants to grasp the classical alternative. Most of them are disappointing due to an absence of plan, an absence of style or the presence of too many styles, and the absence of decoration in the form of fountains and sculpture. Strip most campuses of their trees and the visual chaos is only too apparent. Still, several show certain architectural devices that can be used to advantage in any formal park. I have in mind the campus of Columbia University in New York City. It is a model in the use of terraces, wide flights of steps, paving, ornamental lampposts, flagpoles with splendid bases, and, of course, fountains.

The Columbia University campus

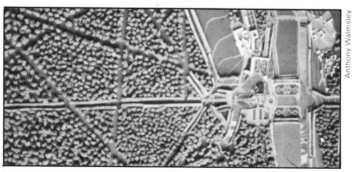

Landscape model, Chantilly, France

was purposely shaped to be an urban campus, much as Chicago's Grant Park is an urban park — as opposed to a pastoral setting such as Prospect Park, which is nature in the city. Olmsted and Vaux, finding the latter ideal not enough for the city, invented the parkway — they invented the word — to link parks with strips of greenery. The first was Ocean Parkway joining Prospect Park, and Coney Island in 1873. Very wide, lined with trees and strips of turf, it was, for them, a step beyond the Paris boulevard. When the Bronx, a part of New York, obtained its park system in the late 1880s it consisted of parks linked by parkways. The Boston Park System, created about the same time, also consists of parks and parkways. On the outskirts of Cleveland, around Minneapolis, along the Chicago lakefront, and elsewhere, similar chains of parks and parkways came into being. Today, with the parkways turned into major highways, the park aspect of these green necklaces has been forgotten.

Another change, beginning in the 1890s, was to pose some difficulty for the landscape architect — the coming of recreation equipment. Some park land, such as the Parade Ground next to Prospect Park, had been purchased for special recreational use. The 1890s saw the introduction of play equipment, first in the form of the sandbox, then swings and seesaws. In the 1900s there were permanent installations for tennis and baseball. By the 1920s such equipment, which by now included swimming pools, was to be seen in more and more parks, and the designer had to make a place for them. Whole beaches were created. One of the more spectacular improvements in New York in the 1930s

Lincoln Park, Chicago, late 19th century

was the making from scratch of Orchard Beach in Pelham Bay Park. Although this creation must be balanced against destruction of the city's parks by highways, this man-made beach remains extraordinary. Often the recreation centers and sports facilities were executed in a pleasing classical style; I have in mind especially those by Daniel H. Burnham in Chicago parks. Unfortunately a certain carelessness has appeared in more recent years and new facilities everywhere seem to be symbolized by the ubiquitous chain-link fence.

Coming to the present it is not quite so easy to find the positive accents. Until recently, there has been a wholesale rejection of our artistic heritage. In getting rid of the faults of the past, much good was thrown away, as Christopher Tunnard observed in *The City of Man*. During the past decade, however, the interest in preservation and conservation of our heritage has grown strong. Gardens such as Governor William Paca's at Annapolis have been brought back. The New York Botanical Garden restored its magnificent conservatory. Even battered Central Park has seen its handsome cast-iron Bow Bridge wholly rebuilt and restored, a cast-iron Ladies Pavilion rebuilt anew, wood shelters, wood bridges, and wood arbors rebuilt and repaired.

In listing neglected resources I begin by naming figure sculpture as part of a fountain; for is there anything more beautiful than water playing on a skillfully modeled nude? Decorated lampposts and park benches are others. In formal parks, the classical devices that are now absent from architects' and sculptors' vocabularies offer a wide selection. And, of course, there is the matter of plants and how to handle them. The use of quincunxes, such as those in front of the De Young Museum in San Francisco, and lines of clipped hedges are but two examples. Above all there is the allée, a double row of trees shading a path. In a number of New York parks rebuilt in the 1930s the allée is the one strong visual note, useful in separating the active from the passive section.

In the informal setting there is need for accepting the lessons of Olmsted and Vaux in the handling of the terrain, the sit-

ing of paths, the creation of glades, and the uses of water. Perhaps their most important lesson, a lesson of the picturesque, is variety in planting. This is certainly one of the most important traditions to be maintained, with the horticulturist on guard against having too many of one species, such as the gingko, the London plane, or the elm. In Central Park a major step forward was taken when the Arthur Ross Pinetum was begun, reintroducing 15 or so conifers that had vanished from the park several generations ago.

The most neglected device of the urban park, especially in the small park or the bit of land brought about by irregular crossings, is the flowerbed. The massing of flowers began in 18th-century classical France; the first elaborate form of flower-bedding appeared in the same country in the 1800s. The first city to give the flower prominence as part of its embellishment was classical Paris of the Second Empire. American cities were slow in discovering the use of the flower for embellishment. Honors for the first notable example must go to Boston, where the Public Garden was begun as early as 1839; it must have been the lone example for several decades. Not until the 1870s did flowerbeds slowly appear in other American cities. New York did not have them on any scale until 1882-1883. Another element of progress was the coming of the conservatory, Chicago obtaining its first municipal one in 1893. Conservatories and the massive use of flowerbeds were very much part of the classical tradition of the American Renaissance. Their presence made possible the Golden Age of Horticulture, which flourished in the public park as on the private estate to the 1930s.

By that decade something strange had taken place: the flower had disappeared from many cities. Of course, the men of the City Beautiful Movement had been replaced by the so-called "practical men." And at the same time the landscape architect turned against the use of flowers, even the use of propagating plants. In New York this attitude was to prove disastrous. Central Park lost its conservatory in 1935, Prospect Park its famous one in the 1950s.

The first sign of a reversal of this dismal trend came in the 1960s in, of all places, Washington. Mrs. Lyndon

Johnson brought flowers and flowering shrubs in quantity to the nation's capital. One spectacular result came about when Lafayette Park was placed in the care of the White House horticulturist. Anyone who has seen the park in spring with its solid blankets of red tulips bordered by blue grape hyacinth knows what can be achieved. The change was given further impetus in 1972 when S. Dillon Ripley, the Secretary of the Smithsonian Institution,

Park Avenue, New York City

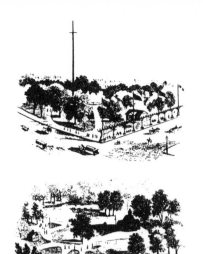

New York City Parks, 1882

founded an Office of Horticulture with a large staff for outdoor and greenhouse work. While the effort is concentrated around the Institution's museums, the best beds are near "The Castle."

Without robbing the nation's capital of the praise it deserves, we must not forget that there are cities, especially in the midwest, that never gave up the tradition as the eastern cities did. Chicago boasts the largest municipal conservatory in Garfield Park. Milwaukee's Mitchell Park shows how splendid flowerbeds stand out in a formal setting. Rochester remains the nation's lilac capital; one portion of Highland Park is covered with one of the nation's largest collections of the shrubs.

As our classical heritage, of which flowerbeds are so much a part, looms larger and larger, there is little question that the flower will return as one of the principal ornamental devices for the beautification of our cities. Now that Washington has seized the instrument it is bound to spread. The return of flowerbeds is a good sign that the future will offer a fresh concept of the urban park as a work of art.

Henry Hope Reed is Curator of Central Park, President of Classical America, and author of *The Golden City*.

The Public Park Needs Reappraisal

We have forgotten an important tradition.

By J. B. Jackson

Once cherished by citizens as a public work of art, source of wholesome pleasure, glimpse of unspoiled nature; admired as the democratic equivalent of the royal garden, the American city park, after little more than a century, has lately fallen on evil days. We no longer love it the way we did. The prosperous neighborhoods that the park did so much to foster now see its presence as a social and economic liability, and its design, its use, its very existence have all become matters of angry debate. How many crest-fallen designers there must be! And crest-fallen recreationists and social counselors and administrators, who find themselves having to reappraise their respective philosophies and come up with fresh and very different justifications for their work.

I hope they start by reexamining their ideas about the origins of the public park, retracing its genealogy. If they do they will discover they have ignored the oldest and most popular kind of play space in favor of the aristocratic garden.

The current interpretation of the history of the park is neatly expressed in the article "Park and Playground" in the *Encyclopedia Britannica* — an article incidentally written by a playground expert, and in its way a gem of misinformation. "The first parks were grants of the royal lands for the enjoyment of the people," it says, "modern parks are gifts from the people to themselves." The role of the royal park or garden was in fact briefly as follows: the first designed parks dating from the 16th century were formal and elaborate gardens, with small wooded areas, created and set aside for the delectation of the court, though on occasion open to a limited element of the public. Early royal parks or gardens were extremely formal, even architectural in

Baseball game near the East River, New York City

design, emphasizing what recreationists deprecatingly call passive enjoyment.

It was the so-called picturesque landscape park, the product of 18th and 19th century England, that inspired the design of the public park in America and Europe. The works of "landscape gardeners" Rauch and Downing and Bushnell and Olmsted were essentially modern versions of the private English country estate laid out as a "picturesque" landscape: a composition of lawns, placed bodies of water, artfully located groves of trees, a would-be natural topography affording occasional glimpses of the wider environment. We know that, of course; but we sometimes forget that this particular kind of park was designed to provide contact with nature, that it was expensive to lay out and maintain, that it too produced "passive enjoyment," and that as a work of art it had to be treated with respectful care; correct behavior was essential.

In other words, the landscaped park, despite its apparent informality, called for a public that was aware of the esthetic features of the design, was in search of a contact with nature, and was socially disciplined. When Olmsted and his contemporaries both here and abroad produced the first large city parks they naturally planned in terms of those restraints. The picturesque natural beauty of the composition was emphasized, the rural, almost pastoral character carefully maintained, and a code of public demeanor strictly enforced — as indeed it still is in many European city parks.

Contemporary critics of Olmsted like to attack his social philosophy. New York City's prolific planner and builder Robert Moses, for instance, refers to him as "an aristocratic Versailles estate landscaper, a notorious WASP in his social sympathies." It is a pointless accusation. Central Park from its first years was used by all classes. Early observers noted with pleased surprise that numbers of working class citizens — "the poor seamstress and journeyman" — were there, along with the rich and powerful.

Why were they surprised? Not because they thought that the poor were out of place in Central Park — though that is what the class-conscious park reformer would like to think — but because they believed, with some justification, that there were other places for recreation that the poor might well prefer.

And in fact there were. Mid 19th century New York City still contained areas offering a much livelier, a much less formal kind of entertainment, and a much less structured environment. Staten Island was a popular resort, and so were the Elysian Fields in Hoboken, New Jersey; and there were other locations, untouched by the garden architect, along the beaches and waterfronts and in the unbuilt-up areas in Manhattan. When the 19th century park enthusiast praised the upper class aspect of the city park he did so precisely because he assumed the existence and availability of other kinds of recreation.

Two Types of Park Land

That is to say, he was aware of something that the contemporary park expert and recreationist has conveniently forgotten: that well into the 19th century every community, large or small, in Europe as well as America, retained sizable areas of land where the common people, and particularly adolescents, could exercise and play and enjoy themselves, and at the same time participate in community life.

The existence of these playgrounds is vouched for by history as well as by tradition. Folklorists find evidence in village after village that a portion of the churchyard and the site of any pre-Christian shrine or temple were commonly identified with youthful sport and games. Some historians suggest that the association between games and places having a traditional sacred character derives from a remote period when the young men of the village were assigned to guard those sites and fight off neighboring invaders. By the Middle Ages the convention was well established: certain spots, usually near the church, were informally set aside for sports and games. But that is not all: these sports and games, deriving as they did from armed conflict with outsiders, retained a violent, competitive nature, were based on notions of territoriality and community status, and were little concerned with the design of the terrain in question or with "a contact with nature." The games were rough and undisciplined, constantly denounced by the Church and the Crown, but quite evidently very popular among adolescents as a way of "de-fending" the community, letting off steam, and achieving personal renown.

Nor were such areas and such sports confined to the village. Every medieval town possessed stretches of land outside the walls, often along the banks of a river where young or active townspeople could enjoy themselves — what the French call *terrains vagues* — pieces of land not cultivated or built upon. Francis I set aside a stretch of the river bank in Paris for the recreation of university students. And in 1222, so we read, the young citizens of London "kept games of defense and wrestling near unto the Hospital of St. Giles in the Field, where they challenged and had the mastery of men in the suburbs and other commoners."

New Englanders, despite the disapproval of the Puritan clergy, hunted, fished, played football on the beach, competed in violent sports with neighboring villages and even frolicked on the common. As for the Southern passion for nonestablishment competitive sports, either in the backyard of taverns or along the road in the open country, there is ample historical evidence of its existence.

The advent of the park movement in the second half of the 19th century produced innumerable "designed" parks in towns and cities throughout the United States, but the popularity of the "un-structured" playground and of unstructured competitive sports persisted. Baseball in its less formal guise, football as a kind of mass confrontation, rodeos, mock war games took place not in the town park but in the so-called grove outside. The landscape architect F. A. Waugh wrote an attractive description in 1889 of the contrast between the formal, overstructured small town park, deserted and forlorn, and the much used grove out in the country near the river.

A Forgotten Tradition

Why have we so completely forgotten this once popular and lively tradition? Why have our parks ignored this important social function: the integration of the young into the life of the community? For one thing, the grove (as the American equivalent to the *terrain vague*) has vanished from the American scene. The expansion of towns and cities has obliterated it and covered it with houses and streets, and tastes in recreation have radically changed. But current philosophies of recreation and park design are also to blame. The persistence of the belief that what the public wants (or ought to have) is "contact with nature" in a professionally designed park, that recreation is at all costs to be "creative," has meant the excommunication of ad hoc playgrounds for adolescents and the public disapproval of any display of physical violence or competitiveness: twin nightmares that haunt the liberal social reformer.

And in the meantime the older city parks have become the victims of reduced budgets, deteriorated neighborhoods, persistent vandalism. They are misused by undesirable and even dangerous elements, and as a consequence less and less used by those who need them. The value of parks is potentially as great as ever. The formal, structured park or garden, the park as work of art for passive enjoyment is essential as an urban amenity — particularly in the downtown, working area. The less elaborate, more "natural" neighborhood park has a valuable role to play in the lives of those who need contact with nature, and in the lives of older people and children.

A. Doolittle. "A view of the buildings of Yale College at New Haven," 1807

A Third Type of Park Land

But is it not time that we acknowledge the need for a third variety: the ample, unstructured, unbeautified, multi-purpose public playground where adolescents can assert themselves and become social beings, defending and serving some youthful concept of the community?

The question is by no means idle; there are in fact signs, still inconspicuous, that we are beginning to try to answer it. Many Western cities, plagued by the misbehavior of a restless and mobile younger generation, are creating sports parks. Parks, that is to say, which are designed for sports of mobility: bicycling, skateboarding, motorcycling, all-terrain vehicles, and even in some cases for skiing and hang-gliding.

They are expensive, unsightly, and still in the experimental stage. Anything more unlike the conventional park would be hard to imagine: noisy, deliberately artificial in man-made topography, used by a boisterous and undisciplined public and dedicated to the violent expenditure of energy and to hitherto unheard of contacts with nature, the sports park seems to repudiate and make a mockery of everything the word "park" has stood for. On the other hand, who knows? It may eventually mature and give the word a wider and more contemporary meaning: the park as a public open-air space where we can acquire self awareness as members of society, and awareness of our private relationship to the natural environment.

J. B. Jackson is a former teacher of landscape history, writer, and editor.

C.D. Weldon. "The Ladies' Lawn Tennis Tournament, Staten Island Cricket Club Grounds," 1883

Urban Recreation

The possibilities never stop.

By John A. Dreyfuss

Big cities are huge playgrounds. Their games are as bland as senior-citizen shuffleboard, as wild as suicidal skateboarding, as sophisticated as chess. But because it is so often taken for granted or noticed by only small segments of the population, the extent of outdoor metropolitan recreation is almost unknown. Yet it is great. And it is growing.

Recreation in urban space is flourishing with the expanding needs and desires of Americans to participate in play for fun and fitness. If you look—no matter where you look—there is recreation in big cities. Show the city child a gutter full of water and you show that child a wild river. Flotillas of flotsam — sticks, paper scraps, old bottles, cigarette butts — become vessels to instant adventure, launched to sink or sail into the cavernous depths beneath the nearest street corner. Sidewalks are fields for play: jumprope, simple as one-two-three, arcane as double Dutch; hopscotch, jacks, marbles. Small fortunes are won and lost and fought over as penny-pitching children measure to the millimeter before admitting that their friend's coin lies closest to the wall.

Stoopball addicts hone their skills, mastering the perfect aim that bounces the Spaulding off the front step and clear across the street for a home run. As soon as the snow melts from eastern city streets, a logical place to find the handle of the family broom is in the young stickball batter's grip as he or she takes a Babe Ruth swat at the ball, striving to get a teammate from a fire hydrant first base around the manhole cover that is second, past third base that looks like a '55 Chevy, and home to the pie plate.

Sometimes a kid needs a change of scenery, since city streets can get monotonous, not to mention danger-ous. Then it's time to adjourn to the rooftops where, to the apoplectic fury of building managers and the consternation of parents, a game of tag takes on new dimensions. While some kids enjoy risking their knees and elbows—and the lives of passing pedestrians — on skateboards.

Southern California surfers originated skateboarding in the early 60s to avoid the doldrums on days when the ocean was flat. The sport advanced from city sidewalks to empty swimming pools to skateboard parks. The parks, which number some 150 from Long Island to Los Angeles, are surrealistic works of concrete art in which young athletes defeat gravity by rolling up the sides of huge bowls and along the walls of immense pipes. They zig-zag through snake runs and tear at 30 miles per hour down slalom courses. And they pay for the privilege: usually $1 to $5 park membership fees plus about $3 for every two hours of rolling around on wood or fiberglass boards that can set them back as much as $150 for a stock model. Price tags on custom boards can soar to more than $400. But the average skateboard—the ones you're likely to dodge on city sidewalks — cost between $30 and $80.

And there are lots of them to dodge. "At skateboarding's peak, a little over a year ago," said Dave Dash, publisher of a slick monthly magazine called *Skateboarder*, "we estimated there were 20 million skateboarders. It's mellowing out now, down to perhaps 15 million."

Hard on the wheels of skateboarders are aficionados of the born-again sport of rollerskating. Gone are the metal clip-on skates, displaced by $80-a-pair shoe skates with polyurethane wheels on precision bearings. It's those wheels that have put rollerskating back on the streets.

Unlike their metal ancestors, the polyurethane wheels give a soft ride, reliable traction, and a lot of maneuverability and speed. So far, California is the focal point of urban outdoor rollerskating. Kids skate to school, bank tellers skate to work, weekend skaters glide along almost any smooth city surface. Skate rental concessions boom in Venice, a Los Angeles beach community where, on a sunny weekend, as many as 5,000 devotees pay $1.50 an hour to walk on wheels.

"Every kind of person skates," said Jeff Rosenberg, president of Cheapskates, Inc., Venice's three-year-old (and therefore oldest) rollerskating concession. "The average age is 28," Rosenberg said, "but we've rented skates to a kid two years old (we stuffed paper in her shoes) and to a man 86 years young. I know of skaters who skate for every reason under the sun: fun, transportation, exercise, because it's the thing to do, even to save energy," Rosenberg said.

On the perimeter of San Francisco's Golden Gate park, concessionaires in vans rent skates to weekend wheelers taking advantage of the city's decision to close part of the park's main thoroughfare to automobiles so skaters and bikers can roll. Rollerskating is eastward bound. The skate concession that started business in May 1978 in New York's Central Park (which is closed to motor vehicles during daylight hours on weekends and holidays) rents up to 800 pairs of skates on a busy weekend.

Rollerskating suffers from the snow. Not so its cousin sport, ice skating, a popular urban outdoor pastime anywhere the temperature slips below freezing. More than 100,000 skaters glide over Rockefeller Center's outdoor rink in New York every winter. The city's parks department manages five open air rinks.

In Chicago, workers in Lincoln Park set up warming huts for skaters on frozen ponds. In some Chicago parks, snow banks are piled around baseball diamonds that are then flooded for skaters. In the middle of Denver, skaters dot City Park Lake every winter, and Washington D.C.'s Federal Home Loan Bank Board Building has an ice-skating concession in its courtyard—a situation that has raised eyebrows and a few voices questioning the propriety of using federal land for free enterprise.

Where there's ice, there's snow, and

Chess game in Central Park, New York City

cross country skiers come out with the snow in eastern city parks. Some of them ski to work when snow removal equipment fails to keep pace with the storms.

Devotees of what has to be one of America's fastest growing and most popular participation sports consider ice and snow their enemies. But, like the Greek historian Herodotus (and, in turn, the U.S. Postal Service, which adapted his words to inscribe on its main post office in New York), they won't be stopped by "snow, nor rain, nor heat, nor gloom of night" — nor sore knees, nor almost anything else. They are the ubiquitous joggers.

No matter the city, joggers brighten the landscape with vividly colored nylon shoes and all manner of running togs as they keep or get fit — both mentally and physically, they will tell you — by running. More than 270 marathons (26 miles, 385 yards each) are scheduled this year in the United States. The number of 10-kilometer (6.2 mile) runs is many times that figure. In 1978 a New York City marathon drew some 11,000 entrants. A "Bay to Breakers Run" of nearly 8 miles drew a like number of enthusiasts in San Francisco.

The popularity of running defies accurate estimation. An often heard figure puts the American jogger population at about 25 million. Whatever the number of joggers may be, probably about three-fourths of them practice their sport in big city streets and parks. Even corporations are getting into the running act. In 1978 *Runner's World* magazine published an ad designed to test corporate interest in running, and received responses from more than 950 companies. Those responses led to a pilot program that has already developed into a nationwide series of runs to be capped by a sort of World's Series of Corporate Running.

"In our pilot program we had 43 different corporate teams, with entrants ranging from vice presidents to file clerks," said Dave Borden, who coordinates the Corporate Cup Association for *Runner's World*. In 1979 we have races in Atlanta, Chicago, Dallas, Kansas City, Los Angeles, New York City, and San Francisco. The top ten corporate teams in

those races will compete in San Francisco," Borden said.

No matter how we play, as Americans become more health oriented, we become more sports oriented. And, regardless of our penchant for health, as our leisure time increases, so does our recreational use of outdoor urban space. The scope of that use is boundless. Under big city skies, one can throw a frisbee (luminous models for night players), ride a ferryboat, serve a tennis ball, drive a golf ball, or hit a handball.

Checkers, chess, pinochle — and other board and card games — are favored by senior citizens in parks across the nation. The next Kareem Abdul-Jabbar is bouncing a basketball on some driveway or playground. Lawn bowlers and boccie ball lovers are rolling spheres across the ground in almost every big city. Bicycle paths wind through parks, bike lanes appear on streets, and in some cities velodromes provide steeply banked race courses required for the fastest outdoor bicycle track racing.

For the less athletic, there is the grand old urban pastime called strutting. It requires putting on one's Sunday best to strut along such thoroughfares as New York's Fifth Avenue on Easter Sunday or

Skateboard bowl, Marina Del Rey State Park, California

Skateboarder magazine

Bevery Hills' Rodeo Drive almost any day. Strutting, which has the advantage of being simultaneously a spectator and participant sport, has an age-old variation called walking. A stroll through Chinatown or SoHo, to an art gallery, in a park, or even around one's own seldom seen neighborhood offers ready recreation for city dwellers.

Children these days don uniforms for a wide range of popular sports like soccer, baseball, and football, or more esoteric endeavors such as rugby, lacrosse, and field hockey. In city parks one can pitch a horseshoe, go fly a kite, eat at a

A day in spring, Sacramento, California

Richard Gilmore, courtesy The Sacramento Bee

picnic, or try to catch a fish, sail a model boat, or row a real one, check in at the band shell to see what's playing. The possibilities never stop.

There are, of course, government studies that say metropolitan areas could use more recreational space. And they are right — more places to play in our cities would be good. But until those places exist, we're doing a lot with what we have.

***

John A. Dreyfuss is the Architecture and Design Critic for the *Los Angeles Times*.

After Winslow Homer. "Skating at Boston," 1859, wood engraving

Cooper-Hewitt Museum

New York City

Fred R. Conrad, courtesy The New York Times

Chess game in Old Town of Berne, Switzerland

Lacrosse game, late 19th century

Adventure Playground, Central Park, New York City

Playground

Notting Hill Adventure Playground, London

Places for Play

The entire city should be seen as a playground.

By Stanley Abercrombie

Play isn't what it used to be. Or, at least, not what we used to think it was. The activities in Pieter Breughel the Elder's 1560 painting of "Children Playing" may still be recognizable today, but our understanding of those activities has changed radically. Once viewed as a time killer or, at best, an energy sponge —a necessary outlet for inconveniently active young metabolisms — play has come to be seen as something both positive and essential.

The first planned playgrounds in America were built in the Boston suburb of Brookline about 1862, according to D. K. Runyon's history of American recreation; their planners were moralists who conceived them as diversions from crime and sin. Jacob Riis in New York and Jane Addams in Chicago, with similar motives, established playgrounds soon after, and by the end of the century there were such facilities in ten American cities.

The current view of play values it as more than a diversion. It is a basic testing ground of human experience, we now see; without it, mature acceptance of the nature of life may be impossible. Jean Piaget and his followers have elaborated eloquently on play as education, and Jacob Bronowski, in his essay "The Imaginative Mind in Science," suggested that "Human beings owe much of their headlong progress in evolution to the fact that they carry out this experimental activity for a much longer time than other animals."

These changes in our attitudes have brought physical changes in our playgrounds, and, despite our having come to take play so seriously, we seem to be providing for play that is more fun than ever. Playgrounds of many types are currently in use, but they can be roughly divided into general categories: the conventional one , the adventure playground, the designer playground, and the non-playground. Mobile recreation vans and interim community playlots are more recent possibilities.

The conventional playground, where most of us played when we were young, is perhaps, the one most in disfavor now. Some of us still have knee scars to remind us of it, for the conventional playground was inevitably paved with some surface more appropriate for aircraft landings than for play. Its equipment — the inevitable swing, the inevitable see-saw, the inevitable slide— was unchanging from site to site and from decade to decade. It was a utilitarian facility, untouched by grace.

Another type, sometimes called the adventure playground, emphasizes variety of use to such an extent that its form is irrelevant to the control of any designer; it is shaped by the children who use it. Such playgrounds seem to have first been proposed in 1932 by C. T. Sorensen, a Danish landscape architect. It was not until 1943, however, in the Copenhagen suburb of Emdrup, that he and architect Dan Fink actually built such a playground. Lady Allen of Hurtwood visited Emdrup soon after and took its ideas back to England, where she became an important advocate of the adventure playground. Rich with junk — cast-off construction lumber, old tires, bricks, ropes, and barrels — and with hammers, nails, and other tools for joining it into new constructions — the adventure playground is to date the most thorough response to our understanding that play thrives on variability. Children benefit most, it seems, from play materials that don't just stand there, but that can be pushed, shoved, molded, tested, formed, and re-formed.

The concepts first expressed in Denmark have spread from England to many other countries. One adventure playground built in Espoo, Finland, in 1971 has a special twist that emphasizes the type's ad hoc character: because of the severe Finnish winter, the playground is open only during the summer, and each season's end is celebrated with a great bonfire that consumes the year's construction.

After World War II, playgrounds began to receive more attention from designers. In one early example — the playgrounds of the 1947 James Weldon Johnson Houses in New York—the conventional equipment was replaced by concrete slabs, mazes, tubes, and platforms. Now, a whole new vocabulary of equipment, generally built of humble materials freshly used, has been developed in the designs of Paul Friedberg, Richard Dattner, and others. New synthetic materials are used, as well, in the tensile grids designed by Berlin architect Conrad Roland. Even sound plays a new part: music-making play environments have been conceived by designers.

Such new equipment is often arranged in new configurations to encourage a variety of different uses. Rather than playing on the swing now, then on the slide, the child is presented with a group of poles near a cobblestone mound and overhung by a grid of steel bars; thus he is invited to invent new types of play incorporating several dif-

Baseball game

Playground, Harlem, New York City

Spain

Playground, Gas Works Park, Seattle, Washington

Brooklyn, New York

ferent landscape features.

Artists are involved, too. In architect Richard Stein's play area on New York's West 90th Street, children can ride sculptor Constantino Nivola horses beneath a Nivola mural. In Atlanta's Piedmont Park they can play among and within the forms of sculptor Isamu Noguchi. And in sculptures proposed by Niki de Saint-Phalle they will slide down huge red tongues projecting from big gaudy faces.

Just as well-designed flatware will not bring better meals nor "designer sheets" bring sweeter dreams, so these new playground designs will not necessarily enrich play. Looking better is not being better. But looking better is in itself something of a virtue, and an attractive, imaginative environment, function

aside, has some value of its own for our children. And at their best the new playgrounds have more than merely a new look; they offer a new variety of activity.

Still another category of playground results from the philosophy that play needs space but not *a* space. It can occur very well on a city street if the street is simply closed to traffic. No special equipment is really needed, and the

street to be closed can vary from year to year or even day to day. This is obviously the least structured playground of all, and it may hold the most promise for giving our children what they need where they need it (close to home).

For any category of playground, a few general observations can be made. First, whether it results from the hackneyed equipment of the conven-

Chalk games

Sailboat Pond, Central Park, New York City

tional playground, the provision of junk, the fixed inventions of the designer, or the accidental occurrences of the street, it is variability that is vital to the best play. The "messy vitality," the ambiguity, the complexity and contradiction in architecture that Robert Venturi began calling for in 1966 may be needed even more by our children than by the rest of us.

Next, playgrounds in the city often need to go directly against the grain of their contexts, for cities are not built for children. Grady Clay, Editor of *Landscape Architecture,* has reasonably warned that "children know best" about their own places. "The continuing, rigid, domineering mastery of children's environments by adults," he says "is socially destructive." But clearly some adult advocacy and interference is necessary, children having notoriously little financial or political clout. (As Fran Lebowitz puts it in *Metropolitan Life,* "Children are seldom able to lend one a truly interest-

ing sum of money.")

Designing for children is further complicated by the fact that it is so rarely a pure and single-minded activity. It is often necessarily combined with parallel requirements: designing spaces to be shared by children of different age groups and by old people; making the space safe for both; making it durable in all weather conditions; yet making it tolerant to abuse from children; and, above all today, having to meet the approval of a community that may not have any deep understanding of the functional requirements. Furthermore, all playgrounds must accommodate our new efforts to include the handicapped.

Another complicating trait of small children is that they seldom travel far from their homes. In 1943, the National Recreation Association suggested that play areas be so located that children would have to go no more than half a mile to reach one. Any standards proposed today would demand a much

more frequent distribution of play areas. And reinforcing the wisdom of a great number of small playgrounds distributed throughout our cities, rather than a small number of large ones, is the relative unpleasantness (and, according to several studies, unpopularity) of large play facilities. Play, it seems, flourishes when it is a bit private, a bit special, a bit mysterious; institutionalized, it withers.

Finally, playground design will continue to change. Paul Friedberg, himself responsible for many recent changes in playground design, imagines what may be next: "As we turn from a work ethic to a leisure ethic, the localized playground becomes an anachronism," he says. "Our whole world will become our playground." And so it may be: our call for more and smaller playgrounds may refine itself into a call for an urban pattern accommodating the essential human activity of play without specific physical containment. This much seems certain: with or without specific playgrounds,

Drawing by Chas. Addams;
© 1974 The New Yorker Magazine, Inc.

with or without special equipment, play in our cities is more highly valued than ever before.

***

Stanley Abercrombie is a New York-based architect and Editor of the American supplement to the Italian design magazine, *Abitare.*

Mobility in Programming

Portable recreation vans produce spatial versatility.

By Catherine Hannah Behrend

Stevenage Adventure Playground
in the outskirts of London

Playground, Central Park, New York City

Open space in the urban environment is a rare and precious commodity—a valued amenity existing in every community—that is to be preserved, respected, and celebrated. Mobile recreation in the streets, parks, and plazas of our cities is a successful means of using that open space without destroying or inhibiting it. The idea is to take limited resources of staff and equipment, put them on a vehicle, and take recreation services to the people.

This kind of recreation programming is flexible and adaptable. Vehicles with different program contents can be scheduled night or day, for long or short periods, on a continuous or discontinuous basis, for old or young participants or both, for 50 or 500. Timing and the potential disruption of open space are two important considerations. But the portability of the vehicle, the equipment, and the program itself ensures that decisions about open space can be temporary and ever-changing.

The arrival and performance of a unit is an immediate and visible event. It is not a promise of something in the future. It is a happening now. People enjoy a variety of experiences right at their doorsteps or in the space they most revere. Mobility is virtually limitless. The personality and complexity of any mobile activity is determined by the space and by the community's interests.

Mobile recreation began when streets and piazzas provided stages for commerce, intrigues, and entertainment. It continued in carnivals and state fairs. Later, mobile cultural facilities were pioneered at least as early as the Virginia Museum's art units in the mid 1950s. Then mobile recreation units, as we know them, were pioneered by Dr. William Ridinger and Robert Wormser at Southern Illinois University in 1965. Their concept of a Cavalcade of Fun at State fairs led to the further development of units and to the Mobile Recreation Research Lab at Southern Connecticut State College, where analytical studies of the interaction of people and vans are conducted. Fran Wallach, who created and directed the first public recreation program in Nassau County, New York, reports in her recent research that there are about 350 mobile vans operating in this country. England and Israel have also adopted the concept.

New York City, however, remains the owner of the largest and most diversified mobile fleet. The city started its program in 1971. With the shrinking capital dollar and the improbability and often undesirability of building permanent structures in open space, it was resolved that the Parks, Recreation, and Cultural Affairs Administration would undertake this program. The reasoning, theories, and justification behind the program continue to be valid.

A mobile event in an urban open space can be a wonderful pivot for community unity and community involvement. Mobile units can be programmed in partnership with the many community and institutional organizations. The scheduling and implementation of programs necessitates community responsibility. The event can draw attention and awareness to the space and be a stimulant to significant recreation planning. With the increase of block associations in New York has come an enthusiasm and a need for fund-raising block parties. Mobile units have been eagerly sought as excellent additions and highlights to such events.

Many communities have designed health units, crime prevention vans, and bookmobiles. Memphis has a Naturemobile. Nassau County has a Fashionmobile. Newark has a Bikemobile. There are even plans in the works for a federally sponsored Energy Mobile. And New York City's Council on the Environment has a Grow Truck, which promotes botanical and greening information. And there is the ever-popular and nationally recognized Jazzmobile directed by Billy Taylor.

Several different types of units are programmed by New York City; they include:

■ The Arts and Crafts vehicle brings crafts projects and artistic experiences to community sites along with an arts specialist who supervises and instructs those present. Some of the projects are ceramics, banners, wood-scrap sculpture, collage, tie-dying, and mask-making. A water tank is built into the vehicle.

■ The Boxingmobile has a portable boxing ring with dressing room, ropes, mats, gloves, head gear, gong, stools, and timer. Staffed by a boxing specialist with first-aid knowledge, amateur bouts and martial arts demonstrations can be presented. Dance performances can also be accommodated.

■ The Cinemobile, equipped with a rearview screen and a film projector, brings a selection of feature films into neighborhoods.

■ Some of the most popular units are the Puppet and Marionette vehicles, which feature original productions. The Playmobile unit, a portable playground on wheels equipped with sliding poles, climbing apparatus, walkways, rocking horses, and basketball rings, is most appropriate for children in areas with no playgrounds. Portable performing stages called Showwagons are often the first types of units purchased by communities. With these units a wide variety of entertainment can be booked, including orchestra and opera performances when the larger stages are available.

■ The Sportsmobile transports a trampoline, tumbling mats, volleyballs, badminton, soccer, barbells, shuffleboard, golf, chess, checkers, and ping-pong onto a street and turns it into an instant recreation area. The popularity of the Sportsmobile led to the development of a Tennismobile. A tennis court with backnets, center net, racquets, and balls is constructed on the street.

■ The Skatemobile can come to any level space and, within minutes, provide a roller-skating rink. For pairs of shoe skates, lyrical music, and street cones, a person trades in his own shoes and begins to learn and enjoy a new recreation skill.

■ The unique Zoomobile is basically a mobile menagerie. The animals, visiting from local zoos and petshops, are brought to many urban spaces. Highly trained staff are informed educators, ready to answer numerous questions about the animals' origins and habitats. The range of animals might be as inclusive as: monkeys, cows, piglets, lambs, goats, snakes, ducks, chickens, parrots, birds, and rabbits.

■ The Swimmobile, a great relief on hot summer days, is a swimming pool on wheels. It is filled from the local fire hydrant. The unit has a filtering system, a heating unit, and a deck on which lifeguards can keep a watchful eye. One community built a Swimmobile in the shape of a large blue whale.

Mobile recreation is an imaginative endeavor. Programs can aid in the revitalization of an open space or help maintain the vibrancy of an area. The choice to go mobile can offer a community flexibility, cost-effectiveness, energy conservation, creative design, visibility, interim programming, and community organization. Let us celebrate recreation at our doorsteps and join in the fun and excitement of mobile recreation.

Besides the use of units at small events, many cities have included them at city-wide street festivals. Boston's Summerthing and Philadelphia's Super-Sunday are prime examples. With city-wide events, entire avenues are

Skatemobile, New York City

Boxingmobile, New York City, Mayor John Lindsay, referee

closed to traffic; portable stages and mobile vans are placed at various points along the avenue. Usually these festivals offer cultural performances by local ethnic communities. The relationship between cultural programming in urban spaces and commercial development has been officially recognized by the federal government. The Department of Commerce has a special assistant to the Secretary who promotes and fosters this interaction.

Catherine Hannah Behrend is Agency Coordinator for Decentralization of the New York City Department of Parks and Recreation. She was the Director of Mobile Units from 1972-1978.

The Search for New Spaces

At what new location can we accommodate which activity?

By C. Ray Smith

Nowhere today is innovative vision more needed than in the creation of urban open spaces. For it is axiomatic that in our cities there are no virgin forests. Even the great 19th century urban preserves had to be reclaimed, created leaf by leaf and stone by stone. The same situation obtains today at every scale and size of open space — from the great park and small playground to the even smaller plaza and garden area. There is no urban land left, we say traditionally.

All that is a myth, says a 1970s study of 106 of the nation's largest cities: "20 percent of all urban land is undeveloped and uncommitted." This is a staggering statement. We have 20 percent more open urban space than we use. Our quest is soon ended. But where is that 20 percent? Why don't we use it? Basically, we do not see it, so we need vision, as well as initiative, in creating urban open space.

The majority of our newly invented urban spaces, according to most specialists in the field, will have a new emphasis on combining locations with how they are used. In the main, new urban open spaces will be new combinations of uses and places, that is, new uses for traditional locations or new places for traditional uses. Sometimes multiple uses will be the emphasis.

Actually, uses or activities are fairly constant. Our open-air urban activities have always included: recreation or exercise, plant care or gardening, animal sports or enjoyment, assemblies and parades, amusement rides and games, resting and watching, eating and drinking, selling and buying, and arts shows and the performing arts. But although these activities have long been traditional, the distinctions between them and the places where we practice them are commonly confused. A park, for example, is not a

place but a use or activity — it is not a where but a how—it is nature-enjoyment of landscape. We could put it anywhere —except where climatic conditions make it impossible.

Some of today's innovative parks are reclaimed and recycled, or composed of excavated materials. The parkland created for the New Jersey Meadows recreation complex, some of it from dumped building materials, is a clear example. And in the Stockholm suburbs, the park called Högdal's Hill is a 55-acre site made of stone and earth excavated for nearby housing towers. In these cases, how the parks are constructed makes them innovative.

Our ideas of parks, essentially, are visions of bringing the country to the city, but one variation is the sculpture park—a combination of landscaped nature and outdoor exhibition hall. Traditionally these have been in open land, as at Frogner Park in Oslo, which features the sculptures of Gustav Vigeland, or at the Sculpture Park in Paris of 1969, designed

Richard Haas. Mural, Boston Architectural Center

Piazza d'Italia, New Orleans

by Jacques Sgard. The Art Park at Glen Echo, Maryland, and Art Park in Atlanta, Georgia, are extensions of this idea.

In smaller urban parks, also—plazas, squares and greens — our visions have traditionally combined the outdoors and art. And in playgrounds, too, combinations of art and recreation are now commonplace—from Hong Kong to Paris.

All these are traditional solutions or decisions about how to use a site. What intrigues us more today is where to find the land in the first place. Where we plan to accommodate activities remains the primary focus—always with the proscription that they be no more than one hour's driving time from urban dwellers' houses. The resulting choices are producing some surprisingly inventive new combinations—adaptive reuses of what we already have.

Among those receiving newest attention are the streets themselves, which

account for 25 to 30 percent of our urban space. Long before the oil crisis, our streets were being reclaimed from the 60-year tyranny of the automobile. The "thoroughfare as park" was the inherent battlecry of urban malls from Kalamazoo to Allentown. The way had been hinted at by the great highways of the 1930s — those Parkways-as-Arboretums such as the Henry Hutchinson in New York and the Merritt in Connecticut. That inventive futurist Arthur C. Clarke has written that, after the loss of our energy supplies, our interstate highways will become our most treasured parkland resource. Streets in town could have the same future.

The New York City Planning Commission's Urban Design Group, which has worked to make our streets more lively with refined sidewalk and plaza regulations, has reclaimed and revitalized Little Italy's Mulberry Street and Brooklyn's Newkirk Plaza as open spaces. Closed off from traffic on summer weekends as a pedestrian mall, Mulberry Street has been spruced up with new signs, street graphics, and banners; with citizen-sponsored planting boxes on sidewalks and window sills; with new street furniture for sitting and shelter; and with occasional festivals—in addition to the traditional San Gennaro week. In recognition of this new vitality, merchants opened some two dozen new restaurants—many with sidewalk cafes— within the first two years of the program.

Related to streets by way of the automobile are the potential parks that Robert Zion brilliantly foresaw in the early 1960s: He urged that by doing away with cars we could do away with parking lots and thereby immediately gain a new vest-pocket park system in the midst of our cities — "the Kinney Park(ing) System," he suggested.

But it is the other places in our cities, those hitherto neglected open spaces that can be combined with new activities — new combinations of the traditional outdoor activities with untraditional new locations—that will make the most exciting innovative spaces today.

Rooftops

The untapped urban preserve continues to be rooftops. Built for protection against the elements and symbolizing the very essence of shelter, our rooftops in general were not considered as another activity level until airplanes gave us a new liberated vision of them. Modest buildings raise up a new level of urban open space to light and air — those basic concerns of all urban planning legislation. We can find ways to make that light and vista available to a wider public on our rooftops. They provide an instant trip into the wide open spaces and could give the freshness and liberated feeling of getting away to the country on the weekend.

Rooftops have, for years, been explored for gardens, and on the roofs of municipal gymnasiums built in the 1920s and 1930s recreation cages are still to be seen. More recently, numerous tennis courts (though usually not open air ones) have mushroomed on our urban roofs. But nowhere have we exploited the potential of these open spaces to the degree that the Japanese have with their game courts.

City Edges

Another large block of neglected urban space is what Bill N. Lacy called "city edges" when he was director of the architecture and environmental design program at the National Endowment for the Arts. Of the 20 percent of undeveloped and uncommitted urban land, a large part is in such city edges—along our waterfronts, canalbanks and streams, reservoirs and flood dikes, levees, jetties, and breakwaters. As shipping has diminished in our harbors, areas are gradually being made accessible to replace the docks and pilings. Nothing like the steps leading down to the waters of 18th century Venice is commonly available to urbanites today. Yet the space is

there — along our piers and lakes, in marshes and wetlands, and on other city edges.

Most of these spaces have been used for traditional parks, but we can innovatively reclaim such lands for other purposes. The national urban parks program has made a substantial beginning in utilizing urban waterfront lands.

A U.S. Department of the Interior study has revealed that "there are almost a million acres of prime, largely undeveloped potential recreation land on islands near America's metropolitan areas." Other uses are also possible, as the Ellis Island immigration center commemoration scheme suggests, and as countless proposals for Alcatraz have also indicated. But certainly, making new suburbs out of them, as at Roosevelt Island in New York, is no way to make urban islands available as innovative open space.

At a narrower gauge, the urban trail movement has stretched out to include the 28-mile long trail near Pasadena, California; the East Bay Skyline Trail administered by the Park District of Oakland; and some of the New York-New Jersey Trail Conference's trails and shelters, which begin in or pass through urban waterfront areas. Chicago's Open Lands Project administers a 95-mile stretch along the Illinois-Michigan Canal. The Chesapeake & Ohio Canal National Historic Park is a waterfront open space along a narrow canal 184.5 miles long.

And in New York City the use of our waterfronts may gain impetus from two small private commercial enterprises — both barge-located facilities beneath the Brooklyn Bridge—the Rivercafe Restaurant with its spectacular vista of the Manhattan skyline and the adjacent chamber music and jazz performances of Barge Music Ltd. The South Street Seaport Museum is another New York waterfront activity of exemplary stature. In addition a major new revitalization program has been announced.

Industrial and Military Sites

Other combinations will consider abandoned railroad lines and streetcar rights-of-way, utility rights-of-way such as natural gas lines and power lines, and

Asphalt Green's Environmental Studies Center (on pier at 90th Street, East River)

easements for underground cables. The Illinois Prairie Path has created a 30-mile long trail following the right-of-way of the former Chicago, Aurora & Elgin Railroad. In Seattle the land and retained equipment from an unused gasworks facility have been combined as Gasworks Park and playground — an ingenious pop invention. And powerlines and aqueducts have been turned into a park in Santa Clara, California. In New York City, an abandoned, 1930s, parabola-arched,

municipal asphalt plant on the East River has been turned into a community-funded youth sports and recreation center called Asphalt Green.

Former military locations also are ripe for utilization as public open space in urban areas. Fort Mason in Golden Gate National Park and Navy Pier in Chicago have led the way. And many New Yorkers eagerly await access to Governor's Island.

New superscale open spaces

Most innovative of all may be the potential for development—both open space development as well as building development—of the large areas of our cities that have been devastated by abandonment, arson, and vandalism in the past decade. That devastation and squalor—in Harlem, in the South Bronx, and elsewhere—are not only symbols of despair but also open lands for hope and innovative planning.

Finally, the age of the theme park—of Disney World, Six Flags Over Texas, and 40 other major parks across the country—has made the potential for the historical districts of our cities to be seen, once again, as the *real* theme parks of our culture. Instead of reconstructed areas, such as Colonial Williamsburg, or invented ones, like Disney's, revitalized historical districts could prove to be great tourist attractions. All of Lower Manhattan, for example, is an open space of such historical richness that it can captivate the most jaded explorer. San Antonio's River Walk, Boston's waterfront and Government Center with the splendidly popular Quincy Market are other models for turning our historical districts into the most real theme parks. If well provided with guidance—clear and available maps, walking tours, information about access to buildings, and so on—such historical urban areas could be the potent theme parks of our age.

What is needed, always, is innovative vision. Perhaps the greatest urban open space—if we will open it—is our imagination.

C. Ray Smith is a design critic, editor, and the author of a recent book about new attitudes in architecture and design, *Supermannerism*.

Conceptual Projects

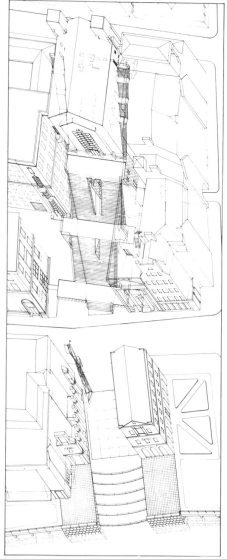

Machado-Silvetti. Proposal for the Steps of Providence, R.I.

John Diele. "Alice's Window," 1974

John Diele. "Karlsruhe, Copenhagen," 1971

Design Coalition, Steven Tilly and Alan Buchsbaum, architects: concept and drawing; Sheila Berkley: play equipment concepts. "The Play Setting"—rocking fork, sand cup, beach knife, slide spoon, cheese tunnels, rocking oranges, inflated cherries, ride-around-rim, berms for rolling

Stanley G. Boles and D. Bartley Guthrie, architects. "Umbrella" proposal, Pioneer Square, Portland, Oregon

B. Wayne Fishback and Peter Pran, Schmidt, Garden & Erikson.
Model for urban development, Gary, Indiana.

Roger Ferri. "Barge Park," floating islands in the waterways of New York

Peter Wilson Associates, Peter Wilson and Jon Evans. Rooftop Landscape proposal

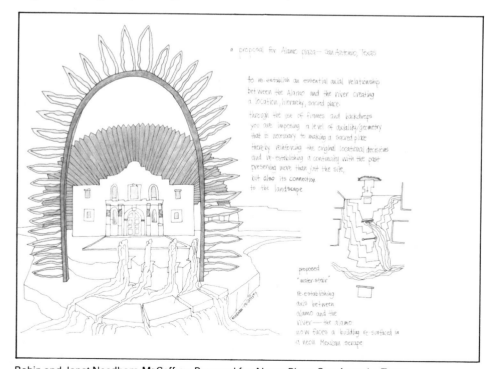

Robin and Janet Needham-McCaffrey. Proposal for Alamo Plaza, San Antonio, Texas

Reclaiming our Waterfronts

A lot is being done to make them more accessible.

By Wolf Von Eckardt

Like crabs, humans like to live near water.

Since urban civilization began 5000 years ago, between the Tigris and Euphrates rivers in Mesopotamia, most cities were built along rivers, lakes, or the sea. In new cities, like Canberra, Brasilia, Reston, and Columbia, where nature forgot, the planners created artifical lakes.

Bodies of water provide not only transportation and food, they can also give us infinite pleasures. They add excitement as well as serenity, definition as well as a sense of space to the cityscape, to say nothing of cool breezes, recreation, and reflections at night.

Our urban troubles started when the industrial revolution invaded cities with its factories, railroads, and slums. Now industry is leaving and there is trouble again, particularly in America, where it is difficult for inner city black workers to follow the jobs.

The flip side of this crisis is that we can now start cleaning up the mess industry is leaving behind. From San Antonio to Boston, from Savannah to San Francisco, cities all over the country are beginning to reclaim their waterfronts, where the industrial mess was worst.

In the 19th century, factories sprang up in the cities because that is where the workers lived, or where — before trolleys and automobiles — they could be most easily housed. Factories sprang up along waterfronts to be close to shipping and because the cotton, iron, and chemical industries, in particular, needed large quantities of water to supply steamboilers, to cool hot surfaces, and to make the necessary solutions and dyes. Lakes and rivers, furthermore, were the cheapest and most convenient dumps for industrial wastes. No one dared object that the manufacturers' "sordid convenience," as Lewis Mumford has called it, poisoned aquatic life, killed an important source of food, and invited diseases.

The railroads, in their day, like the motor roads in ours, were permitted, or, rather, invited to plunge into the hearts of the cities, and, more often than not, severed cities from their waterfronts. The urban shore became an all but impassable jumble of freight and marshalling yards, factories, warehouses, dumps, and soot.

Some ports, particularly those with a preponderance of passenger ships, were more orderly as well as romantic. But the old bustle is dead or dying. The waterfront industries are obsolete. The railroads are largely replaced by trucks. Passengers prefer flying to sailing. The old, congested cities can no longer meet the requirements of modern industry and shipping. "Containerization" — the packaging of freight in containers the size of boxcars, lifted by huge, tracked cranes, and moved by trucks — demands more space than cities can offer.

Much of America's urban waterfront is abandoned, left to rot, and covered by freeways and the concrete spaghetti of their interchanges and access ramps. In New York City, for instance, 40 percent of the waterfront is no longer used for water-related activities.

Chicago is the only large industrial city in America whose citizens fought as early as 1836 to keep their waterfront, as they phrased it, "public ground — a common to remain forever open, clear and free of any buildings, or other obstruction whatever." Seventy-three years later, in keeping with this battle cry, the city adopted a landscape scheme designed by architect Daniel Burnham. Chicago's lakefront park, with its beaches, harbors, drives, and cultural institutions, extends along 24 of the city's 30 miles of shoreline.

Spalding and Roger's Floating Circus Palace, 1852

Louisville, in contrast, sold most of its riverfront parkland to pay off municipal debts. New York City officials thought the East River bank too valuable for parkland. But in 1886, New York built its three-mile-long Riverside Park along the Hudson, part of it over railroad tracks.

In downtown Cleveland, however, you would never know there was a Lake Erie, unless you are rich enough to eat up in "The Top of the Town" restaurant, some 20 stories high. Daniel Burnham's splendid civic mall, supposedly leading to the lake, ends in a dreary whisper of forlorn wasteland, railroad tracks, parking lots, a stadium, a small airport, and "Memorial Shoreway" — a freeway presumably named in memory of the beautiful shore that might have been. In downtown Minneapolis, too, travelers have no reason to know that there is a river. The Mississippi is hidden by an abandoned industrial slum. The last good view of the water was recently blocked by an enormous parking garage.

It would be easy but pointless to go on listing our faults. The British were even more reckless in their industrial towns than we were. And if the water seems bluer on the other side of the Atlantic, remember Venice and what the petrochemical plants in its immediate hinterland are doing to it. Paris, a decade or so ago, rammed expressways into the banks of the Seine where lovers used to

Plan for Baltimore Inner Harbor

walk. Zürich, sober-minded Zürich, almost covered its lovely Siehl River with a six-lane freeway. What we can learn from the older cities in Europe and the rest of the world is not so much environmental protection, but urban design. In Stockholm, Amsterdam, Geneva, Portofino, Ibiza, Rio de Janeiro, and dozens of other great waterfront cities, we can find a good many gracious, joyous, intimate, or ceremonious ways for cities to embrace bodies of water.

An intimate encounter was created in San Antonio, Texas, during the New Deal era. The San Antonio River, which loops below street level through the business district, kept flooding. The engineers proposed to cover up the river bed, put a street on top, and reduce the river to a sewer. The citizens rebelled and insisted that there must be better ways to prevent flood. An upstream retention dam was built and Franklin D. Roosevelt's WPA (Work Projects Administration) enhanced both river banks with delightful walkways that widen at times to small terraces with shops and restaurants. At one point is an outdoor theater. Frequent steps lead down from the bustling business district to this refreshing experience.

The federal urban renewal program, launched in 1949, gave other cities the impetus and money to break through slums and industrial rot to their waterfronts. In some places, the early results were discouraging. In others, urban renewal did extremely well.

It was discouraging, for instance, that in Washington D.C.'s Southwest urban renewal area, the messy but enchanting Washington Channel waterfront was "renewed" into a paved disaster. Before: Fisherboats, fish stores and stands, seafood restaurants, marine supplies, smells, cats, teeming humanity—a sort of "Porgy and Bess" atmosphere. After: A sanitized strip development consisting mainly of a vast parking lot; a motel fronted by a fenced-in swimming pool with parking lot view; big, plastic Muzak-drenched restaurants, and tourist buses. All this is hiding a concrete embankment with a deserted, concrete walkway that is difficult to get to.

In Seattle, the urban renewal agency decided to tear down the old Pike Place Market above Elliott Bay, as pungent, lusty, and varied an emporium as you could find anywhere in America, past or present. Seattle architect Fred Bassetti rightly called it "an honest place in a phony time." But Seattle's citizenry rebelled and overwhelmingly won a referendum that saved the market. The victory has led to careful restoration and imaginative re-use of the gutsy old granite buildings on Pioneer Square and elsewhere on the Seattle waterfront.

Urban renewal, thanks to splendid local leadership and citizen support, achieved a triumph with the redevelopment of Baltimore's Inner Harbor. Begun in 1964, the enormous project of rebuilding 250 acres of deteriorated city around Baltimore's original harbor basin, is substantially completed. You get an impressive view of it from Federal Hill: new piers and bulkheading and a generous park with a promenade now frame the vast expanse of water. The green frame is alive with play fields, kiosks, and a science museum. Waterside restaurants, an aquarium, and a market building are still to come. The water is alive with a marina, boats, and the moored "Constellation," the U.S. Navy's oldest and very picturesque war ship. In the background of this *tableau vivant* is a vigorous skyline composed of old and new office and apartment highrises, sundry towers, and church steeples. New residential buildings and attractively restored old neighborhoods are part of this project. It is deliciously scented by the old but working McCormick spice plant. It is strongly linked to the nearby Charles Center, the heart of Baltimore's downtown.

As this public effort got under way, a private renewal project of a totally different kind, but of equal importance, opened in San Francisco. Here the scent was chocolate. The project, called Ghirardelli Square, grew out of the Ghirardelli chocolate factory, part of which was still a working operation when the "Square" first opened. The original building is whimsical, Victorian, and of cheerful red brick, with a big clock tower, and the airs of a castle by the Bay. The transformation from factory to "Square" was largely the accomplishment of landscape architect Lawrence Halprin, who subtracted some

of the brick, added terraces and an underground garage, and filled the concoction with shops, boutiques, restaurants, and excitement. Ghirardelli might be best described as a one-building Champs Elysees or Via Veneto—a place not just to shop and eat, but to be.

This idea of "adaptive re-use" or "recycling" old buildings soon spread—not only along the San Francisco waterfront. It changed our approach to urban "revitalization" all across the country. It gave the cities a new combination—a combination of historic preservation and sophisticated marketing — with which suburban shopping centers cannot compete. Applied not just to buildings but to whole urban areas, the Ghirardelli approach is somewhat like sensitive gardening. You weed, you prune, you re-plant rather than tear everything up to build a new garden.

The approach was gloriously successful in Boston. Along parts of the downtown waterfront, old granite warehouses built on piers have been converted into apartment buildings. Faneuil Hall and the Greek Revival Quincy Market buildings have been "ghirardellied," to coin an ugly word, into beautiful and lively Faneuil Market. It is a phenomenal success.

The success soon led the developer James Rouse, and his architect, Benjamin Thompson, to venture similarly festive marketplaces in Baltimore and New York. Baltimore's "Harborplace" at the Inner Harbor will be a new building. New York's South Street Seaport Market scheme will restore and adapt four blocks of deteriorating old buildings in the shadow of Brooklyn Bridge. To be completed in 1983, it will also include the South Street Seaport Museum, the leveled Fulton Market site, and two new retail pavilions on adjacent piers.

Some preservationists complain that what results from this approach perverts the idea of historic restoration. True. The alternatives are Colonial Williamsburg or continued decay. The true past can never be restored.

The federal Coastal Zone Management Act of 1972 extended the federal interest in urban waterfront reclamation. In addition to the Department of Housing and Urban Development, and its urban

renewal program, now known as UDAG (Urban Development Action Grants), waterfronts have become the concern of the Department of the Interior. Interior's Heritage Conservation and Recreation Service has just completed "Urban Waterfront Revitalization Study," which details the experience of more than a dozen cities for the benefit of others.

The long, emotion-charged battle over Washington's Georgetown Waterfront seems typical of what happened on most of America's urban shores. Fair Georgetown was cut off from the lovely Potomac River by ugly, obsolete industries, including a smelly rendering plant. Topping the mess is the rickety, elevated Whitehurst Freeway.

It all began in the early 1960's when the highway department announced it would replace the freeway with something bigger and the urban renewal agency announced it would replace the whole waterfront with something better. The citizens of old Georgetown recoiled in horror and the battle ensued, fought with plans and counterplans, feasibility studies, consultant reports, zoning and rezoning, injunctions, law suits, and environmental impact statements. It was citizens vs. the city, highways vs. parks, commercial vs. residential.

In the end no one and everyone won. While the battle brought orderly, official, comprehensive planning to a standstill, developers just moved in and developed, converting old warehouses into offices and apartments, adding restaurants, stores, and hotels, extending the chic of Georgetown in a slightly chaotic and somewhat hectic way. There is much kitsch and some instant charm. And maybe that is the way it ought to be.

Some day, we are promised, there will be a narrow strip of park along the river. The embattled freeway still stands. But there is talk of dressing it up in the flamboyant Victorian manner of Madeira Drive in Brighton, England — with iron fretwork.

Wolf Von Eckardt is architecture critic of the *Washington Post*, and Levin Professor for Urban Studies, Cleveland State University.

Waterfronts

Roberto Clemente Park, Pittsburgh

J. O. Davidson. "A barge party on the Hudson by moonlight," New York

South Street Seaport Museum, New York City

Doge's Palace, Venice, 1857

East River, New York City

Arthur Leipzig

Westminster Pier, Thames River, London

British Tourist Authority

Monongahela Wharf, Pittsburgh

Bill Levis, courtesy Pittsburgh Post-Gazette

River Walk, San Antonio, Texas

Peter C. Papademetriou

Marina, San Francisco

Kent E. Watson, courtesy San Francisco Bay Conservation and Development Commmission

Boston waterfront

Boston Redevelopment Authority

Dreaming of Urban Plazas

Why don't historic images meet our modern expectations?

By Robert Jensen

City Hall Plaza, Boston

We dream of creating open-air spaces for the heart of our American cities, and have built them by the score within the last 20 years. In Boston, Government Center Plaza was completed in 1969 as an urban space reaching out to a whole city. In downtown Chicago three new plazas have recently created a rhythmic procession of urban spaces on Dearborn Street. New York once seemed to acquire plazas similar to these every six months. There are new plazas in Houston and Dallas. New Orleans, that most European of American cities, even has its new and diminutive Piazza d' Italia.

Public reaction to these new plazas has been ambivalent. We are pleased that they have been built, glad they are with us, but from the criticism by planners and writers, and from the simpler judgments by pedestrians and those who use them, recent plazas do not meet our expectations. Those that do — Rockefeller Plaza in New York is a slightly older example — are exceptions. There seems to be a difference between the plazas we build in reality, and the plazas we have in our minds.

It is indicative that we call them plazas or sometimes piazzas. Our own English word "place" won't do. *Place* is derived from the Latin word *platea* — meaning an open space or broadened street — as is the Spanish *plaza* and the Italian *piazza*; but we also place bets, we have places to go, or maybe even a place in the country. The word is at once too common and too diverse in its meaning to designate what we want in an urban center downtown.

So we turn to Spanish and Italian. That is what we want: the Plaza Real in Barcelona, a small pedestrian space like a garden; or the Piazza del Campo in Siena, the singular and unequaled focus

for a whole city. We try to evoke the great open spaces of Europe.

The Campo in Siena is absolutely bounded by buildings and open to the sky; it is an outdoor room. Eleven streets bring people and vehicles into and out of the Campo, yet they are nearly impossible to see from the piazza itself. There is a dominant building, the *Palazzo Publico* or Town Hall, with a magnificent tower beside it, and a variety of other smaller and larger buildings to see. A pattern of nine brick-paved sections springs like a radiating fan from the Town Hall, activating and focusing the piazza's surface. They were first installed in 1347 to symbolize the city-state government that the Sienese called "The Nine." A public fountain, the Fonte Gaia, still bubbles water into a large rectangular pool at the edge of the piazza, the fountain surrounded by sculpture of great historical richness. Jacopo della Quercia's carved panels were finished in 1419 and remained until 1868, by which time weather and touching had almost obliterated them, and they were replaced by good copies.

And the Piazza del Campo is still used now as it always has been. Crowds waited here in 1978 for a new Pope and the celebration to follow, just as they waited in 1260 for news of the Battle of Monteaperti, an early and important Sienese win over the Florentines. The Campo began as the town's central marketplace (the origin of nearly all European plazas) and it is still that, though the daily Sienese market for food has been moved to a clearing behind the Town Hall. Today the Campo is a crowded market for tourists; though large numbers of items are bought and sold, it is principally the aura and beauty of the place that is exchanged. The

Piazza del Campo, Siena

piazza is surrounded by outdoor cafes, which are filled most of the day. In the evenings, between 7:00 and 9:00, you can join the spontaneous parade — the *passeggiata* — as Sienese and tourists alike become one vast outdoor society.

The Piazza del Campo is the quintessential urban space. With its boundaries absolutely defined, with a major building as its focus, with its paving pattern, fountain, and sculpture, it has each of the physical characteristics we wish to affirm in our own urban plazas today.

By contrast, the majority of our own new urban plazas are in front of tall office buildings. They are not made to be the focus of a whole city but to provide smaller open spaces in dense commer-

cial districts: plazas created through a legal mechanism called incentive zoning. Typically, the developer of a new building is given incentives to move the building back from the property line a specified number of feet, so the space in front may be "given" to the street and to the public. The city then allows the developer to build higher than zoning laws would otherwise permit, and usually gives a few additional stories as a bonus. The developer is not simply being generous with this valuable land; he gets more square feet to rent and the city gets a plaza.

Chicago's Civic Center Plaza, First National Bank Plaza, and Federal Center Plaza were created in essentially this way, and much has been done to make these plazas good places to see.

On Civic Center Plaza, a Picasso sculpture is perfectly scaled and placed at just the correct distance from the weathering steel facade of the Civic Center building. Three flags add controlled motion and color; the polite little fountain adds sound and natural texture, as do the few (but large) trees, placed to focus attention on the building. Though rarely filled with people, Civic Center Plaza has an austere beauty, comprehensible from an automobile as well as on foot.

The First National Bank Plaza is more active and informal. Terraces drop gradually from street level to one floor below, where three restaurants and seven shops at the lower level help draw people in. Within the plaza are many trees, smaller plants, and places to sit. An elaborate fountain dominates the center and a mural by Marc Chagall is visible throughout the plaza. There are marching bands, table tennis tournaments, and gymnastic events, to name only a few of the lunch-hour activities.

It is clearly unfair to judge these American plazas against even comparably sized European spaces, much less against the Piazza del Campo. Rich in history, created in times different from our own, often built over hundreds of years, they have earned their integrity (although some European spaces have become mostly parking lots in the last 30 years).

But judge them we do. *Inland Architect* published assessments of the Dearborn Street plazas in 1973 and again in 1975, saying the plazas are not really bounded spaces, that they tend to become high-speed footpaths in which pedestrians are not invited to stay, suggesting that the plazas are in too many ways more like public relations gestures than urban spaces to use.

Perhaps we should admit that the incentive-zoning urban plaza is an architectural device rather than a social device, that it focuses attention on a building and tends to increase the private value of the real estate around it, more than it creates places of social exchange. This should not be surprising, given the methods by which the spaces must be developed. It is mostly luck that buildings around these plazas are located properly and of sufficient height to create a walled perimeter defining urban space. And there is little a city can do if a developer of a property adjacent to a new plaza wishes to remove a building that now, luckily, helps define the plaza and replace it with one that does not. Zoning incentives and controls are weak in comparison with the power of developers.

But strengthening incentive-zoning mechanisms would not aid in creating the urban spaces we want. Enormous government powers were used to establish City Hall Plaza in Boston, for instance, but they didn't help. Built between 1962 and 1969 with the participation of our most important designers and comparable to Siena's Piazza del Campo in both scale and intention, City Hall Plaza today is like a wanted but rather unloved child in the consciousness of Boston. As in Chicago, criticism has far surpassed praise. It is a vast open space, inviting in many respects, that people don't use—though they seem to wish it were used, wish it could be more like that paradigm of an urban plaza we constantly have in our minds.

Our designers and planners understand the physical ingredients that make a good urban plaza, and try to provide them; that is not the problem. And we have the right to our expectations. That is the last thing we should change. The contradiction is deeper, having to do with the way most of us live in the 20th century.

We conduct public and political exchange through television, not in an urban plaza. We have electronic substitutes for physical participation. We receive news and the opinions of the powerful through fat Sunday papers and in weekly magazines, summarized and put in perspective. We rarely go to a special place to hear a speech; we hear it and see it at home.

Perhaps because news and considered opinion are available to nearly everyone at once, we keep our social exchanges more exclusive—at parties and dinners, with people we've invited or places we've been invited to. The evening stroll, the *passeggiata* — an essentially communal and sensual public experience—is not part of our lives.

The much longer distances we casually travel require fast speeds. We tend to keep that private too, in automobiles rather than in public transportation. Regardless of the comprehensibility of the Dearborn Street plazas from the street, it is difficult to be in a car and a plaza at the same time. Plazas require walking; we do so much less walking than before that some people say we may lose the use of our legs.

People come to the centers of cities today to work in their offices. That is a modern use of downtowns: a desk or a room that you stay in, or must move to and from quickly when there are lots of appointments. Plazas in such neighborhoods can usually only be places to pass through, except during lunch.

Market places appear where people live or can get to them conveniently. Most of us don't live on urban plazas, and even if we did it is unlikely that our places of exchange would be in them. Shopping is organized today and indoors at supermarkets and department stores. The best of these places are controlled chaos: specialty shops jambed together and seemingly competing with each other, aisles you squeeze through instead of walk through, excellent merchandise from all over the world. Such diverse bazaars can still be as exciting as they always have been, but they are not in our urban plazas.

The North American climate is often given as a reason we can't create plazas like those in the milder climates of Europe. But our weather is not as significant a reason as those use-patterns cited above for our plazas not being what we want them to be. It is just as difficult to use plazas—or even to establish them — in Los Angeles and Miami, where the climate ought to be perfect, as it is in Chicago or Boston.

Our plaza problem is cultural, technological, and endemic, anchored in the way we live and not amenable to easy solutions. We build our plazas, waiting for the magic to happen, and it usually doesn't. We want to love them and we usually don't. Concealed in the way we live, implied by even the briefest description of what causes us not to use urban plazas, is a sense of alienation from public experience. Because we have lost a part of this pleasure, our need to reclaim it is all the more real. New urban plazas embody our dreams of overcoming the loss.

Robert Jensen is a writer and a preservation architect in New York City. He teaches the history of New York City architecture at Columbia University.

Civic Center Plaza, Chicago

Hedrich Blessing

Pedestrian Malls

Car-free zones are symbols of a new urban spirit.

By Bernhard Winkler and Reinhold Mahler

A city, like an organism, grows and develops in conformity with the cultural habits of its citizens. Growth of automobile traffic is such a development. With few exceptions, it has caught both large and small towns totally unprepared. European cities that have preserved their medieval forms are as incapable of coping with this development as American cities are, although the latter's grid street system is more suitable for motor traffic. Even cities planned and built in recent times offer no valid response to the problem.

The automobile is an achievement of genius—unique in its total support of individual freedom. Nevertheless we indict it as the source of our problem, rather than indicting our immaturity to face its technological achievements. There are levels in this immaturity, observable not

only in the differing accident rates from country to country, but also in differing approaches to traffic regulations. For example, freeway speed limits — apparently approved and accepted by the public in North America — are widely opposed in Europe, especially in West Germany.

It would be wrong to view the use of the automobile in the city as an isolated problem, and it would be wrong to propose the simple banishment of the auto from city streets. Modern economy has become so dependent on the mobility of people and goods that neither loss of human life nor destruction of the city fabric raises questions about the car's development. Only the occasional paralysis of city traffic has led to doubts about the unlimited growth of automobile use. This experience of helplessness, as opposed to the wish for total freedom of movement, has led to a worldwide reaction against the auto in the city. It is a reaction expressed in the creation of car-free streets.

If we are to understand the city as an organism, then we must recognize its diverse symptoms in all their complexity, and treat them with therapies that appreciate the whole. Failure to understand the full nature of our cities, and a belief in operative interventions in order to cure the organism, have sometimes led to mutilation of cities. Divergent interests threaten the coherence of an urban organism, resulting in arrangements where the parts are out of relation with one another — mutually opposing and generating meaningless chaos.

When the unlimited mobility of the car on all city streets comes under a single regulation — a speed limit of 30 mph not to be exceeded, for example — the lack of a differentiation comes close to a law of the jungle. Connecting streets,

business streets, pedestrian streets, parking streets, residential streets, play streets, or simply a mixture of all these, which occurs more often in healthy cities, have completely different needs. These needs can only be met with differing regulations and meaningful design.

Areas for pedestrians were not invented in this century. Vehicles were prohibited in the Greek agoras and the Roman forums. In both cases those were places of special public use, in strong contrast to usual public spaces like streets. At the forum in Pompeii, the surrounding, three-sided colonnade architecturally emphasized its special function. The idea was powerfully geometrical, extended, and surrounded by the most important public buildings. Only the temple of Jupiter, located on the open narrow side, lent the forum its special religious character. By lowering the area a few steps, the space was clearly and finally reserved for the pedestrian. The space was unambiguously defined by its essential public use — religious and pro-

fane. Yet these were Roman cities that had an individual forum for each function — bread market, meat market, religious assemblies, and so on. In this way the forums differ significantly from today's pedestrian zones, which very seldom have special purposes.

One wonders then why in so many cities of different types and sizes, just any street of some importance is given prominence by conversion into a pedestrian mall. Functional and practical reasons do not suffice to explain the phenomenon. In one small German town, for example, it was unanimously decided to install a pedestrian area, but it was impossible to find a suitable street to carry out the decision.

Streets are often torn out of a city fabric and promptly declared pedestrian malls. However, there are a number of satisfying solutions in which a pedestrian area can be considered as a component of a general city development process.

Pedestrian zones are the first signals and physical symbols for a new under-

Pedestrian mall, Munich

standing of the city. This understanding views the city less as a functional structure and more as a living space for human beings. Because pedestrian zones are the symbols of a new spirit, they are of utmost importance. When they emerge as part of a comprehensive and coherent plan, they are universally accepted and spontaneously welcomed. They are a prerequisite for a new experience of public space free of noise and of traffic dangers. We know this from the American shopping centers, which differ essentially from pedestrian malls. The latter are almost always installed in a city center, where man looks for identification with his city. Besides comfortable shopping, almost all European pedestrian malls have produced a marked business growth. But it is the direct and original experience of the city as a community setting that cannot be overestimated in creating a pedestrianized area.

In this way pedestrian zones become important spaces that involve people emotionally with their city. This is the only real justification for the result, which cannot be rationally dismissed, that a pedestrian zone brings considerable advantages to those businesses already there. One cannot discount the cooperation of these local business interests, which is a prerequisite to the realization of these areas.

In Munich, the pedestrian mall we designed is extremely wide considering European circumstances. There were intensive discussions about how the vacuum caused by banning the car would be filled with people. Finally an architecture competition for the design of the complex was announced. Economic and social relations could only be realized by intensive cooperation between the City of Munich and the Chamber of Commerce. Both influenced the design in essential and positive ways. A team was formed of city officials, planners, the designing architect, and all 74 adjacent owners as the client. Due to this cooperation it was possible to allocate the restaurant islands in a correct way as well as to limit commercial activities outside existing shops to a reasonable amount.

The public was kept continuously informed about design problems by newspapers and by a public opinion poll in which 35,000 citizens participated. By these means the population became well acquainted with the transformation of the old city center into a pedestrian area. From its initial popularity during the 1972 Olympics, uses were determined; then

regulations for users were established. These regulations are respected by the public and controls are nearly superfluous.

Perhaps the most important part of the mall's planning was the city's insistence on several preconditions. Having decided that the mall should be supported by an improved public transportation system, the authorities made plans to integrate it with the two subways under construction for the summer '72 Olympics. All other public transportation was also scrutinized and then updated or rerouted. Construction started on an *Alstadtring* (a perimeter highway around the city for through traffic) which distributed traffic to and from the center of the city via side street feeder roads. Finally, the city banned all but emergency, maintenance, and service vehicles from the mall itself and regulated their schedules.

The construction logistics for the mall were every bit as stringent and impressive as its planning requirements. For a while, both the subway and mall were simultaneously under construction, yet merchants had been promised that they could conduct business as usual — and so they did. Throughout construction, delivery and customer access were maintained. An architect visiting Munich during this time said that the subway seemed to be built without ripping up anything, that there was often no sign of construction at all. In any case, there were inspections by the city to assure that anything detrimental to local businesses was stopped and, every two months, the city

restudied and coordinated the construction schedules. Construction included not only the subway and its entrances along the mall (there are almost a dozen of these), but extensive work in utility lines and services for the mall—much of it underground.

Munich is an example of careful, comprehensive preparation and planning under ideal circumstances of town planning. A great many of the pedestrian areas that work well in several countries of the world have built a common confidence in the possibility of humanizing our cities. Based on this confidence, plans and activities are proceeding everywhere to work toward a humanitarian city and begin to comprehend the city as a whole.

The pedestrian zone as a positive collective city experience is the basis for the next step in development. This step is already recognizable in its beginnings, and will lead to a more meaningful structuring of public city spaces. It is evident that a pedestrian zone is proper only for special situations and is only meaningful where it helps fulfill man's need for identification with the city. In each case it is, nevertheless, possible to define and to build city space for specific situations and meanings and to adapt automobile traffic accordingly. In purely business streets it will play a different role from that in streets with mixed uses; in residential areas it will only have a semi-public character; and where children play and where people look for relaxation, it will surrender all of its rights to the pedestrian. The unfriendliness and unattractiveness of many cities is primarily a problem of the urban street, which has in most cases been reduced to its technical function. It is not a question of separating the city into functional units, but rather of designing it differentially according to the manifold behaviors of its citizens. Traffic in its differing forms is an essential part of this design.

Architects **Bernhard Winkler** and **Reinhold Mahler** are Professor and Associate Professor, respectively, at the School of Architectural Design at the Technical University in Munich. Mr. Winkler's office won the competition for the design of the Munich Mall.

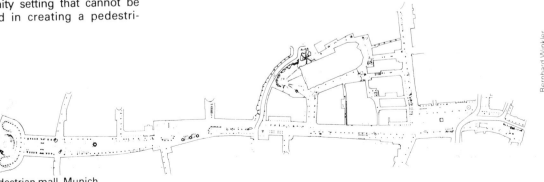

Plan for the pedestrian mall, Munich

Plazas and Pedestrian Malls

Pedestrian mall, Providence, Rhode Island

Trenton, New Jersey

Glenmore Plaza, Brooklyn, New York

Nicollet Mall, Minneapolis

Ghirardelli Square, San Francisco

Captain's Walk, New London, Connecticut

"The Park in the Sky," Los Angeles

Piazza del Duomo, Milan

Piazza del Campidoglio, Rome

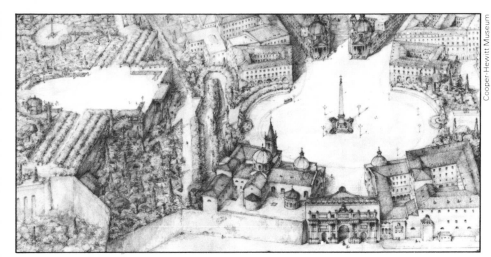

Ernest Farnum Lewis. "Piazza del Popolo and Pincian Gardens," 1910, pencil and watercolor drawing

Father Demo Square, New York City

Images of Special Places

Memorable streets characterize neighborhoods.

By Richard B. Oliver

The experience of a district or even an entire city can be encapsulated or synthesized into the particular experience of a single street (or collection of streets), and the activity, buildings, and other sights along it. Not many streets have this transcendent quality. Most streets are, in fact, unprepossessing and unremarkable places that are of importance only to local residents. Inhabitants of an area may share a communal feeling or a sense of neighborhood that is focused on a local street or streets. Occasionally, one of those streets will transcend its local meaning and acquire interest and importance to the surrounding city and even to the world at large.

Such streets have acquired their renown as visitors came to see that the street space was a place in which one could begin to understand a larger entity. Such street spaces, then, are both ordinary and special, they possess both local and widespread importance, and they form the setting for a special kind of drama: the interaction of locals and tourists.

This interaction is important to both parties: the presence of the tourist confirms for the local that he lives in a special place; the presence of the local provides a clue to the lifestyle of the area. And all of this is enacted in an open space that is usually not radically different from similar spaces nearby, and that no one had designed to act as they clearly do—as tourist attractions. Yet these streets where locals and tourists confront each other play an important role: they are the ordinary spaces of a district or a city through which one moves to view that district or city as a special urban wonder. Moving through these street spaces, one gains an image of the city composed of impressions of the street itself, its spaces, and the things encountered along it.

It is well known that San Francisco is famous for its cable cars. What is more easily overlooked is that a large portion of the image people have of San Francisco is derived from riding the cable cars. Daily, tourists and residents alike ride these crotchety, charming little machines up and down hills and through a series of street spaces that seem, on the surface, to have little enough reason to be remembered as a single entity. While the cable cars are a legitimate form of transportation for locals, for tourists they are not unlike a Disneyland ride; the space through which they move is not unlike a theme park.

San Francisco is often referred to in the Bay Area as "The City," as if there were no other. It is a distilled and heady mixture of urban delights, and the evidence is found in the street spaces traversed by the cable car, especially along the route that connects Hyde and Beach with Powell and Mason. That route links the venerable Buena Vista Cafe, Ghirardelli Square, and The Cannery on the waterfront with Macy's, The Emporium, and the BART subway system stations on Market Street. En route, the cable car climbs Russian Hill, then Nob Hill, and finally descends steeply into the commercial center of the city. There it passes Union Square. It also stops at the hotels—the St. Francis, the Sir Francis Drake, the Fairmont, and the Mark Hopkins; it stops at the top of the serpentine block of Lombard Street and within a few blocks of Chinatown and Grace Cathedral. Along the route, the passenger is offered dramatic vistas north toward Alcatraz and Marin County; east toward Telegraph Hill, the Bay Bridge, and the Berkeley hills; and west to Pacific Heights and the Golden Gate Bridge. In short, if one were to ride the cable car from Hyde and Beach to Powell and Mason, one would move through typical streets of

bay-windowed vernacular houses, see many of the special sights, and experience the unique topography. Altogether this conspires to create the popular image of the city known as "Bagdad by the Bay."

The linear street spaces that are unified by the presence of the cable car and that encapsulate an image of San Francisco do not form a simply shaped entity, like a contained plaza. The spatial dimensions of the whole are especially ambiguous although the dimensions of any one piece of the street are more clear. But what makes the street space defined by the

Donald Macintosh

San Francisco

cable car route so especially vivid and interesting is all of its other dimensions besides shape, such as color, texture, ornament, signs, breezes, sun and shadows, and the manner in which all of these dimensions, including both size and shape, seem to suggest the fabric of the city as a whole as well as the street as an entity. It is in this surprising way that seemingly ordinary and unremarkable street spaces play a powerful role in one's memory of a place and, by extension, one's sense of place.

San Francisco is a special and unique city—popular enough to be celebrated in

dozens of tunes — and its most memorable street spaces have the power to induce a sense of excitement and even reverie. But other cities have similar, if less highly charged spaces. In many cities, there is an informal pattern of roads used for "Sunday drives"— a pattern that unites a series of spatial impressions and scenic outlooks into a cohesive sense of place. Again, the streets involved may be spatially unremarkable, but they may wind through exclusive neighborhoods, engage dramatic topography, reveal typical landscape, or provide views of notable civic structures.

San Diego established an official 52-mile "scenic" drive that was simply a popular route that "Sunday drivers" had used for years. The drive includes the highest vantage point in the city, the rugged coastline of La Jolla, the famed harbor and its companion bay, the major city park, and a host of cultural institutions including the historic Old Spanish Lighthouse and "Old Town." Traversing the 52-mile scenic drive would take the tourist through the city he wanted to see and the city he would later want to remember. The medium for this process would be the varied but sequential spaces of the road itself together with the events, places, and vistas encountered en route. The process can be likened to choreography and the street space to a stage set.

A few cities in the world are characterized by a great diversity of individual neighborhoods and, in these cities, streets can act to define a particular district that may in turn contribute to a multifaceted image of the city. New York is one such city, and its theater district is famous the world over as a symbol of New York. Tightly concentrated on Broadway north of 42nd Street and on the side streets from Sixth to Eighth avenues, the district is located on a set of streets that are ordinary components of the Manhattan grid system, part of the vast abstract pattern that covers almost the entire island. When the theaters are not open, the streets seem not much different from many nearby streets. But for those few moments before the curtain goes up and after it has come down, the streets of the district coalesce into a cohesive though oddly shaped open-air plaza teeming with theatergoers. At such moments, the street spaces transcend

their ordinary character and reinforce the image of New York as "the Great White Way."

In contrast, there are other New York districts with appeal that is more metropolitan than worldwide. A tour of Spring Street and West Broadway in SoHo would give the outsider an impression of the cast-iron district that has become famous as the focus of a fashionable lifestyle. The impression, of course, would not be fully fleshed out, and in many respects would be inconsistent with that of the local resident. But nevertheless, the two street spaces do act as the setting for image gathering about the district as a whole, by locals and outsiders alike.

Similarly, a street can act as the focus of an ethnic neighborhood or "village." For instance, a trip to Little Italy to eat Italian food would, in fact, be a trip to a restaurant or cafe on or just off Mulberry Street. Here the outsider would experience the dimensions — the rich smells, sounds, and sights — that confirm the presence of an ethnic community. The Italian community of New York is popularly symbolized by the collection of cafes and restaurants along Mulberry Street, and all the more so in autumn during the festival of San Gennaro, when the street is transformed into a brightly illuminated fair.

In at least two other American cities — Philadelphia and Boston — the open space that is the stage for an Italian community is an open-air market. The Italian market in South Philadelphia and Haymarket in Boston cater to and are used by local residents as a source of fresh food and other products, and in this way the markets are authentic places. In addition, because an open-air market today is such an unusual urban phenomenon, both places also have acquired the qualities of a tourist attraction. Outsiders visit both markets not merely to purchase fresh food but also to connect with and enjoy an actual remnant of old and traditional patterns of living. In both these examples, the markets are extensions of the street space with patrons often spilling out into the areas normally used by vehicles. When the flea market along the Portobello Road in London is in full swing, pedestrians totally usurp the place of vehicles, and in flea markets in Paris, New York, and elsewhere, mer-

Portobello Road Market, London

chants and patrons take over space usually reserved for the parking of cars. Similarly, one of the great open-air markets in the Western Hemisphere takes place each Saturday in the ordinary street spaces of Oaxaca, Mexico.

The open-air market, indicative as it often is of the presence of an ethnic culture, also helps to create another kind of image. In this third case, the street space is the medium for obtaining an image, usually romanticized, of the city's past and its heritage. The narrow streets of the French Quarter in New Orleans, for instance, are encompassed by 19th-century brick buildings adorned with lacy ironwork verandas, filled with the sounds of jazz, heavy with humid air and pungent odors, and inhabited by denizens at once proud and a little threadbare. The impression received in a tour of the district is one of a sultry, sophisticated, and decadent golden past. The urban delights of New Orleans are at once attractive and wicked, raucous and genteel, concentrated and small scale, elusive and yet specifically tied to the shimmering, evanescent architecture,

the dimensions of the narrow streets, and the glimpses of lush cool garden courtyards hidden away. This tight pattern of street, veranda, and walled garden is rendered all the more vivid in contrast to the open civic splendor of Jackson Square and the irregular pattern of the French Market facing the Mississippi River.

The French Quarter is virtually an island — a fragment from the past — in a much larger city that is in many ways indistinguishable from other contemporary American cities — an impression confirmed by one trip in from the airport. But in the popular imagination, New Orleans is synonymous with the French Quarter. The urbane, if slightly seedy qualities of the street spaces of Bourbon, Royal, Decatur, St. Ann, and others give substance to an image of the Quarter, which in turn is parlayed into an image of New Orleans.

In this last kind of image, the street is very clearly the vessel for communal memories that are widely held. Often these memories are indistinguishable from myth, and only dimly suggest the reality of what once existed. But no matter, because the image of a city's past, and of its present, which is embodied in a few of its streets, allows the public to have a powerful and affectionate hold on a place, and by extension on themselves.

The architect Louis Kahn was fond of describing a city as a place where a young boy could wander the streets until he found what he wanted to do for his whole life. Kahn was extolling the street as the vehicle for discovering the opportunities of a place, and he was doing so in a metaphorical as well as literal sense. By extension, I have tried to suggest that the seemingly modest and unassuming streets of a city are also the medium that enables the imagination to connect vividly with and remember a city by — its physical setting, its districts and special concentrations of culture, and its heritage.

Richard B. Oliver is an architect and Curator of Contemporary Architecture and Design at the Cooper-Hewitt Museum.

Favorite Open Spaces

What is your Favorite Open Space? Why does it appeal to you?

Watercolor by Jean-Michel Folon

St. Peter's Square, Rome, and the square outside Santa Maria Novella in Florence.

I suppose the most impressive open space in the world is St. Peter's Square, but of course it hardly works at all as the traffic goes round the outside. I like very much the square in Florence outside Santa Maria Novella, but it has to work too hard and is always full of traffic, so one can hardly see it as an open space.

Lord Kenneth Clark
Author, art historian
London

Out There.

Because we don't know what's out there.

Michael Collins
Astronaut
Undersecretary
 the Smithsonian Institution

Brooks Vaughn, courtesy Gateway National Recreation Area, National Park Service

The space that you see when you are on the ferry boat, half way between the South Ferry station and Staten Island, facing Manhattan.

Christo
Conceptual Artist
New York City

The Sea.

Always changing, giving back the light of the sky in myriad refractions, alive with the weather, full of food, dangerous, luring, eternal.

One of my favorite man-made places is the Piazza Navona in Rome. Its oval shape lets in the sky. It is a social space. People walk there, eat there, gather there for fairs and celebrations. There is the exuberance of the baroque church and the baroque fountains; there are whispers of a past, even to chariot races. Constant motion in a serene setting.

John Hersey
Author
New Haven

U.S. Naval Observatory, courtesy NASA

My favorite open space is the universe.

R. Buckminster Fuller
Architect, designer, inventor, writer
Philadelphia

The circular park surrounding the Polish city of Krakow.

It was created by the removal of the ancient wall of fortification that protected the city in previous centuries. There is not another space like it. It is a pedestrian green space that is small enough to provide human contact like the *paseo* experience of Latin countries, but large enough to offer good air and protection by trees. The Ogle-thorpe squares in Savannah are a second favorite. They combine an 18th century plan with 19th century houses — the best of all possible worlds. It should be a model for planning the reconstruction or rebuilding of our cities.

Kent Barwick
Chairman,
Landmarks Preservation Commission
New York City

André Kertesz

Kolkozian Market in Boukhara, Ouzbekis-tan, USSR.

It is an enclosed space, a welcoming space, in brief, an urban open space in that old Judeo-Moslem holy city, above all others for the conquerors of Central Asia. There are the piles of goods, the colors, the smells, the noise, the uproar, the booming gaiety, the disorder (all sophistication and tradition), the shouts, the light, the movement, the rites ordi-nary and sacred. In brief, life recaptured, life like nowhere else.

After the curiosity, after the wonder in front of those countless spices with countless plays of color, rest and relaxa-tion at the restaurant, opened and cov-ered, abutting the stalls, part of the mar-ket, smoke filled. A full hour under the cool sun, half lying on "bed-benches" ouzbeks, blue as the sky, tasting oily rice and unforgettable shashliks.

Truthfully, an urban open space when it is a success is only sensations, impressions, intuitions, flitting images, total well-being, and only barely per-ceived. No words can describe all of that. Only experience counts.

Gilles de Bure
Author
Paris

Ilene Berg, courtesy National Zoological Park

The National Zoological Park and two old squares — one in Prague, one in Madrid.

The National Zoological Park in Washington, D.C., has open space with trees, grass, interesting animals, and the people always seem to be in a jolly, happy mood. It is a pleasant place to visit, it is a pleasant place to rest.

Now, something I would not be ac-cused of being quite so biased about is the old town square in Prague, Czecho-slovakia. It is cobblestoned completely across and has a couple of fountains. I have spent several happy hours sitting at the little outdoor cafe sipping Zubrovka and just watching the people. It is kind of a bustling and vibrant place with an air of stability and antiquity even though it is a World War II reconstruction. Perhaps be-cause I could withdraw quietly and enjoy all the little things occurring is what made it so pleasant.

I have also enjoyed a similar square in Madrid. It was an arcade surrounded by shops. In the corner, there was a little outdoor cafe where I sat and drank the wine of the country and watched the pi-geons and the people. Again, I was able to withdraw and yet participate. There was a sense of activity and life.

Theodore H. Reed
Director, National Zoological Park
Washington, D.C.

Roofs.

Like hilltops, they receive sounds from all sides. They give people not only the best views but a solitude without having loneliness necessarily in it.

John Cage
Composer
New York City

In Rome: Piazza Navona for its openness and civility.
In Buenos Aires: Plaza San Martin for its green urbanity.
In New York: Rockefeller Center Promenade and Plaza for the intensity of its life.

All these spaces are very successful at accommodating urban life. It feels right to be there, they rest us or recharge us. The architecture is secondary to the life they make possible. The best ones are impossible to compare with each other, they are entities unto themselves.

Cesar Pelli
Dean, School of Architecture
Yale University

Hyde Park in London, the Bois de Boulogne in Paris, and Le Bois de la Cambre in Brussels.

In my mind an urban open space should allow the inhabitants of a town to enjoy the charm, peace, quiet, and beauty of ideal rural districts. These three areas come very close to this definition.

The last two are similar, being nearly in the town, easy to reach, and sufficiently big to give one the impression of being in the country.

Woods, large areas of grass, and above all water create the perfect outdoor environment. No games or organized entertainments are to be found in these areas, leaving to commercial enterprises the lot of running Fun Parks.

The southern side of the Brussels Bois de la Cambre joins the Forêt de Soigne, one of the most beautiful beech forests in the world, where horse riding is practiced all the year around.

Nature at its best in the midst of a town is a luxury to be cherished, for once it's gone, it will never be replaced.

Prince Antoine de Ligne
Brussels

Piazza Navona.

As a civic plaza containing Bernini and Borromini and as a neighborhood plaza with children and market stalls; for its formal variety and spatial cohesion; for its "golden air" reflected from its orange facades; and for my memories of spaghetti alla Matriciana at Mastrostefano's, opposite the fountain, with good friends.

Robert Venturi
Architect
Philadelphia

Paley Park in New York City.

Although it is not very open, I think it makes a wonderful use of a small space to give relief from the city heat to both passersby and users. I feel it is an inspiration in beautiful and innovative use of a small area.

Katharine Graham
The Washington Post Company
Washington, D.C.

Roger Williams National Memorial in Providence, Rhode Island.

This small national memorial park was conceived in 1959 as an integral part of a plan to restore the historic College Hill section of Providence. When completed, within the next few years, it will be an open-space gem in the heart of the city.

At one time the core of the original settlement of Providence, the land encompasses the very neighborhood where Roger Williams lived and worked, and it includes the approximate site of the town spring which, for a time, was the center of community life. This park will be a fitting National Memorial to Roger Williams—a man whose devotion to the principle of freedom of conscience has such a profound impact on American thought. I am sure it will prove to be a favorite open space for residents and visitors alike.

Claiborne Pell
United States Senator
Rhode Island

Forecourt Fountain outside the City Center in Portland, Oregon.

With its cascades of waterfalls surrounded by trees, it provides a real feeling of the Pacific Northwest. During the hot summer the people of the city come to enjoy the cooling atmosphere and dangle their feet in the water. It's a unique example of combining city and country.

Mark Hatfield
United States Senator
Oregon

Central Park in New York City.

It seems impossible that it should be there, but there it is, and despite many influences that have tried to ruin it over the years, I am sure it will survive and be a great haven for busy city dwellers who are sick and tired of concrete and asphalt.

Theodore M. Hesburgh, C.S.C.
President, University of Notre Dame
Notre Dame, Indiana

Art Park in Atlanta, Georgia.

One of the most delightful open spaces I have ever encountered is Art Park, a wonderful playground designed by Isamu Noguchi for the people of Atlanta. The beautiful balance of colors, shapes, and forms in the landscape is only surpassed by the high-spirits of the children who play there and the adults who enjoy it. Art has been used to create the perfect atmosphere in this space.

Joan Mondale
Washington, D.C.

In England what can rival Kensington Gardens? In Europe the Piazza San Marco?

Roy Strong
Director, Victoria and Albert Museum
London

Piazza San Marco in Venice.

I like it because it has four steps at the base of the San Marco column on which you can sit alone or with a girl, all night long, watching the sea. I would like to see the square in Mecca with the big black stone because it means so much to so many people and I've never been there.

Ettore Sottsass
Architect, Industrial Designer
Milan

Grants' Tomb, New York City

Close by the Hudson shore on Manhattan's West Side occurs a small urban concentration of Picturesque Park (Olmsted's Riverside Park), Standard Cathedral (Riverside Church), Rectangular City Park with Oriental Overtones (Sakura Park), and Eclectic Monument (Grant's Tomb). And right in the middle of it all is what some may find to be a shattering disturbance of the architectural equanimity and others may see as a marvelous ethnocultural efflorescence. It is also the nearest approximation for those who have never felt the embrace of Antonio Gaudi's benches in Barcelona's Güell Park. It is in fact a continuous seating arrangement circling Grant's Tomb; a winding, twisting, oozing mosaic-color-music event of broken and whole ceramic tile in a multiplicity of animal, vegetable, and mineral patterns. It is lastly a city artifact challenge of the most stimulating kind.

William Alex
The Frederick Law Olmsted Association
New York

Two harbor-view promenades — one in Marseilles, one in Brooklyn.

Two promenades, linked by similarly breathtaking harbor views but separated by nearly 5,000 miles of sea are the Promenade de la Corniche in Marseilles, a mile and a half of serpentine road and walkway that hugs the bayfront cliffs south of that city's Vieux Port, and our own Brooklyn Heights Promenade, five precious blocks of tranquility overlooking the harbor and Manhattan's skyline. Users of the Corniche take advantage of a unique two-tier design that permits those strolling along the upper level to be unaware of the protective wall that guards the edge at the lower level. The Heights Promenade offers another distinct advantage: it's here in New York and only a block from where I live. It's a remarkable place.

Elliot Willensky
Commissioner
Landmarks Preservation Commission
New York City

Madison Square in New York City.

It lies like a cool pond beside the dry riverbed of Fifth Avenue. For the person coming south this open space is particularly welcome, for he has been tightly confined by the avenue since leaving Central Park. Marking the perimeter of the square are some of Manhattan's most marvelous man-made pinnacles: the Flatiron Building, Metropolitan Life Insurance Company, and New York Life. With its curving walks and fine old trees and its skyscraper-high escarpment of marble and limestone, Madison Square celebrates at once both nature and art.

David Lowe
Author
New York

The South Bronx.

It's got more open space than any city in the world. You can see for miles. The only thing that compares with it, in my memory, is Berlin just after the second World War. I said at the time that the Germans really knew how to use open spaces. Of course they couldn't have done it without the help of the Americans and the Russians. I think that everybody who has anything to do with urban planning should make a visit to the South Bronx before they start designing their own spaces.

Art Buchwald
Author
Washington, D.C.

Turtle Fountain Riverside Park and The United Nations Plaza in New York City.

Paris, Rome, and London are, of course, all dotted with open spaces that work. So is Tientsin. Our favorites tend to be those that work as pleasure (such as parks), as purpose (such as docks), or as both (such as markets). One of the most urgent needs for urban open space is the need for small children to be able to get safely distant from parent or guardian. In New York, even before the vistas were blocked by architecture, the freespace was blocked by hazards. Yet surely the freedom to be relatively alone and away is basic to growing up. For this reason, when my children were young, I liked the Turtle Fountain area at 79th Street in Riverside Park, which was unfortunately dirty most of the time, and the plaza at the United Nations, which was too sterile ever to get dirty. Both offered parent and child a chance to get far away from each other while remaining comfortably within sight.

Ralph Caplan
Writer and communications consultant
New York

Big zoos, the Bronx Zoo in particular.

Great natural habitat zoos offer unparalleled variety and refreshment to urban dwellers. They are probably the most heavily and effectively used open spaces we have. Education as well as recreation are provided and they are enjoyed by visitors of all ages and walks of life. In New York, the Bronx Zoo offers a healing respite from noise and bricks and glass and steel and from rectangles and traffic. Importantly, their strange and beautiful, intrinsically interesting creatures provide us with a unique perspective on the human condition.

William Conway
General Director
New York Zoological Society
New York

Greenacre Park in New York City.

I like it for the grace it brings to the life of the city around it. The physical amenities are a large part of th.is — honey locust trees, flowers, chairs and tables, the food buffet, and the pleasantly noisy waterfall. But what is best is the response of people. People are nice to each other at Greenacre, and they are nice to the park. Their enjoyment is contagious.

Laurance S. Rockefeller
Conservationist
New York City

Fulton Ferry Landing, Brooklyn, and The Museum of Modern Art Garden in New York City.

First there is the park at the foot of the Brooklyn tower of the Brooklyn Bridge, where one can view the Manhattan skyline — the greatest man-made natural formation in the world. It offers the most exhilarating experience with its constant flow of river traffic — as exciting at noon as at midnight. Equal is the garden at The Museum of Modern Art, where, totally surrounded by New York City, one is so close to the trees and beautifully placed sculpture. It is a powerful experience.

Margot Wellington
Executive Director
Municipal Art Society
New York

The courtyard at the Anthropological Museum in Mexico City.

It has a large spiral column that widens at the top to shield a courtyard below. Under the column is a fountain, which creates a breeze that cools the area. Nearby is a rectangular pond with goldfish and rushes.

Tammy Grimes
Actress
New York City

Architectural Details

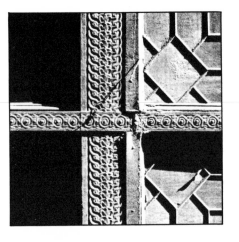

Except as noted, all photos by Mark Feldstein

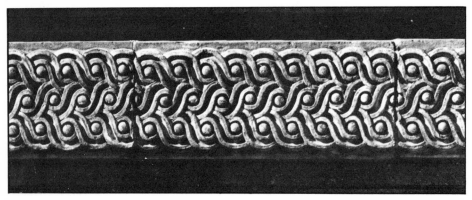

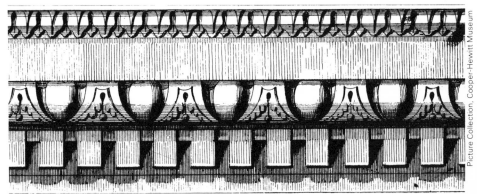

Picture Collection, Cooper-Hewitt Museum

Architectural Elements

The street is made of sticks and stones.

By Gerald Allen

For centuries streets have been lively, varied, and interesting urban open spaces, and of all urban open spaces they are, of course, by far the most common. The effects that they make, the pleasures (and sometimes the pains) they give, have a lot to do with the architecture. Just what are the architectural elements in the street? The answer to that question, not surprisingly, depends on the answer to still another more basic question: just what is a street? Obviously, a street is a linear surface — sometimes straight, sometimes curved, and often paved—on which people and things travel back and forth from somewhere to somewhere else. But unfortunately this definition also serves quite well as the definition of a road, and streets are not roads. The difference is that streets are always in towns and cities, not in the country, and, by virtue of that, they always have buildings and other man-made compositions—architecture, in other words — on either side of them. These are what make them streets. Architectural elements, then, are not just a part of the street, they *are* the street, and they give it its special character.

Wall Street, Peachtree Street, Fleet Street, Beacon Street, Sesame Street, and the Street Where You Live: all are memorable a great deal less for their pavings and curbings and lamp posts than for what goes on around them. What is "on" them, we say in America, meaning what is along the edge. The English, more accurately, say what is "in" them. A certain doctor is *in* Harley Street, and a certain shop is *in* the High Street, correctly implying that both the pedestrian and vehicular passageways and the buildings alongside, with the doctor and the shopkeeper within them, are parts of an ensemble that is the street.

John Nash, architect, Chester Terrace, London, 1825

Elm Street, Lumberton, North Carolina, about 1910

But its parts are nonetheless distinct. The roadway and sidewalks are a general and public realm. Almost anyone is free to be there, and, once there, one is free within certain agreed upon limits to do or say what one pleases. Beyond this realm a strict division occurs. In the case of residential streets, it is a division between public and private. In the case of other kinds of streets it is a division between the generally public and the public for very special purposes—a restaurant, for example, or a stationery store or museum or courthouse. These divisions, naturally, can occur in many different ways, since in towns and cities—and, in fact, in society at large—there are many different things to be divided up. It is architecture that announces the occurrence of these divisions, and it also signals their specific quality.

The reason architecture has traditionally held so enduring a fascination for people is that it uses physical materials like sticks and stones to construct a veritable language that we can read. Architecture, in other words, has meanings, and these are made legible in several different ways. One is that any given piece of architecture refers itself, in its shapes and details, to other things, and therefore it achieves a part of its meaning by analogy. Buildings are almost always "like" other things—other buildings of the past, most obviously — and thus the occurrence in any particular building of a pointed arch or a Corinthian column or a wall of glass or a cheap, barnlike metal roof allows us to understand its meaning relative to all the other buildings that also have any of these things. Another way in which architecture allows itself to be read is by giving physical form to certain circumstantial, highly particular human activities — the very ones, in most cases, that caused a given building to be built in the first place. Once built, it serves not only as a vessel in which these activities can occur, but also as a sign that they do. The architecture of the street is a good case in point.

A row of Georgian houses from the early 19th century in London, for instance, provides at a glance significant clues to the kinds of lives that were meant to be lived there. The houses have a formality and urbanity that comes from their size and from their allusions to the architecture of Greece and Rome; they make razor sharp the line between public and private; and, since they are almost all alike, they express a general agreement about just what a house in the city should be. By contrast, a row of houses in a small town in North Carolina, from the early 20th century, radiates an altogether different style of life. Here the allusions to past architecture are simpler, and the houses are more varied from one to the next. Most important, perhaps, is the fact that the line between the public and private realms is gently and complexly blurred, suggesting an easier and possibly more relaxed intercourse between individual families and the community at large. Here instead of a single line there is a series of layers. A row of large oak trees forms a buffer zone between the roadway and the sidewalk; green grass accompanies the transition from the sidewalk to the houses. And where do the houses themselves start? At the front doors of the actual buildings, or at the edges of their capacious porches, furnished with rockers and swings?

One might well ask what else one would expect to find on a grand street in London at one point in history and on another street in a small Southern farm town a hundred years later. Nothing else, of course, since the point is not that these two streets are different, but that architecture almost singlehandedly *tells* us that they are, and suggests how.

Another example of architecture thus speaking to us is a famous medieval street in the town of York in England. Here the hustle and bustle of commerce in the Middle Ages, the energetic elbowing and jockeying for position, take direct architectural shape in the way the buildings pile themselves together to make a street that is, coincidentally, known as the Shambles. In Edgartown, on Martha's Vineyard, another commercial street straightens out much of this confusion in

The Shambles, York, England

a stricter and perhaps more puritanical way. Here the messages are ones of discrimination and propriety. As in the Shambles, a collection of commercial buildings weave themselves into a dense texture, but each one remains nonetheless distinct and encloses something of its own: an office, a shop, or a bank. Together they help enclose the street like walls on either side. They appear, however, almost to have been selectively eroded by the continuous flow of pedestrian traffic along their facades. The shops, with their heavy traffic, have big glass windows and deep doorways that invite entrance. The offices, more resistant to erosion, sport smaller windows and doors that limit their exposure to the street and give the impression that access is permitted only when it is necessary.

It is worth noting, again, that all of these urban phenomena—in London, in York, in North Carolina, and on Martha's Vineyard — are, in the broader sense, streets. All have what we standardly think of as *a* street running down the middle, and this carries almost none of the special messages of each place but is instead merely the setting from which to read them. (It is also worth noting, incidentally,

that while this is generally true it is not always true. The famous polychromatic sidewalks of Rio de Janeiro, or the nineteenth-century cobbles of a street in a New England factory town—or, for that matter, the mere remnants of ruts in a dirt street in an abandoned town in New Mexico, signaling that this was once the Santa Fe Trail—all are "architectural" in that they, by their physical composition, particularize the general and public pathway, allowing us to read from it specific intentions and specific connotations.)

Usually, though, the pathway remains unspecific, and the key messages, the messages that tell us where we are and what this is, come at the critical seam between it and what lies at its edges. The obvious ways in which this seam can be stitched have already been seen: a hard line (as in the row houses in London), a softer and more layered look (as in the houses in North Carolina), and a selectively open and closed format (as in the main street in Edgartown). Also seen have been the variety of architectural images that each of these abstract formats can have: the classicistic splendor of the London street, the chaotic vitality of the Shambles in York, the simple and literally colonial correctness of the street in Edgartown, and the down-home, naive, and fraternal effusions of the houses in North Carolina, with their big porches — in summer their most important rooms — ranged right up front for all the neighbors, and all the town, to see.

Beyond these, the variations are almost infinite, as one would indeed suppose, since the variety of individual and social phenomena architecturally to be expressed are that too. A street in the South Bronx in New York, for instance, with its tenements with their socially important front stoops, shares something with the London row houses and something else with the houses in North Carolina, resulting in a quite different kind of communal conviviality from either. A house in Cuernavaca in Mexico —elegant and verdant to a fare-thee-well within—proffers a really uncaring facade to the street. Aside from its unprepossessing front door, its only gesture is a wrought-iron-grilled window—there, one

would guess, simultaneously to allow the inhabitants occasionally to look out and to prevent marauders from getting in. By contrast—but still in a similarly Spanish idiom—a house in Santa Barbara, California, enclosed by a white stucco wall, has as its entrance a similar wrought-iron gate, inviting introspection, and, with proper credentials, even entrance from the street.

Main Street, Edgartown, Martha's Vineyard, Massachusetts

Architectural elements like these *are* the street, and architectural elements like these have meanings. It therefore follows that streets, too, have meanings. What are they? They have to do with society, with its sense of its whole self, with its sense of its component parts, and with the orderly division and juxtaposition of these. Streets, with their provision for the general and the public and with their provision for the particular and the private, are a physical, formal, and architectural metaphor for all of these things. The way in which each of these things is related and intermingled, emphasized or muted, in any particular street is what we read when we see it. It is worth noting, too, that when people, as the phrase goes, take to the streets — when revolutions occur and when chaos reigns — it is because these finely tuned relationships between all the parts have gotten out of whack and must be discarded. Thus one must begin again from the general, and one must again build a new street.

Gerald Allen works as an architect in New York, is an editor of *Architectural Record* magazine, and is co-author of *The Place of Houses* and of *Dimensions: Space, Shape and Scale in Architecture.*

Street-Life Activities

Kubler Collection, Cooper-Hewitt Museum Library

Lawrence Halprin

Matt Anderson

D. Gorton, courtesy The New York Times

David Kenneth Specter

British Tourist Authority

Arthur Leipzig

Karin Bacon

Kubler Collection, Cooper-Hewitt Museum Library

Robert Perron

Hubert C. Birnbaum

Bernard Pierre Wolff

Ann Stewart

German Information Center

Street-Life Activities

Our liveliest celebrations are outdoors.

By Karin Bacon

A city is defined by its outdoor spaces and what happens in them. Acceptable activity on the streets of Aspen, Colorado, in the mid-1950s consisted of either washing your car or watering the lawn. Anything else was loitering. The main street in Charlotte, North Carolina, empties like a sieve at 5:00, when the business people pour down the hill to the parking lots. A street in Phoenix, Arizona, is like a superhighway into the desert. "Street life" in Los Angeles means bumping into people in parking lots outside supermarkets.

These are lonely experiences for me, an avid New Yorker hooked on a rich diet of big-city street life. Just the two miles of park where I run most days is shared — often simultaneously — by other runners of all descriptions, owners and their pets, teenage skateboarders, aging bench sitters, Hispanic volleyball players, bag ladies and men, T'ai Chi enthusiasts, the Columbia University track team, promenaders, transistor radio aficionados, Jill Clayburgh and her dog, park maintenance crews.

The streets of New York and other centralized cities are the cheapest show in town and often the most compelling. They are a source of energy, of information on styles, politics, and unfamiliar cultures, a focus for seasonal changes. Most important, they are an arena where the individual rituals that structure our days become social acts. Dense, incongruous, eccentric, and anarchic as the streets of New York City appear, there are surprisingly ritualized patterns of behavior — group activities that we not only enjoy but need.

When virtually any kind of individual activity is conducted in public space — from sunning, stoop-sitting, garbage-scanning, gossiping, bargaining, peddling, running, begging, and campaigning, to peoplewatching, parading, window-shopping, hustling, cruising, lunching, turning on, getting to school, walking the dog, game-playing, gambling, preaching, rollerskating, museumgoing, marketing, lining up, and even just hanging out—it is influenced by the presence and participation of other people. Ticket lines are a visible identification of consent regarding the impact of a hit show. The action outside the New York discotheque Studio 54 is a miniature enactment of the apparently exciting competition of trying to make it from being an "out" person to an "in" person.

Other street life develops from basic activities, such as shopping, but the particular language, noise level, dress, speed, and density define the special character of each neighborhood. Shopping on Saturday afternoon on New York's elegant Madison Avenue is an exhibition of stylish consumption, a display of people clothed like the manikins in the

On the steps of St. Patrick's Cathedral, New York City

boutique windows, strolling leisurely down the street, flowing smoothly in and out of the art galleries and the shops. In contrast, shopping on Sunday on New York's Lower East Side is a noisy and intense body-to-body mixture of Spanish bargain hunters and Jewish merchants, a crush of pickle barrels, underwear, yard goods, and hawkers beckoning from shop doorways.

There is probably a promenade of some sort in every city of the world. Paris has one of the most famous — the walk along the bookstalls that line the banks of the Seine. On Barcelona's Ramblas, where stalls selling birds, flowers, and newspapers line Europe's most vibrant pedestrian street, there is a 24-hour turnover of strollers, beginning with the early morning workers who overlap with the

late-night prostitutes when both are buying coffee and the first newspaper of the day. As the day progresses the street is characterized by the women going to market, the men taking an aperitif before lunch, the after-lunch coffee, the before-dinner *paseo*, and the after-the-movies *paseo*, which becomes increasingly wild and colorful as the night progresses. On Sunday mornings whole families come out in their best clothes to discuss the soccer matches and, of course, to be seen.

On Saturday nights, just as gay men stroll up and down Christopher Street in New York's Greenwich Village, groups of men and women walk in opposite directions in Oaxaca, Mexico, around the town's central bandshell, thus allowing for repeated eye contact and much flirting. Even Los Angeles has its Sunday brunch promenade along Ocean Front Walk, which characteristically includes rollerskaters, pogo sticks, and skateboards as well as pedestrians. Music — played on earphones, radios strapped to the chest, or suitcase-size transistors carried by the most expert skaters — unifies the strolling and rolling with a ritual disco beat.

Although popular activites such as the transistor disco dancing that sprang up in Central Park this summer can instantly transform the image of a place generally, the way people perceive an

The Boulevard, Paris, New Year's Day, 1869

outdoor area is developed over some period of time out of a history of personal experiences meshed with the mythology that has attached itself to the place. The Ramblas, for example, has quite naturally emerged as the staging area for political demonstrations during recent upheavals, for over the years it has become well established as the polis of the city, the center for exchange of ideas.

Now as the 1970s draw to a close, the nation's corporations see outdoor activity not as a political threat but as an opportunity to create a positive image for themselves. Several banks in Chicago now pay performers to animate their plazas during lunch hours with music and dance. Minneapolis businesses have jointly hired an agent to schedule local performance groups on multiple downtown plazas. Exxon provides substantial funding for New York Philharmonic Orchestra concerts in the parks and community festivals on Lincoln Center Plaza.

Developers and city councils are also beginning to catch on that the popular term "livability" must include plans for outdoor activities as well as designs for traffic patterns and beautiful buildings. The Special Events Office of Baltimore, for example, is insisting that potential developers of the waterfront area include performance stages in their plans. The City of Chicago promoted itself in a big way this year when it spent $1.5 million from the municipal budget for a free ten-day festival of music that went from noon to midnight on nine stages. Historic districts like the Strand in Galveston, Texas, are staging special events with historic themes to dramatize and draw attention to new restorations.

The outdoor performances that result could not be produced on indoor stages because of interaction with the total environment. Air traffic provides unexpected punctuation, the audience on the next blanket concentrates all too loudly on opening a wine bottle, but when the orchestra plays the last strains of the "1812 Overture" and fireworks exploding into the sky move the very earth you sit on, the interaction of the whole environment is thrilling in a way a concert hall could never be.

Not surprisingly, the streets of New York City seem increasingly packed with sax players, college-bound (or escaping) violinists, woodwind quintets, electric guitarists, mimes, jugglers, singers, fire-eaters, magicians, hustlers, and card sharks, not to mention characters like the human jukebox, who hails from San Francisco, the home of the street-performer movement. These artists have found that Sunday museum goers are a particularly receptive audience since they are already in the mood to relax.

Not all street performances are inten-

Hot dog vendor, New York City

tional. Who hasn't been an unwilling focus of attention at least a few times, racing down the street after a letter that the wind has whipped away, stumbling in a lurking pothole, sneezing, arguing, or even just yawning loudly? Street happenings can instantly change the space and freeze pedestrians in their tracks. Two kids drum on the mailbox, oblivious to all but the desire for maximum noise, their delivery bikes parked neatly at the corner. A woman with brilliant red hair, wearing a fake leopard skin poncho over her purple blanket, arranges her dozen bags and parcels in a circle covering most of the street corner and sits like a queen in her castle. Such impromptu performances by the young and the old, the sane and the mad provide an amazing humanistic education.

The overlap between fantasy and re-

ality on the street is perhaps clearest during a movie shoot. I have found myself walking through a group of extras unaware until I saw the stars, differentiated from the rest of the pedestrians only by the movie lights and their startlingly familiar faces.

If movie shoots are the ultimate in making you see your everday environment as a performance setting, our celebrations and festivals are occasions when you can step into the fantasy and become the performance. And as with all street rituals, participating in the event rather than watching it creates a powerful sense of community, a fact that has been understood and used by people in power, for better or for worse, throughout history.

Celebrations can be more liberating than other street rituals because they are more formally structured. Once you know the rules and what you are celebrating, you can be spontaneous within that framework. Immediately a bond is established among celebrants that breaks through big-city paranoia and allows for more free communication. More than any other street ritual, there is an emotional intensity to celebrations because the senses, especially the kinetic sense, are heightened, because, as one woman at the Macy's Thanksgiving Day Parade put it, "I can feel the drums in my stomach."

In some countries, the act of celebration has been developed to a fine art. In these societies, more cohesive than ours, a festival can extend for days of intricately scheduled ceremonies and spectacles interwoven with processions, parades, and so much dancing in the streets that it seems the whole town is performing a giant work of choreography. Some of our best-loved festivals have been imported

Snow sculpture, Central Park, New York City

Saxophonist, New York City

and, despite local adaptations, still retain many of their original features. Festivals allow communities to reinforce the ethnic image of their own neighborhoods as well as to step off their home turfs and make their claims to parade through the city's shared spaces. Thus, for example, despite opposition, New York's Fifth Avenue remains identified with national parades.

In cities where constant change is a fact of life, annual parades and celebrations lend a sense of durability and continuity with the past. The ephemeral magic of spontaneous happenings is buoyed by the repetition of annual community traditions. Incongruity and friction between people is balanced by the affirmation of recognizing shared human activities. Vital energy is generated by street rituals when strangers interact with each other and their environment brings them together as spectators and participants. An elderly woman in a red hat outside the Plaza Hotel on New Year's Eve stated it simply when asked, "Why would you go to Central Park tonight rather than stay at home in a nice warm apartment?" She replied without hesitating, "Contact with people, touching people. That's why I live in New York."

Karin Bacon is an independent designer and producer of outdoor festivals and celebrations, and the Director of the Events Company.

A Guide to Peoplewatching

What people do on the street is instructive—and fun.

By William H. Whyte

The best theater in town is on our street corners. But you must know how to look. What we usually see is what we expect to see— other people milling about, waiting for the light to change, the stock crowding scene of documentaries on the urban plight. Look carefully, however, and you will discover a surprisingly rich social life and one with many distinctive and predictable rituals— reciprocal feet, 100 percent conversations, three-phase goodbyes, girl watchers playing girl watcher, shmoozers, and straight men. It's all there right under our noses, if we know where to look. Here are some tips.

The 100 percent conversation

Our research group, the Street Life Project, began studying how people use city spaces by watching people who stopped to talk on the street. How far, we wondered, would they move to the side to get out of the way of the main pedestrian stream? With time lapse cameras we tracked their movements at several street corners for many days.

They didn't move out of the way. They stayed in the stream or moved into it, and the longer their conversation, the more likely it was to be smack in the middle. In other cities, and in other countries, people show the same inclination. What attracts them most in a city is other people, and contrary to what they may say, it is at the busiest, densest places that they most like to congregate.

Department store doorways

Athwart the flow in and out of a busy store is an ideal place for prolonged conversations. In New York, Alexander's air door at 58th and Lexington is one such, and since it air conditions the street corner in summer you will see many group conversations, people just standing there, handbill passers, and the like. Our charts show that the number one spot is the geographic center of the corner.

A block away is Bloomingdale's. Its south entrance is one of the most congested spots in the world to negotiate. It is physically impossible to enter or leave the store; the doors are intricate, require great agility and excessive foot pounds of energy to open. The twelve-foot-wide sidewalk is jammed with 100 percent conversations, street people of all kinds and, at the rush hour, a bank of vendors start selling leather bags or belts or whatnot on the curb right in front. More people will jostle and press in. "One for five dollars, check 'em out," a vendor yells. The volume on the transistor radios goes up another notch. Soon the crowd will be in a true buying frenzy.

On a research trip to Japan we made comparable studies of the doorway of the Mitsukoshi and Takashimaya department stores in Tokyo. The activity was strikingly similar. Conversations, leavetakings, and meetings were clustered directly across the major in-and-out traffic, and save for the bowing, people's rituals were much the same. The Tokyo stores, however, seem more aware of the social function of their entrances than ours. They furnish benches or ledges for easier waiting, ashtrays, and such. They are also much cannier about vendors. They swipe their game; they put out sidewalk food stalls, come-on displays, and, on days when the street is for pedestrians only, chairs and tables for dining.

Step sitting

People also like to block steps by sitting on the most heavily traversed part of them. On the steps of the Metropolitan Museum of Art, perhaps the best in New York, a favorite place is directly in front of the entrance doors. But people sit all over. The Museum encourages them to by welcoming pick-up musical groups, jugglers,

Steps of The Metropolitan Museum, New York

magicians, and such, so there's usually a good show out front and a warmly appreciative audience. Some of the neighbors are not as tolerant and at their behest cops will occasionally come on the scene to chase away vendors. But this is part of the street theater too and so is the return of the wily vendors, to applause.

Plaza steps can be good too. The plaza of the Seagram Building, in New York, is especially interesting. Since people usually take the shortest cut, the main pedestrian flows across the plaza are diagonals from the entrance to the corners of the steps. But the corners of the steps are precisely the places most favored for sitting, talking, picnicking, and on a good day the blockage is so complete that a pedestrian has to look sharply to spot the few places left where one can set a foot to. But it is an amiable congestion and no one seems to mind.

A great series of steps are those leading down to the plaza of Chicago's First National Bank. They work as an amphitheater. At lunchtime on a nice day there will be well over a thousand people there. Some will be sitting in front of the show that the bank usually programs. But the best show is often on the steps— layer after layer of people looking at people looking at other people.

Reciprocal gestures

People in 100 percent conversations often engage in a secondary, silent form of communication. They reciprocate each other's movements, or the mirror image of them. One man may turn slowly on his heel a half turn clockwise, then slowly back. Pause. The other man turns slowly on his heel a half turn counter-clockwise. It isn't always as pat as that, of course, but there is a kind of symmetry when conversations are going well and it is quite noticeable in arm and hand motions.

Another form of reciprocity is straight man and principal. While one man is telling his story, perhaps very animatedly, the other listens passively. But not for too very long. If the principal overstays his turn, the other man becomes visibly restive, starts shifting his feet, and sometimes will declare a shift of roles by reaching out and touching the other's sleeve or shoulder, or, if need be, giving him a sharp jab with the finger. In New York's diamond district on 47th Street these exchanges are an art form. Men, by the way, touch each other more frequently than women do.

The prolonged goodbye

Look for people on the verge of parting. Often they are just beginning, and the full ritual will be a three- or four-phase affair, with each goodbye progressively more emphatic until the last, convulsive one. If you want to distinguish the false goodbyes from the real one, here are two tips: (1) watch the feet; they are the giveaway; (2) don't be fooled by the look at the watch; it is only premonitory.

Shmoozing

On the sidewalks of the garment center on Seventh Avenue in New York you will see knots of men standing by the curb, sometimes so many of them that you have to join the handcart pushers out on the street if you want to walk. The men are talking "nothing talk" they will tell you, idle gossip, opinions on current topics, sports, but they make a communication network that passes trade news with the speed of light. They tend to form up on occupational lines, and sometimes include retired men who have commuted back to keep in touch.

Shmoozers can be seen wherever there is a passing parade to look at. In greatest numbers they will be found in front of office buildings with a large back-office clerical force, like banks and insurance companies. They usually form up just after noon and the most common pattern is the line abreast. This is the most functional for watching and this they will do in a sort of amiable silence, visibly amused by the human comedy passing by. When they go to more circular, face-to-face patterns they will provide an interesting variant of reciprocal gestures. Watch for the man who is slowly rocking up and down on his heels. As long as he does this no one else will. When he stops, as if by some tacit compact someone else, after a pause, will begin slowly rocking up and down on his heels.

Shmoozers are fairly consistent in choosing locations. They show a strong preference for well-defined places: the edge of the curb, facing inward, or, for example, by flagpoles. They are also very pillar-tropic, obeying perhaps a primeval instinct for something at their backs. Rarely will they stand for long in the middle of large spaces. Shmoozers are also consistent in the duration of their sessions. They are either fairly brief—four or five minutes, or fairly long — fifteen to twenty minutes or more. Some groups are of the semi-permanent floating kind, with a constantly shifting cast, and will last the whole lunch period.

Girl watchers

The first shift begins around eleven with the hard hats. They lunch early, often on the sidewalk itself, and as they quaff their beer and eat their sandwiches they watch. They watch so demonstratively, with much horseplay and banter, as to suggest that their chief interest may not be the girls so much as the show they're putting on of watching the girls. Notice how they egg on the older men of the group. The girls are the foils.

White collar girl watchers in New York's Wall Street area are almost as demonstrative and frequently signal their approval with whistles and remarks. Favorite spot: the high ledge at Chase Manhattan Plaza overlooking the parade on Nassau Street. In midtown, for some reason, girl watchers are apt to play it more coolly, more appraisingly, and to affect a slight disdain.

But with all of them it's pure macho. We have never seen a girl watcher make a real pass at a girl and if a spectacular one comes by them they will betray their vulnerability. Watch for the involuntary tics, the quick tug at an ear lobe, the primping of the hair. (An excellent place for observing such reactions on Fifth Avenue is the poolside ledge at the Corning Building at 56th Street.

Pedestrian maneuvers

The bigger the city, the faster people walk and New Yorkers are at the top. They walk fast—men average between 250 and 275 feet a minute—and they walk adroitly. Notice how well they signal intentions—a slight hand move to the right, a wave of a folded newspaper; in these fractions of seconds thousands of collision courses are averted and New Yorkers will rarely bump into each other. It's the out of towners who give them trouble, with their maddening slowness, their ambiguous moves, their tendency to walk three and four abreast, sauntering and dawdling. It's like playing against an inferior opponent and throws New Yorkers off their game. The Rockefeller Plaza area is a good place to observe the conflicts.

Boston's pedestrians deserve a word too. Partly because of their training in the twisting and narrow streets downtown, they are a very aggressive lot and will bully cars to a dead stop. They are also great shmoozers, and even on cold winter days you will see them lined up in a patch of sun, observing.

Another pedestrian skill to watch is the entering of a building. It is not easy. The customary revolving doors and double sets of swinging doors have been engineered to require vast expenditures of energy. But people get around this. They head for the door that's ajar and they will queue up behind such a door rather than go open one themselves. For this reason congestion is at its height *before* the peak of the rush hour. At peak there will be so many people pushing through that all the doors will stay open and the crowd goes through quickly and easily.

A marvelous place to observe these various maneuvers is Grand Central Terminal. With its many entrances and its intricate crossing patterns, the concourse provides an ultimate test of pedestrian skills—and a spectacle of no little beauty.

Chair choosing

The two places that many people find the most pleasant, quietest, least crowded in New York are Paley Park and Greenacre Park and there are similar spots in most cities. They are in fact the most crowded and often a bit noisy. That they don't seem to be is due in part to their movable chairs. Observe how people manipulate them. In more cases than not, they will move the chair before sitting on it. Sometimes there is a clear functional reason; they want to get into the sun, form a group of chairs for conversation. But many times there is no clear reason, and after all the moving this way and that the chair may end up precisely where it was in the first place. But the moves are important just the same. *You* are making them. *You* are affirming your independence, and even if you take back the move it was pleasant to make it. The moves are also social communication. With a move of only a few inches you acknowledge other people's presence and your wish not to intrude upon them. These exercises in civility are a pleasure to watch.

What kind of day brings out the most people? Surprisingly, it's not the crisp, sparkling days in the 70's. It's the hot, muggy days—just the kind you'd expect would make people want to stay inside their air-conditioned buildings. But it is then that you see the most people sitting and picnicking and shmoozing— a point that proponents of megastructures and totally enclosed controlled environments would do well to ponder. If there's a lesson in streetwatching it is that people do like basics — and as environments go, a street that is open to the sky and filled with people and life is a splendid place to be.

William H. Whyte is a writer and an observer who studies the ways people use urban streets.

J.N. Hyde. "Running the gauntlet, New York City," 1874

Lunch hour, New York City

Fortunate Accidents

Unplanned spaces provide unexpected pleasures.

By Brendan Gill

In all modesty, I would be happy to have history accept as Gill's Law the proposition that when open spaces in cities come into existence by chance they nearly always prove more satisfactory than open spaces that are the consequence of foresight and careful planning. This dictum, gloomy news for urbanologists, appears to hold true for temporary open spaces as well as for permanent ones; it is certainly the case that the demolition of old buildings as a result of the current building boom in midtown Manhattan has opened up vistas that many of us would like to imagine as sites for future parks and squares instead of what they actually are — deep holes in the ground, soon to be the multi-story basements of high-rise office buildings.

These temporary open spaces have something to teach us before they disappear. Whether we are conscious of it or not, the amenity of that volume of unexpected light and air has a salutary effect on us; we are drawn to visit a construction site not merely to watch men gouging out a great pit with dynamite, backhoes, and trucks but also to catch a welcome glimpse of the city's past just as the city's future threatens to obliterate it. We see that the city's past, in terms of urban design, could have been far better; we see, more poignantly, that the city's future could have been far better than it is going to be. The damnable gridiron of streets and avenues with which we have been struggling on this narrow island for upwards of a hundred and seventy-five years remains unyielding; it is an iron virgin that seeks always to squeeze us to death, and it appears that there is no way of outwitting this instrument of torture except at an unacceptably high cost. Such open spaces as we have are small in

Demolition, East 53rd Street, New York City

scale and lack emotional nourishment; as the buildings that surround them grow ever bigger, the amount of nourishment the spaces provide will grow ever more meager.

This brings me to the advantage of accidental open spaces over intentional ones. In New York, my ideal example of this phenomenon is Broadway. What a mercy that it existed before the gridiron was thought of and that its vagrant sidelong progress up the island from the Battery to Spuyten Duyvil could only be accommodated to! A series of makeshifts fitted the old highway — the main route between the bustling small city of New York and the upstate village of Albany — into the plat of the great city to come, and such clumsy-seeming makeshifts proved in every instance to be charged with unusual life. Over the years, where has the celebrated energy of New York best manifested itself, if not at Union Square, Madison Square, Herald Square, Times Square, and Columbus Circle? At these freakishly shaped open spaces, people have always felt a natural tendency to mingle and make merry and spend money; here have sprung up our grand hotels, our theaters, our restaurants, our cabarets.

Every city has its accidental open spaces, and without exception they strike me as showing off each city at its most likable. Given that this is the case, what conclusion can we draw from it? Alas, we cannot simply *will* accidents into existence, for then they would no longer be accidents. The most we can hope to do is remain open to the possibilities that accidents provide and to draw up plans that are humanely capable of change. Alastair Reid says of his calling as a poet that to succeed at it one must put oneself in the posture to be struck by lightning; and then hope. What we need in cities is to be fruitfully struck by lightning, and not once but a hundred times.

Brendan Gill is a contributor to *The New Yorker* magazine and President of the New York Landmarks Conservancy.

The Mall, Central Park, New York City

Macy's window, New York City, 1884

Urban Strollways

There are new worlds to be explored.

By M. Paul Friedberg

What intrigues me is the notion that our streets are a vast, untapped resource, not an empty vessel but a multitude of potential experiences—physical, historical, and theatrical. Yet the majority of us are unaware of this. We are oblivious to the fact that streets are the largest single resource of open space; almost one third of our city is comprised of them. You and I inhabit and use this conduit system, which serves so many masters and which was planned, designed, and built well before our time. As each of us walks, we have our own way of experiencing and interpreting this activity; no two people go to the same place and see the same thing in the same way. It is this possibility of limitless and overlapping layers of interpretation that is so intriguing to me. What I want to suggest is that we open up this storehouse of unseen and unrealized experiences, of meanings and activities to us all.

Not all of us have the ability, need, or even the occasion to translate the streets' variety of information. Sometimes it can be done for us by sharing an experience with someone else. I once walked through New York's Central Park with its curator, Henry Hope Reed, and although I had been to the park many times, I had never seen it through Henry's eyes before. His knowledge of the park's designers, Olmsted and Vaux, illuminated hidden meanings, compositions, and details that were unavailable to the uneducated eye.

What I began to understand was that there are many ways to view a park. Any open space is a "state of the art" of its time. It reflects the technology, the social and cultural norms, and the values and objectives of its time. Upon closer observation, the values and sometimes even the idiosyncrasies of its designer or creator become visible. If you looked through Henry's eyes, you could see the attitudes and values of the late 1800s,

Grand Place, Brussels

along with the rich diversity and interplay of the topography and plantings. You could actually hear the music and laughter of the Casino in the Park. Henry was not just a guide, he was a superb conductor with a fine piece of music, orchestrating the environment and surroundings into a multi-faceted symphony. Because of that contact with Henry, my experience of Central Park was enriched, and when I walk through it now, not only do I see the people, I see much much more.

Streets can reveal to us their range of interpretations in yet another way. Thomas Hoving, as New York City Parks Commissioner in the mid 1960s, showed how closing the park to traffic on the weekends dramatically changed the way the park was used. It showed how unnecessary it was to redesign, redevelop, or physically modify our open spaces to further our enjoyment of them; we can simply close them to traffic.

Take these two visions as the living key to the past through the present, and combine them into one idea—strollways —walking as an experience. Let us design a network of strollways without traffic. Imagine how streets could be seen through the eyes of creative people,

Mime at St. Patrick's Cathedral, New York City

Street market, New York City

M. Paul Friedberg & Partners

ranging from the archaeologist and botanist, to the ethnologist and play director. I'd like to eavesdrop on their visions.

The point to be emphasized is that the best way of preserving and expanding street life is not necessarily by altering its form and patterns permanently. By doing this the streets tend to become static and immutable, resisting the kinds of interpretation and participation that give them excitement and meaning. Instead, let us make the most creative use of the environment by only temporarily altering its pattern and pace. Let the street remain a theater, a marketplace, and a playground, but let's encourage it to become more than just a sum of these parts and serve all of our needs, either simultaneously or at different moments.

Without making any permanent changes, let us carry this idea a step further and design a series of strolls. On a holiday, a Sunday, or even in the evening, we can bring in those people whose views and insights we admire to compose for us a series of strolls, illuminating and defining the rich layers of history, diversity, and experience in our streets. At present, there are a

number of guide books, cassettes, and other devices that are helpful, but they are limited; they don't open up to pedestrians more than a few of the most obvious buildings and monuments. Why not have them discover the entire city? On the appropriate day, traffic could be blocked off from the entire length of a strollway. Special pavings, plantings, or graphics might be used to identify its path and strollers would be free to go about on their own or to celebrate with their guide.

What is more clearly embodied in the form and texture of a city than its past? We can design a walk through a system of streets, taking the pedestrian down through the different technological, cultural, and aesthetic periods. The city's response to the changing eras can be revealed by the kinds of stone and brick ornamentation in the buildings and by the evolution of street patterns. Anecdotes about the past can be disclosed. While designing a mall in Grand Rapids, Michigan, I discovered that the eccentric geometry of the downtown was a result of personal antagonism between two early landowners. For quite some time, the streets of one half of Grand Rapids

never connected with the other half. What had been merely erratic in the past, was now the fact that gave Grand Rapids its character and identity. Although we often forget it, we are living in buildings and on streets; although constructed in the past, they are also a part of our present, giving unique form and structure to the environment around us.

Our city is more than buildings; it is also an arboretum of plants and trees that embellishes and refurbishes our environment. In the past, these gave an identity to certain streets—Elm, Maple, Sycamore, Cherry. Washington, D.C. is as famous for its Cherry Blossom Festival as for its monuments. Some neighborhoods, through coincidence, have large numbers of a single type of plant, such as the azalea, and in the spring they provide a barrage of reds, oranges, and pinks. At that time, people from everywhere come to stroll among the flowers. Botanical strolls could give a special identity to neighborhoods; streets could be articulated and understood by the types of trees, flowering plants, or annuals that grow in them. Towns and cities could be orchestrated so that there would always be a profusion of blooms throughout the entire season. Through organized botanical strolls, creative horticulturalists could give us access to some of the fascinating secrets locked in the evolution of the plant. For instance, do you know that the gingko tree, a common American street tree, has a sex and is prehistoric in origin?

Streets can be appreciated on many levels. My street is rich with resources and historical significance. The architecture of townhouses, once the cheap suburban homes of the middle class, now has evolved into the most elegant form of urban living. With the change in technology, the old carriage houses have become coveted houses for the rich. The politics of the area have diversified the ethnic mix into new forms of social interaction, diverse and in dramatic contrast to its early beginnings. The trees, the shrubs, the flowers begin to insinuate that a botanical stroll can be simply an aesthetic appreciation of the texture, color, and form of nature, for those who desire only the shade and beauty of the tree. It is up to

us to choose the level of meaning we wish to extract from our experience.

If we take a gourmet stroll, the city can become a giant restaurant with an unlimited menu. Picture a bright Sunday afternoon and a walk through an Italian, Scandinavian, or Chinese community, its interconnecting streets closed off to traffic. Each restaurant would serve its specialty, only one course, alfresco. A ten-course meal with everything from appetizers to dessert would go on for one block or 20. Already certain cities have taken to the streets to show off their culinary arts. Ethnic food festivals have drawn thousands to delight in one of the greatest of all human rituals, eating.

Probably the most American of strolls, and the one most often taken, is the stroll down Main Street. As a nation of buyers and shoppers, we see the store as a museum of contemporary crafts and merchandise. With what seems to be a limitless source of energy, we can browse for hours looking at the merchandise— and at each other. No longer do we shop only for subsistence, but for recreation, entertainment, and social contact. Some-

times this joy of shopping even rivals our love for the automobile, to the point that, in some cities, main street is literally closed to traffic during lunch hours. The more adventurous municipalities such as Minneapolis, Madison, and Grand Rapids have permanently altered their main streets into strollways without cars, transforming the streets into the market-place, the theater, the new bazaar, an arena of entertainment and activity ranging from art shows and music festivals to antiques and craft fairs.

The possibilities for the transformation of the street are as limitless as our ability to absorb its experiences. The artist, the sculptor, the musician, and dancer have yet to make their contributions. Our art and music should be a part of the environment and not only housed behind building walls. I want to be able to stroll among Rodins, Calders, Nevelsons, and Stellas, surrounded by theater and serenaded by music.

These can be exciting times. The potential in our streets is limitless. By exploring this vast resource of open space, we can experience not only our immediate environments, but also become a part of a continuum, enlarging our perspectives of who we are and where we live. We can alter our vision by taking a stroll with someone like Henry Hope Reed, who enlarges the context with which we see the present. Or we can be transported, suddenly, through an action such as Tom Hoving's temporary closing of the park to traffic, which pulls us out of established patterns toward a more creative use of our environment.

M. Paul Friedberg is a landscape architect currently working on a development on Pennsylvania Avenue in Washington, D.C. He is also Director and Founder of the Urban Landscape Architecture Program at City College of New York and the author of two books.

By Jane Jacobs

The trust of a city street is formed over time from many, many little public sidewalk contacts. It grows out of people stopping by at the bar for a beer, getting advice from the grocer and giving advice to the newsstand man, comparing opinions with other customers at the bakery and nodding hello to the two boys drinking pop on the stoop, eyeing girls while waiting to be called for dinner, admonishing the children, hearing about a job from the hardware man and borrowing a dollar from the druggist, admiring the new babies and sympathizing over the way a coat faded. Customs vary: in some neighborhoods people compare notes on their dogs; in others they compare notes on their landords.

Most of it is ostensibly utterly trivial but the sum is not trivial at all. The sum of such casual, public contact at a local level—most of it fortuitous, most of it associated with errands, all of it metered by the person concerned and not thrust upon him by anyone—is a feeling for the public identity of people, a web of public respect and trust, and a resource in time of personal or neighborhood need. The absence of this trust is a disaster to a city street. Its cultivation cannot be institutionalized. And above all, "it implies no private commitments."

Revitalizing Streets

We can make our streets enjoyable—if we want to.

By Arne Abramson

The quality of life, the livability of a city, is not measured at the skyline, but at ground level—in the streets, parks, and plazas that make up what is known as "public spaces." These spaces, whether publicly or privately owned, are some of the most valuable land resources we have.

Yet not all of them are successful in their use. Suppose a street shows signs of decay—what then? Unlike the mythological phoenix, a street will not, by itself, rise up out of its own ashes. Street revitalization requires a holistic approach to space design and management — an approach that provides a thorough understanding of public needs. In essence, revitalization must be based on the unique set of characteristics that gives a particular street its identity—not on borrowed ideas and concepts applied without regard to context.

The first step in a revitalization based on people's needs is an analysis of the street with regard to its present use. In general, a street serves as any or all of the following: a public space, a commercial space, an information system, and an avenue of transportation. Each of these functions must be studied and evaluated, both on its own merit and as it relates to the others.

In the past, the process of revitalization has focused on strengthening the commercial base of the city and improving transportation facilities. Lately, however, the idea that economic health is closely linked to the quality of social life in the streets has gained wide acceptance. It has become recognized that sidewalks also function as social spaces where people gather to talk or to meet friends, to stroll and window shop, to buy from vendors, or just to watch others pass by. These sidewalk activities are, in fact, valuable assets of the street. Their very

Stamp Market, Paris

Quincy Market, Boston

existence indicates that people enjoy spending time there. In turn, a constant supply of people serves to add to an image of health and vitality, contributing to a business district's shopper volume.

Many of the streets that need revitalization have failed to take such social activities into account. Either no pedestrian amenities exist, or the placement of the ones that do exist tends to discourage the very usage they were intended to support. For example, along major shopping streets, a variety of seating opportunities should be provided. Careful consideration must be given to their location (relative to established use patterns), the number actually needed, and the effect of the overall appearance of the street when they are not in use. Waste receptacles and kiosks for general information should be placed at areas in the streets that receive the most use, such as bus stops and intersections. Trees, planted to provide shade and character, should not be located in places where they might disrupt pedestrian flow, such as intersections or crosswalks.

In short, the ability to maintain a relatively smooth pedestrian flow while providing for socially oriented amenities is integral to the success of the street as a public space.

Facilities such as retail shops, arcades, banks, restaurants, and theaters are valuable economic resources. Their effectiveness in generating pedestrian activity is an important factor in the maintenance of a strong retail center. In order to continue to attract shoppers, however, these facilities must, in addition to satisfying consumer demand, present themselves in a visually effective and stimulating manner.

Thus, much of the work done in commercial street revitalization serves to supplement basic marketing with aspects of design. Research has shown that people tend to walk faster past storefronts that have stark facades and windows. Recommendations could, depending on local characteristics, include emphasizing the architectural qualities of significant historic buildings, encouraging storefront designs that are visually open

to the sidewalk, drawing attention to an area with the use of banners or awnings, and planning for consistency in storefront improvements. In addition, improvements might include a special, unobstructed windowshopping area along the building line; positive and creative regulations regarding vendors; development of off-peak cultural and entertainment programs; and development of an evening lighting program that draws attention to evening-use centers such as restaurants and theaters.

In essence, the goal of commercial strip revitalization is to provide shoppers with a comfortable environment to which they will want to return, both during and after normal shopping hours.

A comprehensive graphics program is a significant factor in the success of any downtown revitalization effort. Perhaps the most chaotic aspect of downtown areas today is the clutter and visual confusion created by overuse and poor placement of signs. While great sums may be spent on revitalization, commercial and traffic signs usually go untouched, reducing the total impact of the improvements. An improved graphics system can be one of the most effective ways to bring about the pedestrian and vehicle changes that a street improvement plan promotes. Additionally, it serves to improve the street visually.

Street revitalization efforts should, therefore, include the development of a comprehensive graphics system — one that takes into account both the design and placement of signs. Traffic, commercial, and informational signage should be redesigned to present relevant information in a clear, concise manner and placed only where necessary, thereby avoiding much of the clutter.

The overall effect of this would be to facilitate a smooth flow of pedestrian and vehicular traffic.

A street's most obvious function is as a carrier of people and vehicles. The most common complaint of "urbanophobes," however, is congestion — waiting in traffic, bumping into platoons of people while walking down the street, pushing through crowds, and so on. For the most part, the problem is not simply that there are too many people. Congestion arises

Bourbon Street, New Orleans, 1868

out of conflicting user group requirements — those of pedestrians, cars, buses, and taxis. The question becomes one of how to accommodate these various groups and still maintain a smooth flow of traffic.

In seeking to improve general traffic flow, three areas need to be examined: distribution of space between street and sidewalk; conflicts between cars and buses; and vehicle/pedestrian conflicts. Successfully dealing with these issues is often the difference between congestion and vitality.

Consciously or not, the concept of automobile transportation has dominated American urban planning. As a result, many major streets, through design and management provisions, give clear preference to vehicles. For example, traffic signals are synchronized for cars. This results in a mass of people waiting for the "walk" signal. When the light turns green, a platoon of people travels down the street, thus causing congestion. Vehicles, which typically carry slightly over 50 percent of a street's travelers, are given 66-75 percent of the street space. In particular, parking lanes, which occupy roughly 20 percent of a street's space, have been found to serve less than 5 percent of the street's users. The

overcrowding of sidewalks is an obvious result of such space distribution. Further contributing to sidewalk congestion are the placement and design of bus stops: people waiting for buses often interfere with the pedestrian flow and those who want to browse and windowshop are often discouraged from entering stores by people standing in the alcoves of buildings while waiting for buses. More often than not, the result of this on both economic and street activity is negative. Improvements to remedy this could include altering traffic signals to allow for a smooth, continuous flow of pedestrians; widening sidewalks (with varying widths to reflect pedestrian flow densities); and the provision of special bus stop areas.

Conflicts between cars and buses result when buses continually slow down and pull in and out of traffic to pick up passengers at bus stops. This constant entry to and exit from the traffic flow contributes to congestion. Remedies for this might include restricting the use of the street to buses and emergency vehicles at certain hours of the day or establishing exclusive bus lanes.

Major vehicle/pedestrian conflicts occur at crosswalks. Often, the "walk" cycle isn't long enough to allow people to cross the street before cars begin moving

into the intersection. An easy remedy to this situation is to adjust the traffic signals to an interval that allows adequate time to cross the street.

Thus, revitalization of a street as a transportation route deals with the sidewalk as well as the street. Efforts are made to improve the allocation of space between sidewalk and street, as well as vehicular and pedestrian flows.

The revitalization of a street is a complex process that must deal with the coordination of a variety of interdependent aspects: pedestrian and vehicular circulation patterns, the effect of storefronts and other commercial facilities on pedestrian activity, and the effectiveness with which the street functions as a public space are the major areas of analysis when planning improvements. While design changes alone cannot bring people into an area, changes that respond to people's needs can be a major factor in users' enjoyment of and subsequent return to a space.

Arne Abramson is a Project Assistant at Project for Public Spaces, Inc.

Portobello Road, London

Portobello Road, London

Open Spaces—Open to All

Let us not forget the handicapped.

By Edmond J. Leonard

Urban open spaces can provide a refreshing escape from the tedium of big city monotony. Their benefits, however, are universally beneficial only if open spaces are accessible to and usable by all people, including handicapped individuals.

The exterior environment can make less subtle the difference between a disabled person who is shut in by fate and one who is shut out by design. The person who is blocked by design barriers from participating in community life because of physical limitations cannot know the spiritual uplift, the inspirational release that comes from the sudden change of environment that is provided when open spaces are carved into cityscapes. Without the independence to travel these neighborhood paths, a handicapped individual's union with neighbors and integration into the neighborhood are cruelly thwarted.

Open spaces can and should be available for enjoyment by everyone, whether viewed from a wheelchair or on crutches or a cane, whether experienced with diminished or lost sight or hearing. To start with, there should be at least one path of travel that does not have steps and that has a suitable surface for wheelchairs. The minimum clear width of walk surface must be 36 inches. If gratings are located on walks, they should be designed so that cane tips or wheels do not penetrate the spaces.

Such an accessible route of circulation should allow a disabled person to arrive at, and enter, an open space from a public transportation stop or from an accessible parking area or passenger load-

Ed Sullivan, courtesy United Cerebral Palsy of New York City, Inc.

ing zone. The route of circulation ought to be free of obstructions or protruding objects that might reduce the maneuvering space for persons in wheelchairs. Street furniture such as telegraph poles, signs, mail boxes, fire hydrants, benches, and water fountains should be located beyond the minimum width of the path, both for the benefit of persons in wheelchairs or on crutches and walkers, and for those who are blind.

Wherever the route crosses a curb, a curb ramp must be provided with a slope that is not steeper than a 1 foot rise in 12 feet, unless a steeper ramp is unavoidable because of space limitations. For blind persons, the approach to the ramp needs some type of surface change, to act as a cue or warning.

Many small parks and grassy plots have walks that rise and fall with the contour of the land. Ramps ought to be the alternative to steps to meet such level changes, with handrails on both sides for those ramps that project some distance. If the sloping walk or ramp borders on a drop-off, then a curb or wall that prevents people from slipping off the ramp should be included in its design.

Picnic, play, and game areas need to have tables and other equipment and furniture that can be used by persons in wheelchairs. The height of checker tables, for instance, should be from 28 to 34 inches, with knee space provided underneath to roll a wheelchair into a comfortable position.

Lighting in open spaces should take into consideration the intensity of pedestrian use, hazards present, and relative need for personal safety. Occasional rest areas off the traveled path can be enjoyable and helpful for all pedestrians, but especially so for those with handicaps that make walking exhausting.

Communication barriers can be minimized by signage that accommodates persons with low vision problems. Size, color, and graphic layout can be critical, as well as location of the sign. Raised or indented characters or symbols, which can be read tactually, afford an opportunity for

Ed Sullivan, courtesy United Cerebral

the visually impaired to read directional or warning signs.

Potentially dangerous plants, such as those with large thorns or poisonous fruit, may present a hazard when placed immediately adjacent to major walks. Seed pods, berries, or fruit that may produce a slippery surface ought to be removed from walks. Branches that overhang walks can provide a dangerous barrier, especially for blind persons, and should be pruned to prevent eye or face injuries.

With proper design and construction of outdoor elements, increasing numbers of people in our society can be encouraged to lead more productive lives. In the past, provisions to assure barrier-free site design have been largely neglected. While this inadequacy has not been intentional, it is a reality that handicapped people face daily. Those given the responsibility of shaping the exterior environment should be aware of the design needs of all people.

Edmond J. Leonard is Program Director of the President's Committee on the Employment of the Handicapped.

Urban Identities

The spirit of the place remains the clearest design guide.

By Ian McHarg   From a telephone interview.

Open space has always been conceived of as a component in a humane city. However, as long as we believe that nature is to be dominated and exploited as only a backdrop to the human play, we are not going to give it much importance.

In the relationship of urban open space to urban architecture, the most reasonable thing is that the two be complementary and indivisible. One of the sadnesses of Modern architecture was that, by and large, it was anti-nature. It assumed generally that the outdoors was simply a podium upon which the building stands and that the landscape was really a kind of exterior decoration. Landscape was really denigrated as only a decorative background for building.

It is much more reasonable to think about the landscape as an important component of expression of the region itself and of the place within which buildings exist. Open space is continuous; buildings are instances in space.

For example, it is difficult in Denver not to see the mountains. They are the biggest statement, within which is a plains city, within which there are river systems, and so on. The hierarchy of the elements and all of the ancillary spaces should speak to that same identity. There'll be variation in identity, clearly; but they should all be of an identity that ultimately says, Colorado—the ecosystem of Colorado, its pre-eminence in terms of the whole experience, the backdrop and everything else.

That would hold in another way, obviously, for San Francisco and New Orleans and for the City of New York. The great thing about New York is the business of looking at the ends of the streets and seeing the bloody rivers. There is the horizon. There's the East River on one side and there's the Hudson on the other.

That's absolutely extraordinary. I always have a sense of it; maybe because I sense it, I am conscious of it; even though I can't always see it, I know it's there; and it's always a reference point for me.

I did a park for the Lower Manhattan Plan about 15 years ago where we proposed to fill out from pierhead line to bulkhead and make a continuous park from the Holland-America Line pier all the way down to the Battery and then up the East River to the Brooklyn Bridge. They are filling out to that bulkhead now. It would be an important element of New York's identity in the sense that the city comes to a park that defines the edge of the river; then comes the river. That would be a major identity. There would be other things that would amplify that as an idea. All of the things within should somehow speak to the larger statement of identity. That's hard to express in New York, but it's much more obvious in San Francisco or New Orleans or Denver.

Philadelphia is a little bit more subtle, but probably easier to do than New York, because it's a physiography and also because there's a penetration of the rivers, which go right through the fabric of the city. They are continuous. Not only the Delaware and the Schuylkill, but the Poquessing, Tennypack, Wissahickon, and so on. That great pattern of rivers—most of which even now do have a kind of natural expression—produces a network. So you always have a reference to the larger landscape.

Houston, too, has a marvelous opportunity. First of all it's an old prairie, but it's the edge of an oak-pine forest with water oaks that are 250 feet high, willow oaks, and yaupon. It is a rich vocabulary. The millionnaires in Houston know this because they live in Willow Oaks; they live in just exactly that environment. So Houston, too, has an identity and this could be found. It would take more skill there, obviously, than it would in Santa Fe or San Francsico, but you know, nonetheless, there's still a challenge, still an opportunity.

Also part of a city's identity is lots of elegant urban open spaces. The Museum of Modern Art garden in New York may be the best example of urban landscape architecture. It's an incredibly elegant and effective design of open space. It's a lovely mini-park and one of my refuges in New York. Just to go into that space is an enormous gratification. It may be the best thing Philip Johnson has ever done.

However, one of the tragedies of Modern architecture, which absorbs landscape architecture, is the conception of the International Style. An office building is an office building. Whether it is in San Francisco or Los Angeles, it doesn't make any difference. It's the same bloody stupid building wherever it goes. It is not responsive to place and it is not responsive to people. That was believed to be generically true.

Of course, it was generically *untrue*, and it really is, in biological terms, a heresy. Everything we know about plants and animals is that they are place-specific. Over long periods of time plants and animals have specifically adapted to the absolute specificities of environment. This is revealed in their present form, color, and texture—and of course all of the process. But this has not been true of Modern architecture. There we simply eliminated difference and emphasized unity, uniformity, and universality.

Of all the things that suffered, the landscape has suffered most—because the identity of places is immediately revealed by not only the physiography, but by the plants and the animals as well.

This should be exploited.

I would like to be able to go to any city in the United States and be blindfolded or be dropped in from a helicopter by parachute—so I'd have no way of knowing—and be able to identify where I am not only because of the plants and animals but the buildings too — the whole thing. The natural identity of the place would be idealized and formalized and abstracted by designers. Still, the identity would be there. It would be amplified by abstractions, not eliminated. This doesn't mean to say that everything has to look like a natural landscape at all, but the natural landscape should be the palette from which people select, and then represent, abstract, and idealize. Everything should be an application and an evocation, indeed, of the identity of the place — the *genus loci* again.

In the U.S. we have such an extraordinary diversity of environments. What a palette one has to think about in view of millions of environments from Santa Fe and San Francisco to Houston and Philadelphia. This idea of identity is for me the most important generating idea.

Ian McHarg is an urban planner, landscape architect, author, and Chairman of the Department of Landscape Architecture and Regional Planning of the University of Pennsylvania.

Art Without Museums

Outdoor sculpture and murals brighten the scene.

By Martin Filler

The impulse to decorate public spaces with painting and sculpture is old and basic, and its origins are lost in the proverbial mists of time. In the West, the rise of urban civilization around the Mediterranean brought with it the institutionalization of public outdoor art. In the cultures that flourished there in the millenia before Christ, such art was seen as a manifestation and extension of the might that caused those images of gods and men to be molded, carved, and painted. Art of this sort grew up independently in these early urban societies, and the rule of the Hellenes, and later the imperial Romans, brought the practice of public outdoor art to the whole of the civilized Western world.

After the hiatus of the Early Middle Ages, a revival of this European tradition of public outdoor art came, as did so much else, during the Renaissance. This rebirth of the classical tradition included a return for inspiration in architecture and urban planning to styles and practices dormant for centuries. Not least of

these retrievals of older traditions was the reinstitution of sculpture as an integral part of the way cities were designed and built. In many areas of Europe, these new public artworks were the first to be executed since the fall of the Roman Empire. While still expressive of the power of the state, the new efforts differed from those of their precursors in that they also expressed a freer, more humanistic view of man and his place in the world. Delight and pleasure (concepts not unknown to the Romans in private art) were now seen as legitimate goals of outdoor art for the people. Furthermore, the deployment of sculpture and painting became a codified part of a neo-classical tradition that prevailed in architecture and urban design with rather little modification until the beginnings of modern architecture in the 19th century.

Outdoor art has always been more common in those climates in which such art could be assured of a reasonable chance of surviving exposure to the

elements. Thus wall paintings have been more prevalent in Italy than in Iceland, mosaics more usual in Spain than in Sweden. But rare is the region without some tradition of outdoor artwork, be it the richly ornamented façades of Northern European guild halls, or the illusionistic painted architecture of the towns along the Ligurian Coast, or the folk paintings to be seen throughout Southern Germany and the Austrian Tyrol.

In America, however, outdoor art for much of our history was limited to what was necessary to provide a link to that earlier classical tradition. If our capital city was to be based on Baroque city-planning forms, then it must also have statuary at appropriate points to give authenticity to the borrowed scheme. An American courthouse square came to need a statue of a hero as much as the Campidoglio did, but that, for the most part, was as far as Americans usually went in the production of outdoor urban art during our first hundred years.

The largely unplanned growth of our northern cities during and after the Civil War, however, left us with an urban fabric far different from those earlier, idealized visions in the classical tradition. With rare exceptions—such as the City Beautiful movement at the end of the 19th century— little attention was paid to the necessity for an aesthetic component in our urban areas. Though war monuments and grandiloquent sculpture set-pieces proliferated in our cities in the years between the Spanish-American and First World Wars, another generation had grown up before outdoor urban art was to receive any significant public support. That came about during the years of the Great Depression, during which painters, sculptors, and artisans were left idle by

the collapse of private patronage; this was one of the first effects of the economic catastrophe. But starting in 1934, the New Deal, through its newly formed Work Projects Administration, gave America its most ambitious and creative publicly sponsored arts program ever. The fruits of it can still be seen in virtually every city of any size across the country. The sense of renewed social purpose, of reawakened civic pride, and the inestimable sense of psychological uplift that this public arts renaissance created marks one of the high points in the sponsorship of the fine arts in the United States.

Although the Second World War effectively ended the WPA's role as chief underwriter of public arts projects, the post-war years did not see a complete reversion to the situation as it existed before the New Deal. Government sponsorship, often on the state and municipal level, continued the creation of public art at public expense — though in diminished degree. The urban renewal (some say removal) movement that changed the face of our cities in the 1950s and 1960s furthered the cause of art in the open spaces that were characteristic of most of the redevelopment schemes of those decades.

Murals

But it was during the 1960s that the fine arts in this country were to be discovered at last by a mass public. That dramatic change was both the cause and the effect of the unprecedented sums our federal government began spending in support of cultural affairs.

One of the most active groups that was born during that period is City Walls, Inc., which was begun in 1968 by artists Allan D'Arcangelo and Jason Crum to bring fine art to parts of the city where

Hubert C. Birnbaum

José de Creeft. "Alice in Wonderland," Central Park, New York City

Vest-pocket park, New York City

there had been none before. The haphazard real estate development of New York, along with its shifting patterns of construction and demolition, had left the city with a great many blank walls. Not all were desirable (or suitable) for use as ready-made advertising billboards, of the sort that had made Times Square the first great example of public, superscale Pop Art. Over the past 11 years City Walls has commissioned more than 52 city walls, in order to "enhance the visual environment, to create imaginative transformations, and to give a sense of pleasure and delight," in the words of Doris Freedman, director of City Walls, Inc. Ranging from Richard Haas' illusionistic cast iron facade painted on a blank side wall of a building that became an instant landmark in the city's SoHo district, to Alex Katz's brilliantly congruent squares of heads high above Times Square, to Alan Sonfist's lyrical grove of trees on a wall in the decimated reaches of the West Bronx, City Walls' efforts have largely succeeded in doing what the group intended to accomplish.

The high-art approach of City Walls, consciously based on aesthetic appeal and the endorsement of artistic achievement, is counterbalanced by the populist philosophy of some of the first wall-art projects done during the 1960s. These were politically motivated protest murals that began to appear in black neighborhoods of Boston, Chicago, Detroit, New York, Newark, Philadelphia, and the Watts section of Los Angeles as part of the social unrest that swept through our inner cities after 1964. City Arts Workshop, the other major wall-art organization in New York, is like City Walls, a product of the *annus mirabilis*, 1968. But City Arts is the embodiment of the prevalent attitude of this period that art should be a participatory, communal experience, and this kind of wall art is quite the opposite in all but final intent from City Walls.

City Arts Workshop murals are planned and executed by the people of the communities in which these works are done: they tend to be in poor neighborhoods, and their subject matter most often contains explicit social or political messages. Instead of the cool, geometric abstractions or perceptually playful *trompe l'oeil* works done under the aegis of City Walls, the City Arts murals writhe with indignation, exhort solidarity or protest, and place the importance of aesthetic content far behind those of group involvement, personal expression, and the acting out of the creative process.

A number of notable examples of high-style wall activity have been done in other cities across the country. These efforts include a mural-cum-vestpocket park in Philadelphia, designed by Bauhaus-trained artist Herbert Bayer, financed by the Atlantic Richfield Corporation, and donated to the Philadelphia College of Art, which now occupies the company's former headquarters building. The wall painting, entitled *"Horizons,"* was conceived as an entity with the adjoining park: an illustration of how

art on the environmental scale encourages interrelationships among various media. In Boston, Richard Haas has executed his most ambitious commission on the vast blank wall of the Boston Architectural Center. The mural depicts an imaginary sectional cutaway view of a grand, neo-classical edifice, and has become a distinctive visual landmark on the Boston skyline. Even small cities have joined the trend: Stamford, Connecticut, has a nostalgic recreation of the city circa 1900 painted on two right-angled walls above a parking lot in its heavily demolished downtown urban renewal area, a rather poignant (and pointed) reminder of the city that once was there.

Sculpture

For the most part, though, sculptural projects have been even more numerous than wall art in the United States. Perhaps this has something to do with the more concrete nature of sculpture (often perceived as more "real" and permanent than outdoor paintings by many patrons of the arts). Certainly it has as much to do with the availability of blank walls fronting public spaces, which are not common in all cities. In New York, through the efforts of the Public Arts Council of the Municipal Art Society, some 23 sculptures have been placed on temporary display at various public sites around the city. Works by such sculptors as Robert Bladon, Clement Meadmore, Louise Nevelson, Kenneth Snelson, George Sugarman, and Arthur Weyhe have provided imaginative alternatives to the stock conventions that represent the outer limit of artistic adventure in the minds of many people.

Cities such as Chicago, with its tourist-attraction Picasso head and the scarcely less popular Oldenburg baseball bat, have come to recognize that the general public is ready for something a bit more unusual than the equestrian pigeon-magnets of days gone by. Philadelphia now sports a snappy Oldenburg clothes-pin directly across from its Victorian city hall, a juxtaposition that would have been unthinkable 20 years ago. Curiously, though, the commissioning of public

sculpture for a specific setting in this country has never been a particularly successful enterprise (as a visit to our most sculpture-filled city, Washington, should convince us). The placement of independently created, large-scale sculpture in open spaces often works much better than officially sponsored works. The reasons for this are as obscure as the true nature of the creative act itself, but the new spirit of experimentation abroad in the land brings at least the hope of a more effective way of providing better outdoor sculpture.

What now remains to be done for the continuation of this kind of public art is for us to enact nationwide the kind of compulsory patronage legislation—a "1 percent for art" law— of the kind already on the books of some 23 cities and counties in the United States. Baltimore, Chicago, Kansas City, Philadelphia, San Francisco, and dozens of other cities now require that 1 percent of all new construction budgets be set aside for some work of art to be placed on or around a building. For, if we are to keep our cities habitable in the face of the most severe challenges to the future of urban life in the history of our country, then we are going to need all the help we can get.

Martin Filler is Editor of *House & Garden* magazine.

Jean-Pierre-Louis-Laurent Houël. "Public Monument for a Paris Square," about 1802, pen and gray ink, brown wash and pencil

Outdoor Art

Claes Oldenburg. "Clothespin," Center Square, Philadelphia

Philadelphia Convention and Visitors Bureau

Rudolf Siemering. "Washington Monument," Philadelphia, late 19th century

Robert Perron

William R. Devine, courtesy Chase Manhattan Bank

Louise Nevelson Plaza, New York City

Bill Levis, courtesy Pittsburgh Post-Gazette

Fountain, Point State Park, Pittsburgh

Kenneth Snelson. "Forest Devil," Mellon Square Park, Pittsburgh

Wall of Schmidt Music Store showing Ravel's *Gaspard de la Nuit,* Minneapolis

Araonel de Roy Gruber. "Steelcityscape," City Hall Portico, Pittsburgh

Jean Dubuffet. "Group of Four Trees," Chase Manhattan Plaza, New York City

Isamu Noguchi. Sculpture, Marine Midland Plaza, New York City

Street Furniture

How can its design be upgraded?

By Carter Wiseman

Consider the fireplug, or the humble streetlight, or the police call box. Or the public trash barrel, for that matter. There are, after all, millions of such pieces of "street furniture" in cities and towns across America. In New York City alone, 13,513 outdoor telephones and 63,000 parking meters punctuate the view of the streetscape. Yet the forms of these objects are generally so nondescript that to the average passerby they are all but invisible when he is not making a call or buying another fifteen minutes of relative security for his car. In fact, the most intense attention paid to these ubiquitous urban artifacts is usually by dogs.

We are all used to thinking of cities as made up of buildings. Most of us are oblivious to the design and equipment of the spaces that separate those buildings. It is a costly oversight. I cannot count the number of times on a steamy summer day that I have searched in vain for a shaded bench, or at least a ledge without anti-personnel spikes imbedded in it to discourage vagrancy. Or the number of times I have struggled to hold down a piece of notepaper as frigid winds tore at it through the exposed cowl of a public telephone, drowning the operator's voice in the bargain. Or the number of times I have tried to angle my camera to eliminate a gangling, sign-encrusted streetlamp intruding on the view. Whatever the numbers, they add up to too many.

The streetscape need not be the hostile environment it nearly always is in this country today, and there are abundant examples to remind us that in the past it wasn't. Take, for example, the graceful fluted lamp-posts that have survived from the 19th century in some parts of Boston and Washington. The Los Angeles twin-globe model, while certainly not high art, is far meatier to the eye than its modern equivalent. Or take the ornate and admirably comfortable cast iron and wood benches designed by Frederick Law Olmsted to provide respite in and around his masterful parks.

The supply of European survivors is, predictably, richer. Paris still retains a handful of Hector Guimard's wondrous Art Nouveau Metro gates. (New York has one too, but it resides as a relic in the garden of The Museum of Modern Art.) And what would the Piazza San Marco be without its richly ornamented light fixtures? Even the simple sculptural bollards used to discipline horse-drawn carriages — and now, just as effectively, cars—in the small towns of Spain are reminders that age does not equal obsolescence.

In San Francisco, New Orleans, and Boston, successful efforts have been made to preserve some of our own venerable street furniture. And as part of its "Main Street" project, the National Trust for Historic Preservation has helped retain still useful sidewalk hardware in such diverse communities as Madison, Indiana; Galesburg, Illinois; and Hot Springs, South Dakota. Last January, New York City's Landmarks Preservation Commission blocked demolition of one of the city's three remaining old subway kiosks. And the Commission is now seeking funds for a city-wide survey that for the first time would include street furniture among the candidates for protection.

But most recent design leaves much to be desired. Not so much in the new plazas and special renewal districts being created in many cities. There, zoning and funding restrictions make it possible to insist on at least minimal design quality. The problems lie in the much larger area covered by the public right-of-way itself.

A classic example of how bad street furniture design can get is the horde of hexagonal concrete trash bins that came clunking into New York City some years back. Their worst offense was that they didn't do their job (the holes were too small to accommodate much more than gum wrappers, and the lids could be opened only with keys, which the sanitation crews were constantly losing). But their slanted, belligerent bulk was more appropriate to Albert Speer's West Wall than to New York's streets. (The bins are now, mercifully, being hauled away, but at 500 pounds apiece, it is slow going.)

Another designer's fantasy gone amok is the doughnut-shaped seating at the Federal Reserve Building in Minneapolis that threatens to wedge the posteriors of unwary pedestrians permanently between upper and lower rings. More common are the endless, joyless variations on the goose-necked streetlight that are standard in most major American cities, and which never fail to remind me of the death-ray weapons in "War of the Worlds."

What stands in the way of better design at street level? One problem is that people with the appropriate background are seldom found where municipal design decisions are made. "The ultimate urban designer is the Director of Public Works," says Rai Okamoto, Director of Planning for San Francisco. "That person should, of course, have adequate design talent and experience, but that is almost never the case." Michael Parley, Deputy Director of the Urban Design Group of New York City's City Planning Commission agrees. "People trained in design are just not in the positions in government to make much of a difference," he says. "Most of the decisions are made in individual political fiefdoms." And the result is that most of the designing is done by engineers.

Not the least of the deterrents to better work is the prospect of having the end-product destroyed. At considerable expense, an enterprising New York block association some years ago erected a handsome brushed-steel notice board on its corner, only to see the glass smashed

Paris

New York City

and the crisp surface dented by bricks and broomsticks within months. Faced with the same sort of problem at far greater scale, the New York Telephone Company recently halted the manufacture of its enclosed booths. All new sidewalk phones are being mounted on pedestals that, while less vulnerable to vandals, are open to the weather and are impossibly noisy.

Another frequently heard complaint among designers and city officials alike is lack of funds. "We don't have the money to maintain the property we already have, let alone embark on much new work," says John Hart, an architectural associate with New York's Urban Design Group. The problem has become particularly acute in recent months in California. "We're suffering from the effects of Proposition 13," explains San Francisco's Okamoto. "It's not just a matter of volition anymore, but of resources. When you talk to people about improving the appearance of the street, they are likely to say that other things should have higher priority."

Just how much impact lower budgets have on the actual appearance of street furnishings is open to question, however. According to Ekkehart Schwartz, head of urban design for New York's Department of Highway Operations, "most contracts for, say, benches or lighting, involve so much money that making them look attractive usually means only a small added expense."

Regardless of the sums involved, by far the most deadening influence on qual-

New York City

ity design work is government bureaucracy. A recent survey conducted by New York City's Urban Design Group shows that 29 separate governmental and private

New York City

organizations are involved in the initiation, funding, production, and maintenance of different elements of street furniture. In some cases, the passage of a design from conception through execution can be harrowing. To cite what is admittedly a worst case: the application of a restaurant owner who wants to erect a sidewalk cafe must go through the Department of Consumer Affairs, the Landmarks Preservation Commission, the Bureau of Franchise, the Department of Highways, the Building Department, the City Planning Commission, the local Community Board, the Borough President, the Board of Estimate, and the Fire Department. Normally, the process takes between 14 and 18 months, but after three years of struggle, one Manhattan restaurateur (whose 80-page application was returned at one point because he had abbreviated the word "Incorporated" to "Inc.") simply gave up. "It wasn't worth it to me," he recalls. "Some people manage to get approvals, but either they're better at filling out applications than I am, or they have friends where it counts."

In the face of such obstacles it is reasonable to ask how the design of objects on the street can ever be upgraded. One man who claims to have some answers is Harold L. Malt, the author of *Furnishing the Street* and currently director of the planning program at the University of Miami's Department of Architecture and Planning. "There are plenty of well-designed items available," insists Malt.

"It's simply a matter of making people aware of them and showing them where they can be had." To that end, he has, with the aid of a grant from the National Endowment for the Arts, produced the *Streetscape Equipment Source Book*, a comprehensive catalogue of high-quality street furniture that is made available to architects, planners, and others involved.

Competitions and catalogues are a step in the right direction, but a more frequently mentioned solution to the dearth of good design is some form of municipal review board with the training to recognize good material and the power to demand it. New York and San Francisco in their art commissions already have such bodies. In both cases, however, their influence is limited largely to passive approval, and they are often consulted too late to make more than superficial alterations in a project. "If there were some sort of local task force to review design questions early on in the process," says Jerome Butler, Chicago's City Architect, "it would do much to improve the look of America's cities." While wary of the potential for dull, uniform design inherent in such a proposal, San Francisco's Okamoto concurs in principle. "You can't legislate good design," he says, "but there should be some sort of hierarchy so that we could at least sort out the visual static we are subjected to and then concentrate on the forms."

Even without powerful review agencies at the local level, America's streetscape is not entirely barren. The simple but elegant light standards that went up in New Haven, Connecticut, in the early 1970s remain a durable example of how thoughtful design can bring visual unity to urban spaces. The free-standing sidewalk clocks, clustered lighting, and large planters at Nicollet Mall in Minneapolis give substance to that overused term "urban amenities." And the globe lights and ample seating around Boston's Government Center provide visual allure and pedestrian relief in the shadow of the massive state buildings.

Certainly one of the best examples of how to combine practicality and aesthetics in the field of street furniture is the series of bus shelters introduced in New York three years ago. Designed in consultation with

the city's Art Commission (an encouraging if rare example of how constructive such bodies can sometimes be), the shelters have two sides, one of which is clear glass, the other of which consists entirely of a light box for advertising. The spare lines and subdued copper hue of the structures are a pleasure to the eye, the roofs keep off rain and snow, the clear walls provide protection without isolation, and the enormous illuminated ads contribute entertaining splashes of color to the parade of street activity—not to mention substantial revenues to their private owners. So successful have the 500 original shelters been that the city plans to erect another 4,100 of them (although how soon remains uncertain because of a dispute between the originators of the idea and a second company that has been awarded the new contract).

Clearly, inefficiency and ugliness are not obligatory attributes of street furniture in this country. But we have a long way to go. Only recently I was reminded of just how far. During an autumn trip to Europe, I stopped off to see a Viennese friend who had just returned from an extended stay in New York and Texas. During the course of my visit, my host brought out some snapshots of his American adventure. There were the usual photos of conventional landmarks and tourist attractions. But also among the collection were several shots of more mundane objects: trash cans, shapeless to start with, but now bent and bulging where they had been beaten by the sterns of countless sanitation trucks; stark "no parking" signs left tilted at grotesque angles by marauding automobiles; and faceless phone booths fouled by grafitti.

To my friend, who is an artist and is used to the lush Baroque forms and imperial order of his native Vienna, these American artifacts evidently qualified as picturesque. To the dogs, it's all the same. To the rest of us, well, we deserve better.

Carter Wiseman has written on architecture and urban affairs for *Harpers, Newsweek,* and *Horizon.* He is presently Senior Editor of *Portfolio* magazine.

Street Furniture

New York City

Paris

Copenhagen

Hamburg

Paris

Paris, 1850

New York City

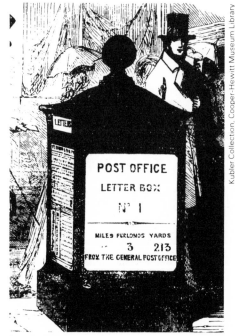

London, 1855

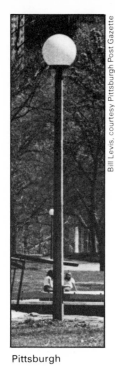

Bill Levis, courtesy Pittsburgh Post Gazette

German Information Center

Bernhard Winkler

French Government Tourist Office

Italian Government Travel Office

Landesbildstelle

Steven Baratz

Pittsburgh

Berlin

Munich

Place de la Concorde, Paris

Florence

Germany

New Haven, Connecticut

David Kenneth Specter

TELEPHONES

BELL SYSTEM

David Kenneth Specter

Sy Rubin

phone

CAFE

Kubler Collection, Cooper-Hewitt Museum Library

New York City

New York City

Paris, 1850

canopies Buildings Dept.

commercial signs Buildings Dept., City Planning Commission

enclosed cafes Board of Estimate, Buildings Dept., Bureau of Franchise, City Planning Commission, Dept. of Consumer Affairs

sidewalk cafes Board of Estimate, Buildings Dept., Bureau of Franchise, City Planning Commission, Dept. of Consumer Affairs

sewers Dept. of Highways, Water Resources

gratings Buildings Dept., Dept. of Highways, Transit Authority

curbs Buildings Dept., Dept. of Highways,

art Art Commission

benches Art Commission, Dept. of Highways

bicycle racks Art Commission, Dept. of Highways

carts Dept. of Consumer Affairs, Dept. of Highways, Police Dept.

information kiosks Art Commission, Dept. of Highways

trees Parks Dept.

subway entrance Dept. of Highways, Transit Authority

stands Buildings Dept., Dept. of Consumer Affairs, Dept. of Highways

telephone booths New York Telephone Co.

fire hydrants Art Commission, Fire Dept., Water Resources

traffic signs Art Commission, Dept. of Traffic

trash receptacles Art Commission, Dept. of Highways, Sanitation Dept.

refuse Sanitation Dept.

mail boxes Post Office

planters Art Commission, Parks Dept.

street lighting Art Commission, Bureau of Gas and Electricity

police call boxes Electrical License Board, Police Dept.

meters Art Commission, Dept. of Highways

sidewalks Borough President's Office, Buildings Dept., Dept. of Highways, Transit Authority

bus shelters Art Commission, Transit Authority

Building Zone

Sidewalk Zone

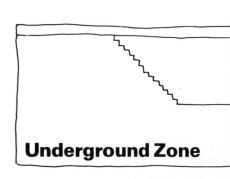

Underground Zone

New York City Street Study: Design Approval of Street Structures

Original drawing by Jack Hart and Patrick Too, Urban Design Group, Department of City Planning, New York City.

At a busy intersection in a typical large American city there are many unrelated elements. The drawing above is based on a series of charts prepared to demonstrate the complexity of administrative procedures for determining the location and design, and for providing funding and maintenance for these structures, with the ultimate objective of simplifying the procedures. This drawing shows 38 structures and a list of agencies responsible for approval of their design. Twenty-five of the items must be approved by 2 to 5 businesses, utilities, or governmental departments. Funding, location, and maintenance may come under the jurisdiction of other agencies.

As a result of the study, the New York City Department of City Planning has begun to prepare new simplified procedural guidelines. These are now completed for the approval and supervision of sidewalk cafes.

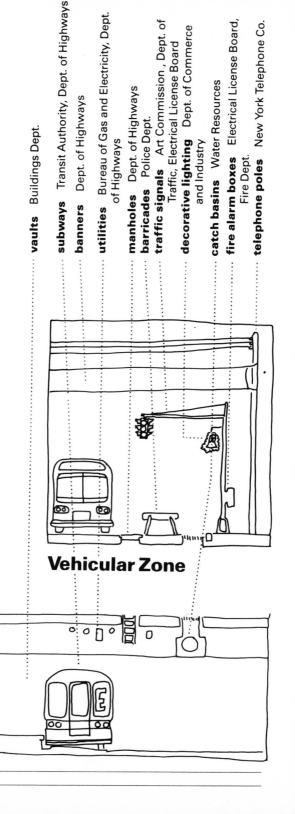

vaults Buildings Dept.

subways Transit Authority, Dept. of Highways

banners Dept. of Highways

utilities Bureau of Gas and Electricity, Dept. of Highways

manholes Dept. of Highways

barricades Police Dept.

traffic signals Art Commission, Dept. of Traffic, Electrical License Board

decorative lighting Dept. of Commerce and Industry

catch basins Water Resources

fire alarm boxes Electrical License Board, Fire Dept.

telephone poles New York Telephone Co.

Vehicular Zone

Urban Environmental Design

New assistance is being given to local governments.

By Andrew F. Euston, Jr.

In March 1978 the Department of Housing and Urban Development formally introduced urban environmental design as an administrative cost eligible for Community Development Block Grants. This step reflects the emergence—and success—of numerous local interdisciplinary urban environmental design practices. They deserve wide application and more deliberate integration within public management at local levels.

Urban environmental design is the term for the interdisciplinary decision-making at local levels of government that guides public and private investment in physical development. The phrase is intended to shift emphasis from aesthetics to design focused on people, livability, and quality of urban life. It consists of interdisciplinary administrative and policy processes for improving the quality of new development, rehabilitation, restoration, and neighborhood preservation. It benefits the public interest in housing, transportation, pedestrian systems, the working environment, and the full range of physical settings that comprise the human habitat.

In municipal government today there is a rapidly escalating demand for specialized design-oriented decisions. Routine municipal decisions promote or inhibit public and private investments in physical development. Often many separate public agencies have impact on the physical environment of a locality. Fragmented and ineffective decisions are a too frequent result. The public interest in these decisions, which is considerable, includes concerns for equity, economy, performance, and quality. Urban environmental design is a specialized aspect of local government administration that has consequently emerged to cope with these concerns. Design includes the administrative activity as well as the "fat pencil" conceptualization of a development project.

Most of the $400 million in annual Community Development Block Grants for these administrative expenses goes toward activites that should, according to federal law, be of interdisciplinary nature. And this influences the quality and the performance of what is built as much as and often more than what is conventionally conceived of as design. The costs of urban concerns are great. All too often money is poorly spent; unexamined options are closed; private investments are attracted elsewhere; and, in general, the urban environment and the quality of life are diminished.

Urban environmental design is implemented through zoning, tax policy, social programming, capital projects, and a host of other governmental activities. Its decisions bridge the planning for and the ultimate occupancy or use of public and private investment. In the aggregate these are design decisions that determine the location, siting, massing, budgeting, life span, and actual uses of what gets built. They determine the quality of urban life as it is affected by such environmental factors as accessibility, durability, compatibility, amenity.

A number of local governments have adopted interdisciplinary design staffs: in Dallas, the city planning agency has supported an Urban Design Division, which bridges agency lines, to initiate physical development programs, zoning and environmental control ordinances, ecological data systems, and so forth. In Cincinnati, the Office of Architecture and Urban Design has been shifted from urban renewal to public works in an effort to increase the quality and efficiency of design/development management. Seattle and Baltimore have widely dispersed design review, preservation, and development coordination activities administered by interdisciplinary staffs that include design professionals.

In New York City, the Mayor's Development Offices, staffed by urban designers since the mid 1960s, are given the task of coordinating the design and development activities of the dozens of line agencies involved with planning and construction. And in Trenton, New Jersey, an interdisciplinary urban environmental design team has become an important and influential part of the planning and renewal processes.

Slightly more than 43 cents of every dollar that is spent by local government comes from federal sources. However, this massive federal investment has a spotty history in the production of high quality design. Despite improved planning and design standards and greater attention to environmental impact, failures such as St. Louis's Pruitt-Igoe housing recur. Until the 1974 HUD Act, federal design objectives were addressed through environmental impact statements prepared by HUD. The Act has resulted in delegation to local entities those National Environmental Policy Act activities previously performed by HUD, including responsibility for environmental impact statements.

New York City

By Lewis Mumford

Reprinted by permission of Harcourt Brace Jovanovich, Inc., from "Closed Minds and Open Spaces" in the volume *From The Ground Up.* Copyright 1953 Lewis Mumford.

The fact is that one cannot have good architecture, either functionally or aesthetically, unless buildings and open spaces are conceived together. The right interval is as important as the right note or the right succession of notes. I suspect that one reason for the commonplace and unimaginative and sadly shortsighted utilization of this magnificent opportunity is that park operations are handled in one city department, street planning in another, and building operations in a whole series of other agencies, municipal, state, and federal. Because of that division of labor, everyone involved tends to hold to conventional practices instead of applying a fresh imagination toward the conception of an entirely different urban pattern.

vironmental impact statements. This delegation of authority has caused observable alterations in the operations and structures of local governments. Many cities and towns have re-examined the intertwined missions of their numerous line agencies and have regrouped them to achieve greater integration of their activities. This integrative effort is what Urban Environmental Design entails.

A better understanding of the public decision-making that affects the physical environment of cities is needed and can be achieved.

Andrew F. Euston, Jr., architect, is Senior Urban Design Program Officer, U.S. Department of Housing and Urban Development.

Las Vegas, Nevada

Las Vegas, Nevada

Demolition of Pruitt-Igoe Housing, St. Louis

By George Nelson
Reprinted by permission of Little, Brown and Company from *How to See*. Copyright © 1977 George Nelson.

The trouble with matters like visual pollution is that they cannot be measured, *nor can the effects be predicted. If we want to calculate the environmental damage done by, say, car exhausts or factory effluents, we have the people, techniques, and instruments needed to come up with precise answers. The dangers to vegetation, animals, fish, and people can be measured and repeatedly tested. But how do we measure the harm done by a superabundance of billboards? How do we even come to a consensus on the ugliness or inappropriateness of such installations? For that matter, how do we define ugliness? There is no Boyle's Law to tell everyone precisely what beauty is. When such matters are put to the vote, what kind of result comes from the polling of opinions on something not really intelligible to the voters?*

In the United States, we have a useful special example of the problem in Las Vegas. Here the signs along its main strip are higher, larger, more expensive, and more numerous than anywhere else. The result, when combined with the jukebox glitter of its motels and fun palaces, is a densely packed environment more suggestive of a neon jungle than a normal city. Well, how about Las Vegas? Beautiful or ugly? An expression of uniquely American vitality or social sickness? Would anyone come to see this extraordinary sight if the quick-marriage shops and gaming tables suddenly vanished? What does a Las Vegas tell us, for better or worse, about ourselves? Should it be given a Historic Landmark designation, or bulldozed out of existence? I picked Las Vegas because we have all seen it, on the spot or in photographs, and because there are critics on both sides of the fence.

What it comes down to, all too often, are disputes about "taste," probably the most unreliable of all possible yardsticks. If A finds something beautiful, and B thinks it is not beautiful, but okay, and C is convinced that it is the ugliest he has ever encountered, where do we go from there? This is almost always what happens in a society where there is very little experience in seeing. There is always that character who doesn't know anything about art, but knows damn well what he likes. If a public relies on the judgments of a book reviewer, or a film or theater critic, the authority given him seems to be based as much on his experience as anything else. One of the things we can build up, in the absence of reliable measuring techniques, is experience. We do this by looking and thinking about what we are looking at.

Public Graphics

Sandwich, Kent, England

British Tourist Authority

Arthur Leipzig

Chermayeff and Geismar Associates

Unobtrusive information, France

Chermayeff and Geismar Associates

Graphic accident in Soho, New York City

Hubert C. Birnbaum

New York City

New York City

Belgium

Paris

New York City

New York City

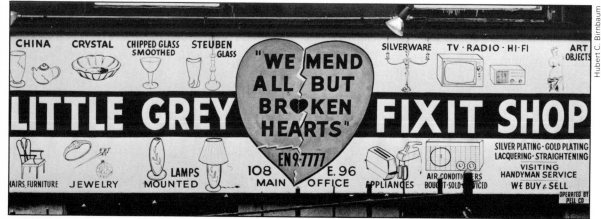

New York City

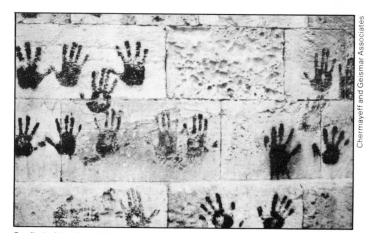

Grafitti of the East, Udaipur, India

Graphic Design in Public

How important is it?

By Ivan Chermayeff

New York City

What makes an urban space worth talking about? Or remembering? Trying to remember all the best urban spaces is difficult. There are not so many, but too many to remember: Bath, Caceres, Piazza del Popolo, Piazza San Marco, Place des Vosges, Trafalgar Square, Louisburg Square, the Ramblas in Barcelona and Figueras.

What's in common? Are these spaces always nice? Even in the middle of the night? In the rain? The last two questions suggest that one criterion for quality is population. People. If they aren't there,

New York City

Pedestrians and sophisticated signs, Copenhagen

is it a desert? If it's too late, too wet, or too cold, an urban space becomes a desert. Which suggests that if a place is a desert too much of the time, then it's not an urban space worthy of note.

Plenty of urban spaces are recorded and photographed, lauded and exalted in magazines. But after 1:15, forget them. I mean 1:15 in the early afternoon. The Spaniards, by the thousands, are walking, meeting and loving, taking coffee, and buying birds until exactly 1:00 in the morning. Not at all like the plaza at IDS Center in Minneapolis, which right after the lunch hour makes one suspect that the plague has hit. At night one knows the plague has hit Minneapolis.

It is people. Children. Dogs. But to have people one needs reasons. Crossroads, meeting place, church, state, shop, restaurant, bar, cafe. All or any have either existed forever or spring up because the people are there. Lots of people. Lots of turnover. The Via Veneto becomes a long space for urban voyeurs. Perhaps the best urban spaces really require pretty girls and warm weather.

Quincy Market in Boston is an excit-

ing urban space because it brings people, enough people, together. They want to be there desperately. People like to go where there are other people. They like to be right. To have made a good decision. To be in. To be chic. To be safe. But that is Quincy Market. Not quite real. For tourists, really. Not quite urban.

Does one go to urban spaces? Are they magnets? Yes and No. They evolve. Manufactured, they leave a slightly phony taste. A freshly contrived, instant urban space is all right. Recapturing a place that was a place, had a reason—fish or flowers, it makes no difference. It is only an observation that reasons make architecture, and architecture makes quality, and quality makes urban spaces worth talking about. So if you can start backwards, you will still be ahead.

New York's Waterside apartment complex is not an urban space. It's a wind tunnel with you as the test victim. Boston's City Hall Plaza could be an urban space if all the rug dealers and pot mer-

Unobtrusive information, Bath, England

chants of Massachusetts or Damascus were invited to pitch their tents.

Cars are bad for urban spaces. Piazza del Popolo survives because of Ristorante dal Bolognese's superiority over Fiat.

Again, urban spaces are people! There are some fairly ugly urban spaces that are great to be in because they are alive with people. There are a few urban spaces that are great even when there are no people. Not many. A tiny few. And that's when architecture counts. Like a Louis Baragan house: narrow stair, dangerous if possible, with no railing, which takes one to a narrow corridor which takes one to a little door, which opens onto space! Space surrounded by high walls and covered by a view of a graphic blue sky. The architecture of space with materials and reasons, where wishes won't do. It also takes time. More than we have, maybe.

Building lettering, 18th century, Amsterdam

tables, sell the tickets. Locksmiths, garages, designers all need to be found in case of emergencies.

When visual enrichment is at its most memorable, it is really more often than not from other sources. Pigeons, umbrellas, heavy snowflakes, shadow, and sunlight. Graphic qualities are often at their best when they are uncalled for, accidental, and anti-social. The peeling of paint, the patina of wear from passing feet on manhole covers, letters painted over drainpipes and corrugations, political slogans, preferably in languages one

can't read, are usually interesting and, in their own small way, contributing. Unfortunately, it is very difficult to put the mix of graphic life into predictable piles. Cheap plastic chairs are acceptable; cheap plastic signs are not, perhaps because no one can sit on the signs to block one's view of them.

Signs and symbols, Copenhagen

Graphic design's real contributions to the urban environment fall into one tradition or another, protected by trades and skills passed on for generations, and then further protected by zoning restrictions, eliminating illumination and restricting sign sizes, which otherwise bury architecture. Without restrictions or policing we have chaos and anarchy. Some people love Las Vegas and Times Square and Piccadilly. Not in the daytime. Only when neon counts.

Grafitti is single-minded, oblivious, and unconcerned. It may be exciting sometimes, but there should be no faith in it. It symbolizes frustration, sickness, and sadness, not the hidden depths of talent lurking in the minds of juvenile delinquents.

The standards of graphic design are

highest when they are functional street-markings; international and national warnings to workers, pedestrians, schoolchildren; and instructions to stop and go and slow.

After the functional comes the classic. Flags and banners.

After that one is left with temporary fairs, street festivals, souks and markets, and graphic designers' paradises like Amsterdam, Copenhagen, and half the towns in Switzerland, festooned as they are with nice chocolate boxes and other graphic delights.

Ivan Chermayeff is a graphic designer and partner in both Chermayeff & Geismar Associates and Cambridge Seven Associates.

Modern, classic, Copenhagen

Peeling graphics in Harlem, New York City

Where is graphic design? Very low indeed on the totem pole, where it belongs. Very unimportant. Times Square and Piccadilly and downtown Tokyo are not much as urban spaces. Best not to stay too long. No reason to anyway. Like graphic design generally.

Imagine any average urban corner without signs. Just picture them gone. No signs. No advertising. Better? Certainly. One of graphic design's jobs is to fill in. Tell the people what's going on, and distract them from the stream of cars. There are messages to deliver. To fill the

Graphic architecture, England

Street Signs, Paris

Urban Air Quality: Problems and Prospects

Although much remains to be done, the air is getting healthier.

By David Cohen and Herbert Luger

The average person breathes 35 pounds of air each day — six times as much as the food and drink normally consumed in the same period.

By the early 1970s over 200 million tons of waste products were being released into the air annually. Slightly over half of the pollution came from the internal-combustion engines of cars and other motor vehicles. Roughly 22 percent was emitted from industrial sources.

Cars, powerplants, and industry are the lifeblood of all major metropolitan areas. And, in fact, very few large cities comply with all federal clean air standards. Air pollution is, more often than not, an urban problem.

Air pollution is associated with the increased number of cases of emphysema, bronchitis, asthma, lung cancer, and numerous other respiratory diseases. It is also connected with diseases of the heart, and with certain incidences of impaired mental performance.

Children, as scientists have discovered, seem to be especially vulnerable to adverse health effects caused by air pollution. Minority groups, because of their large concentrations in urban areas, are also disproportionately affected.

Illness caused or aggravated by air pollution costs the American people billions each year. Part of this is spent in medical treatment, lost wages, and reduced productivity. Even more money is lost through property damage. Air pollution corrodes buildings, damages personal property, and harms parks, forests, and crops. In all, dirty air costs over $21 billion a year, far more than the dollar amount estimated to abate it.

In recent years, however, the fight to clear the skies has been making steady progress. This is attributed in part to the

New York City

passage of the Clean Air Act of 1970 (amended in 1977) and to the environmental programs carried on by the individual states and by the tireless efforts of countless citizen groups.

The United States Environmental Protection Agency recently released data showing that, although much remains to be done, the air is getting healthier. From 1972 to 1977 sulfur dioxide levels dropped 17 percent; carbon monoxide levels were cut 20 percent; and particulates — smoke and dust — decreased 8 percent. Effectively an estimated 18 million fewer people were being exposed to levels violating health standards in 1977 than in 1972. Nitrogen dioxide levels have also decreased. And, although Americans were doing more automobile driving during this period, smog levels have remained stable, if still unacceptably high.

"While America's air has gotten cleaner," EPA Administrator Douglas M. Costle states, "we're still a long way from having ideally healthy air throughout the country. The problem of urban smog is the most difficult before us."

Since much smog is auto related, society faces a basic tradeoff in its transportation systems. The romance with the automobile must be weighed against the desire for better health.

Emission control devices on cars; driving less, in favor of mass transportation; walking, bicycling, car pooling, and so forth; urban transportation control plans; inspection and maintenance programs for checking vehicle emissions; continued controls for industrial sources, such as the use of scrubbers at power-plants — all of these measures are tools in the battle for clean air. And, of course, there will never be a substitute for an informed, active citizenry.

David Cohen is an Environmental Specialist and **Herbert Luger** is Regional Librarian, both for the Environmental Protection Agency.

Burning old auto batteries, Houston, Texas

New York City

By Bernard Rudofsky

Street dirt is still one of the conspicuously appalling sights in American towns. It is a virulent form of the old evil, aggravated by the packaging industry that unloads an increasing volume of instant trash upon us. Yet from all the evidence, natives are unaffected by it. Just as the syphilization of a race imparts some degree of immunity and seems to lessen the disease's manifestations, so does constant exposure to dirty streets blunt one's sensitivity.

To most old-world nations, clean streets are of utmost importance; a good many might even be accused of making a fetish of cleanliness. To the confirmed litterer, no spectacle is more absurd than the sight of somebody's sweeping the street in front of his house, a practice by no means restricted to small towns. The weird part of it is that even before the procedure starts, there is no visible dirt, not a scrap of paper around. For all its rusticity, the performance resembles a pantomime, a folkloristic Dance of the Sweepers, interpreted by children and some stout ballerinas. No doubt we have here the ritual of a faith that places cleanliness among moral virtues. What seems to us a morbid preoccupation with keeping clean is nothing short of a state of grace.

New York City

Crime and Vandalism

Sign on an empty flowerpot: These flowers are here for everyone to enjoy.

By Blair G. Ewing and Allan Wallis

Robert Perron

New York City

Kubler Collection, Cooper-Hewitt Museum Library

A mugging, 1857

These flowers were put here for everyone to enjoy.

Sign by an empty flower pot in Greenwich Village.

The streets, parks, plazas, and other open spaces of our cities are meant to be settings for public events, social life, and play, as well as places to facilitate movement and access to air and light. In the last two decades, these urban open spaces have also become—indeed, in the view of some citizens, have become primarily — the settings for vandalism, mugging, purse-snatching, rape and robbery. It is little wonder that people have come to think of these spaces as high risk environments, to be avoided and left lifeless for large portions of the day. The image that many of our open spaces have taken on is not what their designers had envisioned, but what the criminal and the fear of crime have created.

The commission of a crime in an open space or elsewhere requires at least two elements: a willing offender and an environment that offers relatively favorable opportunity to commit an offense. In general, environments that present high risks to offenders of being detected and apprehended, and that also offer a relatively low reward do not attract crime. The path to crime prevention, then, would seem to consist most simply of increasing the risk to offenders or reducing the potential rewards available. Straightforward as this approach appears, two caveats must be added. The first caveat is that it is no simple task to determine the risks and rewards present in a particular environment at a given time. We still know very little about how offenders perceive the environments in which they plan and execute their offenses. The second caveat is that in the attempt to increase risk to offenders we may simultaneously decrease the attractiveness of the environment for its legitimate users.

With these cautions in mind, it may be well to limit the discussion of crime in urban open space to a class of environments within that category, namely, to those designed primarily for passive use by the general public, such as walking, people watching, and eating lunch. These spaces are predominantly in non-residential areas, and include office plazas, shopping streets, vest-pocket parks, and traffic islands planted with benches.

The crimes that occur in urban open spaces are as varied as the spaces themselves. They range from crime against property, such as vandalism; to personal crimes such as purse-snatching and assault; as well as what are sometimes called "victimless crimes" such as prostitution, gambling, and exhibitionism. These crimes do not occur at random locations or times of day. Each tends to follow, on the whole, a distinguishable pattern. This suggests that offenders tend to assess with some care the drawbacks and opportunities for committing a crime in a specific environment. The purse-snatcher, for example, needs an easy means of escape, but is relatively indifferent to public (non-police) surveillance. By contrast, the vandal is frequently deterred by casual public surveillance, but may be less concerned with conditions for escape. Although the crimes committed

in urban open spaces vary widely, those environments have common opportunity characteristics that seem to support crime. These are spaces that tend to be public in the sense of being anonymous. They are used often briefly and only in passing by people who are strangers to each other. They are heavily used, but often only for a few hours of the day. It is usually not clear to the public who is responsible for the protection and maintenance of such spaces. These are environments, then, that attract a sufficient number of people to provide an attractive pool of victims, and a shield of anonymity and indifference that reduces risk to the offender. Crime prevention strategies applied to these spaces must essentially work to alter these characteristics. They must bring the relation of risks to rewards into a less favorable ratio for the offender.

Research conducted over the past decade, much of it under the auspices of LEAA's National Institute of Law Enforcement and Criminal Justice, has identified a number of strategies for reducing crime in urban open spaces. They include four basic approaches to

reducing crime opportunity: target hardening, controlling circulation, surveillance, and providing support activities:

Target hardening refers to designing the environment to be more vandal resistant. Materials that are easily cleaned or less easily marked may be used. Target hardening also concerns the selection of hardware, such as locks and fences, which make it more difficult and time consuming for the offender to commit a crime, thereby increasing his risk, or at least his perception of risk.

Controlling circulation consists of measures that will affect the movement of people through space, so as to slow the egress of offenders and keep them in areas where surveillance can occur, thereby increasing their sense of risk. Circulation may be controlled through the use of physical design features such as planters, benches, fences, or level changes. Security personnel also may be used in combination with these.

Surveillance refers to keeping offenders under observation. This may be achieved by mechanical technique, such as the use of alarms or closed circuit television, through the use of security personnel, or by increasing the ability of people who use a space to see what is going on in it. This form of spontaneous or natural surveillance is enhanced by the removal of visual barriers and hiding places, and by the introduction of adequate lighting. Here, as in the case of circulation control, careful consideration must be given to the use of such landscaping elements as lighting and street furniture.

Support activities consist of amenities introduced into the environment to encourage new uses or give fuller support to existing ones. Support activities may range from food-vending stands, which help to accommodate the noontime luncher, to fashion shows and musical performances, which provide special opportunities for gatherings. Support activities may be employed to attract users at off hours of the day, creating a condition for natural surveillance. Support may also take the form of more actively involving users in the maintenance and appearance of a space— the provision of movable

sculpture, for example, which may be intentionally rearranged by passersby, or the provision of blank walls to be decorated by local groups who may provide a unique and personal identity for the space.

These crime-prevention strategies may appear in large part to be no more than applied common sense. Yet their successful implementation, as evaluative research has revealed, is not as simple as it may appear. Improved lighting may decrease crime on some streets, but not on others. Simply improving the possibilities for natural surveillance does not in itself ensure that citizens will in fact engage in surveillance, or report the crimes that they might witness. The difficulty of effective implementation arises, in part, from the second caveat mentioned before: that in increasing risks to offenders we may also decrease the attractiveness of the environment for its legitimate users. A balance between security and attractiveness must be struck if an environment is to be successful.

An environment might be secured by strictly controlling access with guards augmented by mechanical surveillance. This "fortress city" approach is not only costly, it has the potential effect of reinforcing the anonymity that too often characterizes urban open spaces. A more appropriate approach is to select among methods of increasing security while simultaneously enhancing the involvement of users with the environment by providing activities that people enjoy watching as well as engaging in. A careful and sensitive balance must be struck between the need for security and the need for open public spaces where citizens can enjoy themselves.

Blair G. Ewing is Acting Director of the National institute of Law Enforcement and Criminal Justice. **Allan Wallis** is with the Community Crime Prevention Division of the same organization.

"Air clean enough for you today?"

Drawing by Koren; ©1970 The New Yorker Magazine, Inc.

Community Gardens

An active citizenry is fostering a greening movement.

Except as noted, photos courtesy Liz Christy

New York Daily News Photo

New York Daily News Photo

New York Daily News Photo

The Greening of Cities

There is a difference between surviving and thriving.

By Liz Christy

George Hayward. "Contoit's Garden, Broadway, New York," 1830

In the last ten years, participants in community-sponsored open space projects have gained experience, have matured politically, and have produced a number of open space projects. In the early 1970s, there were but a handful of these projects; now there are over 350 in New York City alone. Some are allotments for individual vegetable or flower plots; some are parks where the community participates in maintenance and management; others are multi-use areas that include recreation. Most have the word "community" in their names followed by "park," "garden," or "farm." Almost every project is uniquely tailored to the needs of the neighborhood, and all require tremendous muscle and determination supplied by volunteers. Imagine urban spaces as fields or meadows instead of rubble waste. This is our new "rural renewal."

People have historically joined together to grow plants for survival or pleasure. The term "community garden" expresses that traditional dependency of the two life forms, linked together by basic needs, benefitting each participant.

In the late 1960s, the number of vacant lots in cities began to increase at a phenomenal rate. The combination of abandonment by landlords and arson led to rows of burnt-out, bricked-up buildings, and later to ugly, refuse-filled vacant lots. As the financial situation worsened, urban renewal and other building plans were postponed; bulldozed areas lay empty. The sight was an incentive to neighborhood groups. City residents looked on the growing decay of housing stock, urban renewal promises, and the fact that parks departments could not take care of their parks. People realistically recognized that nobody was going to take care of the neighborhood, the building, the sidewalk, the tree — if they had one — except themselves.

A number of grass roots, self-help programs took the initiative to bring about a return of greenery to our cities. In New York City, for example, the potential was investigated in the late 1960s by The Parks Council, an established watchdog for parks and neighborhood improvement. In the early 1970s such projects as Ruppert Green, Asphalt Green, and Village Green demonstrated what the concern was all about. Then other organizations began to spring up specifically with this purpose in mind. The Green Guerillas was formed in 1973 as a group of professionals and experienced volunteers working to improve the quality and quantity of green open space. Among other greening-assistance organizations are the Magnolia Tree Earth Center, The Council on the Environment of New York City, the Environmental Action Coalition, and the Horticulture Society of New York to mention just a few. A number of these and other groups work together as the Street Tree Consortium, which pioneered a citizen street tree pruning and maintenance program; it is under the jurisdiction of the Parks Department, which certifies citizens to prune the city's street trees.

These groups were spurred along by all levels of city government and institutions, including The New York Botanical Garden and the Brooklyn Botanic Garden. New York State's Parks and Recreation Department and Cornell University contributed money toward outfitting the "Grow Truck" — a mobile lending service of garden tools and books for citywide use — which is just one activity of the Council on the Environment's Open Space Greening Program.

Then the Bronx Open Space Task-force was organized as a collaboration of groups and institutions concerned about the devastation in the South Bronx. Government listened. The federal government is contributing toward the creation of 15 new park spaces there. And it responded in 1977 with a $3 million Urban Gardening Program to meet the needs of inner city residents. In the same year a Gallup poll showed a dramatic increase in the number of people growing vegetables—from the Bowery Houston Community Farm/Garden to the several hundred allotment gardens sponsored by Cornell University and the Housing Authority of New York City. In 1978 the federal program was expanded to 16 cities nationwide.

Most residents who want to begin an open space project already have a local eyesore in mind. The first step is to find out its ownership—private or public. In New York City, for example, the General Service Administration's Green Thumb Program provides speedy assistance and a cheap ($1 per year) interim 30-day cancellation lease for available city land. If the group needs or wants property/liability insurance, there is a master community park plan through The Parks Council or individual insurance firms.

The next step includes site feasibility and soil analyses. The neighborhood should be canvassed for an assessment of open space needs and desires. In the

1960s, a lesson was learned when many well-intentioned people funded and built play lots in needy areas without consulting the communities. These play lots were destroyed. Communication in all phases of development through posters, signs, and news articles is essential for successful projects. Design, subsequent budget, and phase planning for construction, maintenance, and management usually require professional assistance. Through participation in this process, residents learn the criteria for safe, usable, protected, and comfortable open space.

The first problem in developing vacant or abandoned city lots is soil. Ideally, building demolition should include excavation to a depth of 3 feet and a cover of clean sand and soil. However, since this is almost never done, community groups are faced with the problem of manually excavating highly alkaline building debris and replacing it with expensive topsoil—at present, $18 to $36 per cubic yard.

Throughout our cities, neighborhoods are creating open spaces that are appropriate to their needs. These include recreation for toddlers—with a mudpie box or sandbox, or with a Tricycle Freeway complete with STOP and YIELD signs; or a recycled Volkswagen or motorboat filled with concrete and sunk into sand for climbing and playing; or an adventure playground built by young people under supervision of adults to be taken apart and rebuilt. Some residents may opt for a commons or lawn that can be used for picnics, storytelling, rolling, reading, playing tag, or kite-flying. Surrounded by a path, it can be used for jogging, running, or skateboarding, if properly landscaped between usage areas. Trellises with vines or roses can be utilized for shaded seating. Lily ponds, barbecue pits, amphitheaters are all possible and well within the means of some neighborhoods' priorities and budgets.

Sometimes the simplest form of adaptation is an outdoor living room, complete with sofas and tables for dining *al fresco* when apartments get too hot for cooking and eating. These outdoor living areas may become a social club at night or be developed as "Everyone's

Backyard" or a "Pick-Me" flower garden with a day set aside for nearby residents to pluck flowers for their homes. The benefactors are, of course, also invited to weed, seed, and water.

So varied are the options that we marvel at the ingenuity that has evolved. The list of possibilities includes: recycling centers, compost systems, herb or Biblical gardens, greenhouses, sunpits, domes, coldframes, mini-forests, dog runs, birdhouses and meadows. A mound of earth can be used for climbing, sledding, rock gardening, cycling, reading, digging, sliding, and so on.

Asphalt surface areas have been screened with landscaping. Multi-use potential is determined by the construction, the materials selected, and the design. One city-owned open field parking lot in downtown Manhattan, for example, is scheduled to become "Bumper Park." When completed it will provide for bike as well as car parking; perimeter "green screen" landscaping will cut the glare; during off-hours, games such as tennis or volleyball can be played by simply inserting posts for nets into existing pipe sleeves in the surface. Another possibility is that recreation areas can provide an arena for winter ice-skating. Using concrete aggregate for surfacing and a three-inch high berm or wall of the same material with removable blocks for drainage can ease the space into winter recreation use.

There is a difference between surviving and thriving in our cities. Somehow a partnership must be formed for better management of public parks. Monies must be raised for substantial restoration projects. Whether the present tax-base program is adequately related to each park is a question that should be properly explored and resolved. Possibly those owners who occupy land abutting small parks should contribute directly to the maintenance fund and co-manage the park with the parks department. Every park should have a "Friends of the Park" support organization.

The services and objectives of parks departments might be re-evaluated in light of the responsibility for lands in trust. The usual problems of continuity

and professional management with adequate use of funding deserve study. Comparison with other municipalities in this country and abroad might provide practical alternatives.

A municipality might provide a corps of ironmongers, fence welders, tree pruners, and other specialists to assist local public and private parks in their efforts to maintain their open spaces.

Contrary to what a politician once said about the deteriorating condition of our green space, the parks will not abide, they just rot or barely survive and reflect their devaluation outward into surrounding neighborhoods. The banks that offer mortgages to surrounding homes or buildings have a vested interest in stabilizing their investments. Government and business must recognize open space as a crucial issue and be encouraged to participate because it's the popular new thing to do.

In future urban renewal plans, provision for participatory open space with "rural renewal" opportunities for plants and people is a public mandate. Bending the street grid to provide for more squares, small parks, and mews will soften the city's edges. These small

spaces should perhaps be managed by adjacent private or public nonprofit owners, who would be assessed a fee-per-lot to be put toward maintenance costs. A sense of closure, scale, intimacy, and style is important. New parks and gardens with space for resident-managed garden plots for vegetables, flowers, or other plants should be set aside permanently in every neighborhood.

Comprehensive, long-term planning can only be accomplished with a visionary, empowered agency, with an educated constituency, and with boldness and courage. Master plans that are superimposed on local plans can provide open space transition areas from one neighborhood to another. Greenbelts, linear or curving parks, byways, a series of commons, fields, nurseries, meadows lined by a tree-shaded path are all possible if we are willing to change our stance and work toward these amenities—a tradition of people and plants in partnership.

Liz Christy is Director of Open Space Greening for the Council on the Environment of New York City.

Interim Lots

Spaces are there for the taking—at least for a while.

By Jane G. Brown and Karl Katz

Hot air balloon on Wall Street, New York City

In major cities in this country and for that matter large cities everywhere, there is often a time lapse between one permanent use of a site and a new use of that space. It is not unusual for a building or even blocks of buildings to be torn down in anticipation of new construction only to have the funding for the project disappear.

The space may then remain vacant for months, even years, while new plans are made and investors recruited.

In recent years awareness has grown of the enormous potential for these vacant city spaces. They come in a wide variety of sizes and shapes: lots, dead-end streets, rooftops, river piers, spaces between buildings, walls, to name a few. All over the world exciting projects have been successful in making use of these odd-lot spaces, thereby bringing new life to communities. A few of these projects have been elaborate in design and expensive to produce but for the most part they have been simple, inexpensive ideas that were community inspired and sponsored. Some of them have been, in fact, the work of just one determined individual. Some have been of short duration, such as a site for a day-long street fair. Others are semi-permanent in nature: tennis courts on rooftops, or waterfalls in mid-Manhattan, adventure playgrounds in Stockholm, or a gutted airplane in a vacant lot in Jerusalem, in which children are free to explore and dream about taking off to other worlds.

All of these projects have one thing in common — they have been successful; they have been dreamed up, carried out, and completed. And they worked. This is not a discussion about architectural designs that have never made it off the drawing board nor is it a criticism of those that have. It is simply a small sampling of imaginative ideas for the use of temporarily vacant city spaces:

One of the earliest but still perhaps the classic example of this temporary use of space was illustrated by the Ruppert Green project. When Ruppert moved its operations out of town, the old Ruppert Breweries in Manhattan were torn down and high-rise residential housing was planned. However, there was a substantial delay after the breweries came down before new construction began. With the inspiration and hard work of three young architects aided by some foundation money some of the 12-acre area was grassed over. A rolling meadow and a section for individual gardens were laid out. The housing project eventually began construction and now has been completed for several years, but there was a significant period when part of the space was green and full of flowers, benches, windmills, excavations, and play areas.

Almost simultaneously with Ruppert, small greening projects were cropping up all over New York. One particularly active group to emerge was the Green Guerillas. Headed by the concerned and dedicated young Liz Christy, the Guerillas started modestly with one small vacant lot in the Bowery and developed into a city-wide network with gardens in vacant lots in all five boroughs. Their 'green mobile' moved around the city equipped with cultivator and rototiller and a variety of vegetable and flower seeds.

Adventure playgrounds have been another highly successful interim use of vacant city land. Using whatever materials are readily available — rubber tires, construction materials, plastic, wood, pipes, and so on — children can create their own world, which is usually much more to their liking than a slick designer's playground. This is one area where other parts of the world, especially England, Israel, and the Scandinavian countries, are ahead of the United States. Adventure playgrounds can be messy—mud, bricks, old boards—but they are great fun.

Another popular use for temporarily vacant land is an archaeological dig or exploration. In United States cities local history is beginning to attract attention. Several years ago a section of Bedford-Stuyvesant, Brooklyn, was marked for demolition to make way for a Model Cities housing site. Concerned that some local history was about to be destroyed, an amateur archaeologist recruited the help of local Boy Scouts, Neighborhood Youth Corps, and interested older citizens. Working just in front of the bulldozers, they searched and dug old houses, foundations, wells, cisterns, and attics. Slowly they began putting together the pieces of a thriving settlement of black freemen called Weeksville, which existed

from about 1825 until 1875. The artifacts were all labeled and have since been displayed in local schools and museums. They are now the property of the Society for the Preservation of Weeksville History, which has managed to save two of the original Weeksville houses.

Vacant lots have also been used with great success for open-air art exhibitions, sculpture workshops, flea markets, dog runs, bookmobiles, and Christmas tree farms. There really is no limit to the interim use of vacant city space—except imagination.

The authors appreciate the generous help provided to them by the Billy Rose Foundation.

Jane G. Brown is a writer who devoted two years to research on vacant lots. **Karl Katz** is Chairman for Special Projects at The Metropolitan Museum of Art in New York.

Movie in Brooklyn, New York

SHOE LATCHETS!

"GLASS PUT IN!"

BALLOON MAN.

"FIVE FOR TEN CENTS!"

Community Gardens

Vegetable and flower gardens are sprouting up in cities.

Neighborhood Land Trusts

A community stewardship exists for urban spaces.

By Peter R. Stein

Thousands of vacant and abandoned properties exist in low-income neighborhoods across the country. These garbage- and rubble-filled lots are a blight on America's landscape. By and large, local governments are not in a position to remove this condition, and the burden for improvement falls on the shoulders of people who live in the neighborhoods where these abandoned properties exist. It is often these same neighborhoods that also have the greatest lack of recreational amenities. The vacant land at present may be an eyesore, but creative action can turn this liability into an asset. Community organizations have demonstrated that the ability exists to recycle these unused properties into neighborhood open space re-sources with only minor assistance from outside agencies.

On February 6, 1979, the members of the Unity Place Land Trust in the South Bronx took title to a large vacant parcel as a protective step in securing their control over neighborhood land. This site is in the process of being converted into a neighborhood open space amenity to meet the needs of existing residents and urban homesteaders in the South Bronx.

Urban community organizations have a long history of neighborhood-initiated open space projects. Hundreds if not thousands of community vegetable gardens exist as testimony to their creativity. In addition to gardens, many playlots, playgrounds, sitting areas, and passive green spaces have sprung up in dozens of neighborhoods. These projects are not the result of some city planner's belief that more open space was a necessary ingredient of that neighborhood. These open space projects are the products of time, muscle, and sweat given by local citizens who believe that they know how their open space needs can best be served.

These numerous positive expressions of neighborhood initiative need a sense of security and a process for control. Neighborhood land trusts can serve as the mechanism to provide local residents with the structure and the process to own urban open spaces on a cooperative basis. A neighborhood land trust is a non-profit corporation composed of community residents who act together to own property on behalf of neighborhood residents. It is through this structure of cooperative community ownership that residents are provided the opportunity to participate in the control of the neighborhood landscape.

Land trusts are not a new concept. Begun in various parts of New England over 100 years ago, they have served as effective land preservation tools for rural and suburban communities. Modeled after the "town commons," land trusts demonstrate an effective example of positive citizen action with long-term benefits. Historically, land trusts have been used for conservation of lands that have little immediate use to residents of urban America. Recently, the land-trust concept and other land-conservation tools have made the transition to the inner city. In urban communities, neighborhood land trusts have been formed in a variety of locations as a partial solution to the problems of disenfranchisement and lack of control of urban open spaces. The use of neighborhood land trusts serves both the need for a legitimate expression of cooperative property ownership and as a citizen-action vehicle for reinforcing the cooperative spirit that is so vital to the development of community open space projects. This sense of positive responsibility and community stewardship is a key ingredient in the land trust structure and is incorporated into the legal purposes of the corporation.

A community organization can develop a neighborhood land trust by first researching the applicable state regulations for nonprofit corporations. After consulting an attorney and preparing the articles of incorporation and the bylaws that meet state requirements, the land trust can then file for approval as a non-profit organization. Once approval is granted, the land trust can then begin to conduct the business of acquiring property or other assets in behalf of the community. As an added incentive to receive charitable gifts, the new land-trust corporation should file with the Internal Revenue Service for federal tax exemption. This will enable the land trust to offer potential donors a charitable deduction for the value of the property to be given to the land trust.

As far as legal responsibilities: the land trust is required to file reports with the state and federal regulatory agencies — in most states it is the department of charities or the department of state; in the case of federal agencies, to file the mandated reports with the Internal Revenue Service. Properties that are owned by the land trust are required to be used to meet the charitable purposes set forth in their articles of incorporation. Any proceeds that come from the sale of property, investments, or gifts have to be used to further the purposes of the charitable organization; they cannot go directly to land-trust members.

Neighborhood land trusts are now being used by numerous community organizations in different cities to provide protection and long-term community responsibility for neighborhood gardens, playlots, urban community nurseries, playgrounds, and green spaces. These open space projects and the neighborhood land-trust process are parts of larger mechanisms for community revitalization. Housing, jobs, and education all must have a livable environment in which to flourish. Neighborhood land trusts can help community organizations enhance and protect open space resources that are integral elements to such a livable environment.

Peter R. Stein is currently the Eastern Director of the Trust for Public Land's National Urban Land Program.

Drawing by Steven Guarnaccia

All photos by Maria Grimaldi, courtesy The Horticultural Society of New York

New Directions in Botanical Gardens and Zoos

Their objectives are expanding.

Interviews by C. Ray Smith

If urban parks bring the country to the city, botanical gardens bring the woods to the city—and zoos bring us the wilderness. In both those latter large urban preserves today, the animal preservation and conservation movement is accelerating as fast as science can thrust it.

"We have developed a self-sustaining colony of ruffed lemurs from Madagascar," says Charles L. Bieler, Executive Director of the Zoological Society of San Diego. "Around 31 of them have been born in 1979 alone, and we have sent several to other zoos." The San Diego Zoo has also successfully bred 40 rare Arabian oryx — a delicate desert antelope—in captivity. "None are believed to be left in the wild," Charles Bieler says—and several have been sent to an animal preserve in Lebanon.

"We have propagated a herd of Speke's gazelles from Somali to the

African Plains Annex, Bronx Zoo, New York City

Magnolias in bloom, Brooklyn Botanic Garden

point where it is self sustaining," says R. D. Schultz, Director of the St. Louis Zoological Park. "And we have now begun to place those in other selected zoos," he adds. St. Louis has also developed the only self-sustaining colony of black lemurs in the world in captivity.

"If we don't reproduce animals in captivity," says San Diego's Bieler, "we can't get the animals, and therefore we can't have zoos."

Theodore Reed, Director of the National Zoological Park in Washington, D.C., elaborates, "We know the animals are being killed in the wild and there will soon be none left. And we are also faced with restrictive laws that make it difficult to get animals. So we have to be net producers of them."

For zoo animals, too, scientific techniques such as induced estrus, artificial insemination, and fertility drugs are used. "We have, for the first time ever," says Schultz of St. Louis, "in a total man-

agement program, produced successful births of Speke's gazelles with these techniques. It is a tremendous breakthrough."

Also now, zoos have bigger family sizes and bigger cages, according to Washington's Theodore Reed. Primarily that means open-air cages — without bars and surrounded by dry moats or water-filled moats or by rock barriers. These natural habitats are the result of concern for animal ecology today, but they have a longer history of presenting animals to the public in more realistic settings — since the days of Heinrich Hagenbeck, in Hamburg, Germany, around 1913.

The St. Louis Zoo created its first naturalistic display in 1921; now it has a 3-acre Big Cat Country. Other new large natural habitat zoo settings within larger zoos are the Minnesota Zoological Garden's developed acreage, which is virtually without bars or cages through-

Trail sign, National Zoological Park, Washington, D.C.

The Enid A. Haupt Conservatory of the New York Botanical Garden, New York City

out; the Bronx Zoo's 38-acre Wild Asia exhibit; San Diego's Wild Animal Park—an 1800-acre preserve in the San Pasqual Valley 30 to 35 miles north of the city; and the National Zoo's 3,000-acre breeding farm in Virginia's Shenandoah Valley.

Most of the breeding is done in these new large preserves, but natural habitats provide better breeding grounds only for certain species. For primates, such controlled environments as primate reproduction centers are "even better than large environmental habitats," San Diego's Bieler says, "because they can better monitor physiology, take urine samples, know when the animals are cycling," and so on. But for the hoof stock in Wild Animal Park, he adds, "I think it is proven conclusively that there has been a remarkable difference in animal reproduction up there."

The natural habitat also has proved

to be the best form of educational program that zoos have ever investigated. Such programs are the continuing concern of zoos with regard both to preservation of endangered species and to preservation of endangered zoos.

"You try to teach the kids that animals are a part of the same universe that you and I are a part of and that they deserve a chance to live too," says Washington's Theodore Reed. To that end, zoos have added all sorts of new amenities to educate and appeal to their visitors—labels, graphics, benches, rest areas, and, above all, trains and monorail rides. These "sky safaris" carry visitors over miles of narrated tours at San Diego's Wild Animal Park, the Bronx's Wild Asia, Minnesota's Garden, and at Tampa's Busch Gardens.

In this contemporary reversal of history the animals are out in the open, and

the people are in mobile cages.

Botanical Gardens

In botanical gardens, arboretums, and horticultural facilities, similarly, the preservation of endangered species is being implemented through development programs and public education. The two share the spotlight in the world of botany today.

According to Howard S. Irwin, President of the New York Botanical Garden, "Tomorrow's society must tailor its material needs to the availability of its resources. And the most basic renewable resource at our disposal is the world of plants. To the extent that it is endangered, all other living systems are endangered."

Entrance to the Hagenbeck Zoological Garden, Hamburg

As James R. Buckler of the Smithsonian Institution's horticulture department says, "We have to understand the interrelationship of plants and their environments with the animals and all other living things."

"Without green plants," says Elizabeth Scholtz, Director of the Brooklyn Botanic Garden, "there wouldn't be any life on earth. Man relies on plants. This is something that we teach in classes to school children. And all botanical gardens are becoming aware that they are gene pools of endangered species."

This danger is real. As the Bronx's Irwin says, "There are about 20,000 species of plants native to North America north of the Mexican border, and of that number approximately one-tenth, and certainly no less than 1,500 of them are in various degrees of endangerment or threat of extinction—due to industry and agriculture.

"Of the scientific advances in developing botanical materials," Irwin continues, "a further aspect is using techniques that manipulate a genetic transfer to develop plants that more directly meet our needs. The large botanical gardens that have research establishments within them are working in this direction. To the extent that we impoverish our native flora, we are mortgaging a lot of future options we have in terms of food plants, in terms of land management, and in terms of the cycling of nutrients."

In both of these types of large urban open space — botanical gardens and zoos — preservation, conservation, and education are, today, the critical issues.

Central Park Zoo, New York City

Urban Wilds

We can bring back the vanishing wilderness.

By Elizabeth Barlow

Rye grass

Switchgrass

Angelica

Parsley

No art form remains the same for more than a couple of generations, and gardening is no exception. Since World War II a stylistic evolution has occurred in the field of landscape design: the replication within the urban context of natural plant communities of various types usually associated with wild nature. This seemingly artless kind of landscape planning is in fact a highly sophisticated and scientific ecological reordering to produce landscapes which, unlike traditional gardens, appear to be happenstance, fortuitous, and spontaneous rather than works of horticulture and landscape architecture.

Interestingly, it is Holland, with its extensive man-created landscapes and with the densest population of any country in Europe, that has pioneered on a significant scale the urban wilds concept of landscape planning: both the Amsterdam Bos, a large man-made forest that serves as a major park, and the planting around certain Dutch post-war housing projects as well as the planting along Dutch roadsides. At Bijlmermeer, a 1960s housing project located on the flat polders southeast of Amsterdam, designers have moderated the harsh winds and the inhumanly scaled architecture by creating a woodland screen comprised of trees; under local conditions of soil and climate they form a natural ecological association over time.

At Delft Zuid an urban wild has been created to serve an important social function: to provide a normally regimented people with daily contact with wildness. The director of that project put it this way: "During the weekends many inhabitants of the cities migrate to the countryside, to the woods, the moors, and the dunes, and everyone is delighted to walk on small winding paths, to sit on a bank among high growing weeds, to pick flowers in the field, to play with sand in the dunes, and to run over hills. But at home everything is straight and tidy. Shouldn't we ask ourselves if it is possible to bring a piece of nature into the towns so that we can give the inhabitants some weekend fun during the week too?"

The Department of Social Medicine at the University of Leiden conducted a study of this area after it had been in existence for five years and concluded, not surprisingly, that for children it provided a more suitable environment than a standard playground because of the opportunities it offered for digging holes, building shelters, picking flowers, and so forth. The report also observed the ways in which adults used this outdoors to create personal space.

In England an Ecological Parks Trust was established in connection with the Queen's Silver Jubilee in 1977, and it has supervised the creation of William Curtis Park on a two-acre former parking lot for trucks. To cover the asphalt, a demolition company brought in debris and soil. The impoverished soil provided was actually preferred both for reasons of economy and because it would promote greater species diversity than organically rich topsoil. The soil was then arranged to create various mounds, and a depression was excavated for a pond. Young people in the Conservation Corps and the Bermondsey Boys and Girls Brigade did the planting: native trees and shrubs—Scotch pine, white willow, black poplar, elder, gorse, bramble, and red currant—and a protective nurse crop of alder and birch. This work force hand-graded and cultivated the soil, removing bricks and stones and hand-raking it. The crew then hand-graded the pond basin, lined it with plastic sheeting, protective matting, and soft river sand and gravel. As this park was to be an experiment, some areas were left for natural colonization, while others were hand-seeded or planted with grasses, rushes, sedges, buttercups, angelica, cow parsley, and comfrey.

In this country a notable ecological success story is provided by the creation of Jamaica Bay Wildlife Refuge in New York City. Two man-made ponds rimmed with dredged sand in the middle of the bay are today part of Gateway National Seashore and a haven for a spectacular variety and quantity of migratory and resident water fowl and shorebirds. The refuge was primarily the creation of Herbert Johnson, a New York City Parks Department employee during the 1950s and 1960s. Trained as an estate gardener, Johnson turned himself into a marine plantsman, planting beach grass on the barren sand bars and planting Japanese

black pines, autumn olive, *Rosa rugosa, Rosa multiflora,* bayberry, and chokeberry, as well as various grains such as wheat, oats, and rye.

The sea of waving grasses that once constituted the vast mid-continental American prairie has all been plowed under for farmland except for some fragments along stream courses and railroads. In Chicago attempts have been made to reintroduce prairie ecology, most notably at the Morton Arboretum, thanks to Raymond Schulenberg's dedicated efforts. He and his associates collect native grass and forb seed from remnant prairies; clean, sieve, winnow, and thrash it; sow it in greenhouse flats; then plant it in carefully prepared soil. They subsequently weed the sown areas until true prairie ecotypes have formed. Other attempts at prairie rebirth have been undertaken by the Conservation Department of the Cook County Forest Preserve, which has sown with a Nisbit drill seed mixtures of big bluestem, Indian grass, switch grass, little bluestem, sideoats, grama, green needle grass, Western wheatgrass, and Canada wild rye. Less meticulous in terms of soil preparation and subsequent management than the Morton Arboretum prairie-rebuilding program, these experiments have not yet yielded as true a prairie ecotype but have nevertheless provided congenial habitats for whitetail deer, wild turkey, and other forms of wildlife.

Landscape architects, such as Darrel Morrison in Madison, Wisconsin, have appropriated an urban wilds approach to landscape design. Morrison has used prairie vegetation and "prairie edge" trees and shrubs in his planting plans for Walden Park in the middle of Madison and for the grounds of an insurance company in a Madison suburb.

From all the urban wilds discussed the same conclusion emerges: the creation of native ecological plant communities on disturbed lands or abandoned farmlands is not simply a matter of planting a few seeds and saplings and letting nature take its course. In almost every case the initial maintenance costs are as high as in traditional horticultural situations. While a few commercial seed houses are beginning to sell wild plant

seed, seed and plant collecting is still a major labor for many urban wild landscape creators. Hand-weeding undesirable growth, while the desired plant association is established, becomes naturalized, and can enter into the dynamics of ecological succession, is as time consuming and labor intensive as traditional gardening. Gardening in the urban wilds requires more than a traditional green thumb; one must, in fact, be thoroughly knowledgeable about the prototypical ecology one is trying to establish. This means not only an understanding of the composition, distribution, and micro-associations between species of a given plant community, but also an understanding of the soil(s), climate, and micro-climates of both the archetype and the specific restoration site.

The creation of urban wilds says something about our relationship to our world. This type of gardening would have seemed ridiculous to past generations.

When cities were small and wildness everywhere, raw nature was frequently characterized as "rude" and "horrid." Plants were ruled and made submissive by topiary and parterres. Then romanticism bred an Elysian naturalism with gardens and parks of undulating walks and serpentine lakes. Now in a technocratic age we have come full circle and want to create landscapes that are no longer a vision of paradise but rather that "rude" and "horrid" nature itself. Out of some deep-seated psychological necessity we have begun to domesticate wildness in our cities rather than lose it from our lives.

Elizabeth Barlow is the Administrator of Central Park and the author of *The Forests and Wetlands of New York City, Frederick Law Olmsted's New York,* and *The Central Park Book.*

Comfrey

Bayberry

Gardening in an Urban Environment

Many plant species flourish in cities.

By James R. Buckler

Verbena

Marigold

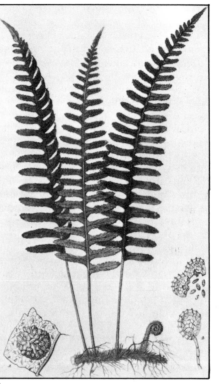

Fern

Ivy

From *A collection of coloured plates of plants and flowers*, Cooper-Hewitt Museum Library

The urban environment presents a unique challenge for gardeners around the world. With the frequent lack of space to grow plants in natural soil in a city, homeowners must turn to window boxes; terra cotta, ceramic, metal, or wooden containers; and the selection of that one specimen plant that is in scale or proportion to the space available. This challenge, unlike that of the rural or large suburban garden where many plants can be used, forces the city gardener to spend more time in the initial selection of the plant(s).

In the past five years Americans have been trying to introduce more and more plants into the city not only for aesthetic reasons but also because plants and flowers in our gigantic concrete, brick, and glass jungle seem to lift man's spirit and introduce a new quality of life. In most other cultures around the world, potted plants have always been a part of the city environment. In Italy, France, and England, virtually every balcony, courtyard, or terraced area is filled with colorful flowers, specimen trees, and water features.

The most challenging type of urban gardening involves the balconies of high-rises and townhouses where plants are subjected to wind currents, boiling sun, and lack of rainfall. These hostile environments can be harnessed so that magnificent flowers, shrubs, and trees can survive. First, make a checklist of the conditions on the balcony or terrace: the amount of light, the views—ugly or beautiful—and the space available to display plants. In gardens of full sun, select such plants as ivy, geraniums, petunias, and/or mixed annuals for hanging baskets;

tubbed bananas; topiary or standard trees of oleanders and lantanas; and larger trees such as weeping willows, small leaf lindens, and weeping beech. For the shaded city garden, select fuchsia, begonia, English ivy, impatiens, or ferns for hanging baskets; rhododendrons, azaleas, Japanese dogwoods, and Canadian hemlocks for tubs.

To prevent the rapid fluctuation in root temperatures in the summer and/or winter, use a one-inch-thick sheet of styrofoam on the sides and bottoms of permanent planters and window boxes.

Collect unique planters such as old whiskey barrels cut in half or used nail kegs for the unusual display of plants. For those who always marvel at the exotic tropicals used on balconies in New Orleans or in Southern Italy, don't be discouraged. Even in the North one can use the same luscious ferns, geraniums, spider plants, bananas, oleanders, and caladiums from spring through fall. These plants can then be moved inside for the winter.

The most critical cultural requirement in city gardening is the soil-water relationship. Plants should not be allowed to dry out to the permanent wilting point because they will not come back. Therefore, a well drained yet moisture-holding capacity soil is necessary. A mixture of two parts peat moss, one part soil, and one part perlite or sand should be used. If weight is of concern on a balcony or rooftop, add additional perlite. If available, add liberal amounts of leaf mold or compost to the soil mixture since these decaying leaf and plant parts help to retain moisture in the soil. Add approximately one cup of ground limestone per bushel of soil to correct any acidity problem from the peat moss. Watering should be done on a daily basis in the summer—except on cloudy days—because drying winds can cause plants to wilt and die. Fertilize the plants every two weeks with a soluble fertilizer such as Peters 20-20-20, Rapid Grow, or any other balanced plant food. Dissolve one tablespoon per gallon of water (or packaged recommendation) and apply to plants.

In planting window boxes or tubs of annuals, use as many flowers as can be stuffed into the container. Many people have been brainwashed that plants should not be potbound, and therefore they are scared of putting more than one plant per pot or putting them close together. This misconception can cause a garden to fail since underplanting leaves too much soil exposed to the drying winds and to the baking sun. It is always wise to fill boxes, tubs, and/or hanging baskets with as many flowers as possible since boxes overflowing with plants will retain moisture and last longer. Fill with combinations of geraniums, begonias, miniature marigolds, coleus, verbena, zinnias, trailing ivies, spider plants, and other exotic tropicals or annuals. This massing of flowers and vines will create a true bouquet of flowers that will be enjoyable from week to week.

Always provide adequate drainage in the bottom of containers by using gravel, broken terra-cotta chips, or crockery. If weight is a problem, save styrofoam packing and use it in the bottom of the window box or other container. Remember, plants can be damaged as much by sitting in water as they can from lack of water. Always water thoroughly rather than sparingly, since it is better for plant roots to get one deep watering rather than many shallow waterings. This will prevent roots from forming too close to the surface and drying out when you forget that one shallow watering.

Trees can also be a valuable part of the urban environment. For streets, the larger specimens such as Norway maples, horsechestnut, green ash, ginkgo, London plane, red oaks, tree of heaven, and Japanese zelkovia can be used. For the small courtyard, balcony, terrace, or roof garden, the European hornbeam, honeylocust (use thornless if available), weeping willow, and linden (basswood) are excellent choices. Smaller trees including dogwood, weeping and standard cherry trees, as well as topiaried trees of boxwood and hollies can be added to city gardens.

With the tremendous interest in returning to natural foods over the past five years, vegetable gardening in the rural, suburban, or city environment has become an important part of the gardener's realm. Even on the smallest balcony, one can grow cherry tomatoes in hanging baskets; cucumbers and climbing beans trained on a trellis; tubs of cabbage and kale; hanging baskets, tubs, and window boxes of herbs. And any other vegetable plant available can be tried in the balcony or rooftop garden. Although most herbs require full sun, don't forget the mints—spearmint, curled mint, peppermint, and others, which can tolerate shade.

Last, but not least, the city home can provide a wealth of blooming as well as foliage plants grown under fluorescent lights. From high light requirement herbs to annuals, indoor light gardens can extend the growing and flowering periods for twelve months. The Indoor Light Garden Society of America, Inc., has many excellent pamphlets and fliers on plants that respond well to light gardening. The basic items needed are cool-white fluorescent tubes (2 or 4) or any of the special grow lights on the market. These should be placed on a timer so that the plants get 16 hours of daylight and 8 hours of darkness for maximum growth.

The proper selection of trees, shrubs, vines, and potted plants in the urban environment can provide a year-round experience of nature's bounty. One needs only to dream about it, buy the plants, manicure, and give them a little TLC — tender loving care — and they will respond and provide a true "Hanging Gardens of Babylon."

James R. Buckler is Director of the Office of Horticulture at the Smithsonian Institution. He is a specialist in historic and Victorian gardens and accessories.

Rooftop Garden, New York City

Cultivating Green Communities

Let's plant a tree for every newborn child!

By Karl Linn

The deepening awareness of the ecological crisis, with its alarming extent of pollution in our air, water, and food, has mobilized people all over this country and the world into green action. Today this movement is becoming a significant political force. It is a grass roots movement to increase the quantities of plants, flowers, vegetables, and trees in our cities and therby improve the quality of our urban open spaces.

Until now, "progress" has focused on industrial development and transportation networks, all considered means to an end. Yet the end—the better life—has never come. Progress, as we know it, has just about destroyed our landscape and the cultural fabric of our residential communities. This growing perspective has led American society to refocus and invest in its residential neighborhoods, the very locus where life is lived.

The growing interest in neighborhoods is also reinforced by another national trend. Large segments of our population have started to react against the wasteful and debilitating overcentralization and bureaucratization of institutions and cities. Neighborhood self-management and economic self-reliance are being explored.

The growing groundswell of the green community has also become possible because of the vast acreage of urban land that has become available and remained depressingly barren for years — since the large-scale urban renewal/demolition assault on neighborhoods of the 1950s and 1960s. The increasing availability of urban land throughout the U.S. allows our dreams and visions of garden cities to become a reality in our lifetimes. The isolated neighborhood park and playground can be linked into networks of safe greenways. Open spaces not only serve for leisure recreation but can be transformed into productive green fields of community-based horticultural and agricultural enterprise. A city-wide support system for green community action needs to be developed.

One of the main activities of the greening movement is community vegetable gardening. It produces less polluted foods and counters the constant escalation of the cost of feeding families. According to the National Association for Gardening in the 1977 edition of *Gardens for All:*

All over the U.S., more than three million individuals and families who have little or no land of their own suitable for gardening are getting together and gardening on an estimated 30,000 organized community garden sites.

Currently, there are more than one million leisure gardens in Great Britain, about one-half million in West Germany, 36,000 in Switzerland, and about 30,000 in Sweden. There are thousands more in Denmark, France, and the Lowland countries.

Urban community tree nurseries, stockpiles of growing material such as the Bronx Frontier's compost operation and depots of recyclable building materials, solar heated rooftop greenhouses, community canneries, and environmental craft workshops are all new components of such a support system. Subsidized training and employment programs could be synchronized with grass roots self-help efforts dedicated to neighborhood greening and building. New training and employment opportunities can grow out of efforts designed to heighten and personalize the quality of human habitat.

This new scale of urban greening makes possible a new integration of the best that city and country living have to offer. In San Francisco half a huge black asphalt-covered schoolyard was transformed into a nature-study yard with a pond and wild vegetation. Tadpoles and dewdrops became part of the elementary school's nature studies.

Until now, capital improvement programs that have allocated funds for the development of public urban open space projects — the massively built and inflexible neighborhood parks and playgrounds — have considered those projects as finite products — to be built in one shot, hopefully maintenance free and vandal proof. Such isolated improvements were overly expensive. Today they draw fire from all surrounding communities, which have to remain empty handed. This early crop of public open spaces was conceived to accommodate rather passive recreational mono-uses, while being maintained by public agencies.

But today the growing readiness of citizens to engage actively in the molding of their neighborhood environments, including open spaces, is supported by new powerful socio-economic forces. The alarming fiscal crisis makes it no longer possible for municipalities to develop and adequately maintain their public parks and street trees. In search of alternative strategies, public administrators support and even solicit the active participation of neighborhood residents in planning, design, construction, maintenance, and even management of neighborhood open spaces. This fiscal crisis also coincides with a maturation process, compelling many people in this country to become more concerned with the creation of a heightened quality of life and environment.

In the midst of growing hardships and hazards, these new trends, nevertheless, carry new possibilities. A new kind of partnership between neighborhood communities and government becomes possible. Collaborative planning activities between both can respond more sensitively to local needs and preferences, giving expression to the richness of the broad range of cultures, races, and lifestyles that make up American society.

Another expression of this evolution is evidenced by the readiness of citizens to affirm their ethnic and racial roots. Residents of an urban Italian neighborhood have begun to develop arbors for urban vineyards. They hope to ship arbor sections to other Italian communities to generate a new enterprise. Puerto Rican and Dominican communities are busy planning plazas and placitas for their neighborhoods to adapt a valued cultural tradition to mainland America.

Despite this promise that can integrate the urban dweller into a more natural habitat of a garden city, many of the current new green uses of vacant land are considered only temporary by government agencies. Ultimately more profitable and tax-revenue-producing development is preferred by city halls. Ironically, successful greening efforts, which enhance the quality of urban neighborhoods, will contribute to their own destruction by encouraging construction of housing and commercial structures on the same land.

Greening efforts also contribute to the displacement of many of their original creators. The enhancement of neighborhoods will price many of the original residents out of existence there. Only a strong green community can counteract this gentrification process and protect the green rights of culturally, racially, and economically heterogenous communities.

There are milestones in historic development that we all remember. These special days and years affect our daily lives through their unique meaning. We get excited about imminent birthdays and holidays, and we prepare our balance sheets and resolutions as a new year approaches. Some nations prepare their future through five-year plans. It is understandable that we would think of George Orwell's approaching 1984, which has come within the range of our own five-year cycle of anticipation. Initially, 1984 was a glimpse into a horrible future designed to caution and mobilize us in our efforts to work for creative alternatives.

Yet the impact of the prevailing economic and ecological crisis, the precarious balance of global peace, topping the legacy of a century besieged with worldwide wars and holocausts, cannot help but make more vivid George Orwell's nightmarish fantasy and extend it to include the image of our planet burned and charred by an all-out nuclear war.

There is also enough growing despair and cynicism in the world that we should be alarmed about the powers of self-fulfilling prophecies of doom. All our efforts at denying these realities have only left us with an ominous feeling of unreality.

Yet as 1984 approaches, we all hope for transformations, to dispel the dark shadows of our lingering nightmare. As we look for springs of hope and sources of strength, we realize that we, the green people, have a special calling. All of us who care for plants, who have made them part of our daily lives and are at home in man-made and natural open spaces, know that we are custodians of powerful life-giving forces.

The dialogue between people and living plants has also become deeply satisfying for us since plants respond to human care. They respond to our attention, emanating a sense of well-being, and instill a reassuring sense of competence. Plants elicit almost the same kind of smile that babies evoke from the sternest faces. Plants, indeed, do disarm.

All of us desire to inform ourselves, to learn, and to be better prepared to cultivate the earth, so that our planet may be transformed into a lush and fertile green field. I am certain that it is this vision, this yearning for a green world that all of us share in common. To connect with our deep-seated craving to strengthen our belief in survival, it is not enough to operate large-scale greening operations. We have to learn to transform the planning, planting, and caring processes into meaningful mass greening celebrations.

We have to stage greening efforts in such a way that they will tangibly and symbolically succeed in uplifting people's spirits. Many individual trees in cities have already been named and adopted by neighbors. A town could plant a tree for each newborn child so that over the years scores of trees and children could grow together. Or memorial trees as "living gifts" could line the streets as symbols of rebirth. To plant a tree today should become more special an occasion than breaking ground for the construction of an inanimate building. Poems should be read, prayers should be said, and music should be played. As thousands of people pile earth around a thousand trees, a community reaffirms its collective commitment to life itself.

My hope is that all those who go to green gatherings will not only learn, but that each will have an opportunity to plant a flower or tree ceremonially. Cumulatively these will become millions of flowers and millions of trees — both symbols and realizations of our growing green community.

I also hope that green celebrations will transform into sapling trees the guns that the millions of soldiers over the world carry on their shoulders; young trees to be planted by the young soldiers of the world. They can become gardeners who learn to cooperate as they join in the common pursuit of tending and greening the planet.

Karl Linn is a landscape architect and Associate Professor at the New Jersey School of Architecture.

James Thurber, drawing

Trees for Use in the City

Reprinted from *Cities* by Lawrence Halprin by permission of Van Nostrand Reinhold Company and The MIT Press.
© 1963 by Litton Educational Publishing, Inc.; © 1972 by The MIT Press.

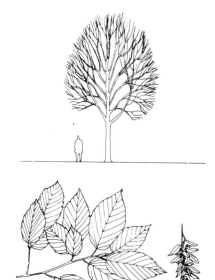

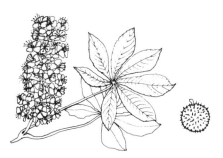
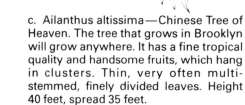
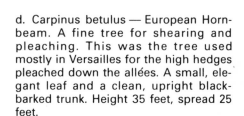

a. Acer platanoides—Norway Maple. A wide round-headed, densely foliaged tree. Leaves are five-lobed, quite large, and deep green, turning a golden yellow in the fall. A fine tree for a symmetrical, clean, impenetrable look. Height 40 feet, spread 35 feet.

b. Aesculus hippocastanum — Horse Chestnut. The famous tree that grows on the Champs Elysees. The flowers bloom like white candles in May, coming out with the lovers. A wonderful tree with a handsome, five-fingered leaf, it grows up to 50 feet high with a 30-foot spread.

c. Ailanthus altissima—Chinese Tree of Heaven. The tree that grows in Brooklyn will grow anywhere. It has a fine tropical quality and handsome fruits, which hang in clusters. Thin, very often multi-stemmed, finely divided leaves. Height 40 feet, spread 35 feet.

d. Carpinus betulus — European Hornbeam. A fine tree for shearing and pleaching. This was the tree used mostly in Versailles for the high hedges pleached down the allées. A small, elegant leaf and a clean, upright black-barked trunk. Height 35 feet, spread 25 feet.

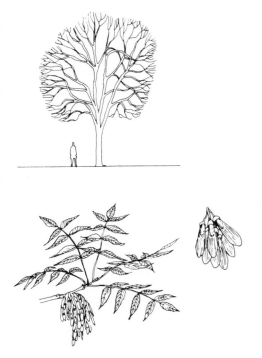

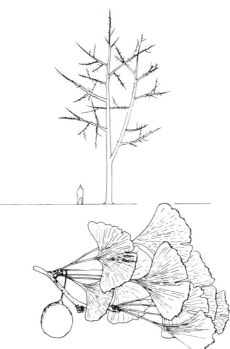

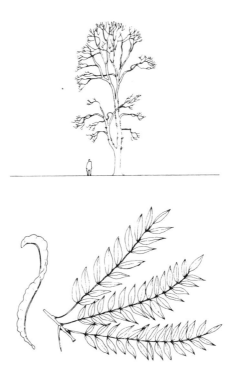

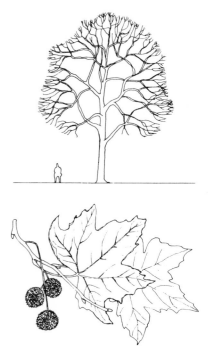

e. Fraxinus pennsylvanica lanceolata—Green Ash. A good, all-around, tough, vigorous tree. The bark is most interesting: marked diagonally, and quite black in color. Height 35 feet, spread 30 feet.

f. Ginkgo biloba — Maidenhair Tree. A living fossil that owes its life to the fact that it has been planted for centuries in the temple gardens of China. The females of this species produce evil-smelling fruits, so use only the male. Height 60 feet, spread 35 feet.

g. Gleditsia triacanthos — Honey Locust. Very high-headed, spreading, umbrella-shaped tree with a beautiful silhouette, deep black bark, and fine textured leaves. Tough and handsome. Height 50 feet, spread 40 feet.

h. Platanus acerifolia — London Plane Tree, Sycamore. The most planted street tree in North America. It can be sheared, pleached, or pollarded with excellent effects; withstands winds and soot admirably. Other excellent sycamores: Platanus orientalis — the Oriental Plane Tree, Platanus racemosa — the California Plane Tree. Height 50 feet, spread 40 feet.

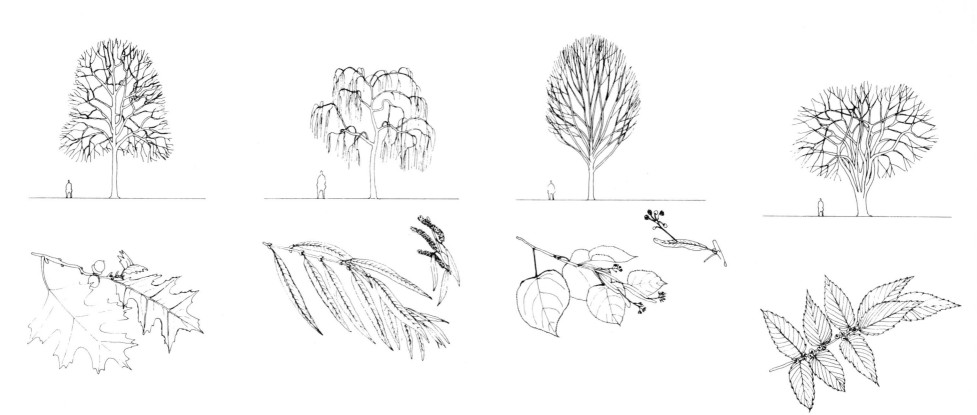

i. Quercus borealis—Red Oak. The best of the oaks for city conditions; clean, handsome, upright, and all-American. A deeply serrated leaf, which turns a brilliant red in the fall. Height 50 feet, spread 40 feet.

j. Salix babylonica — Weeping Willow. Actually a native of China, this willow is not good for a street tree but is wonderful for small parks, playgrounds, backyard gardens. Its long, yellow, whiplike twigs have a fine color when the leaves have fallen. Height 30 feet, spread 30 feet.

k. Tilia cordata — Linden Basswood. The famous "Unter den Linden" tree, an extremely popular street tree in Europe. A beautiful round shape, handsome heart-shaped leaves, and delightful small flowers. The American species, Tilia americana (called basswood), makes some of the tastiest honey in the world. Height 50 feet, spread 30 feet.

l. Zelkova serrata — Japanese Zelkova. Very much like the American elm in its shape and leaf, though smaller, and can be used in its place since it is not susceptible to the Dutch elm disease. Height 45 feet, spread 50 feet.

Selected Reading List

recommended by contributors to URBAN OPEN SPACES

Anderson, Stanford, ed. *On Streets.* Cambridge, The MIT Press, 1978.

Bacon, Edmund N. *Design of Cities.* New York, Viking Press, 1967.

Barney, Gerald O., ed. *The Unfinished Agenda: The citizen's policy guide to environmental issues.* New York, Thomas Y. Crowell Company, 1977.

Bosselman, Fred, and Callies, David. *The quiet revolution in land use controls.* Washington, D.C., U.S. Government Printing Office, 1971.

Boyle, Wickham. *On the Streets, a Guide to New York City's Buskers.* New York, New York City Department of Cultural Affairs, 1978.

Brambilla, Roberto, and Longo, Gianni. *For Pedestrians Only: Planning, Design and Management of Traffic-Free Zones.* New York, Watson-Guptill, Whitney Library of Design, 1977.

Breines, Simon, and Dean, William J. *The Pedestrian Revolution – Streets Without Cars.* New York, Vintage Books, 1974.

Carr, Stephen, and Lynch, Kevin. "Where Learning Happens." *Daedalus,* February, 1968.

Chadwick, George F. *The Park and the Town: Public Landscape in the 19th and 20th Centuries.* New York, Praeger, 1966.

Chermayeff, Ivan. *Observations on American Architecture.* New York, Viking Press, 1972.

Chermayeff, Serge. *The Shape of Community.* New York, Doubleday & Company, 1963.

"Community Design by the People," *Process Architecture.* No. 3, 1977.

Cooper Clare C. *Easter Hill Village: Some Social Implications of Design.* New York, The Free Press, 1975.

Coulton, George G. "Medieval Panorama: The English Scene from Conquest to Reformation," Chapter 44, *Sports and Theater.* New York, W. W. Norton & Company, 1974.

Council on the Environment of New York City. *Design Option Book.*

Cox, Harvey. *Feast of Fools: A Theological Essay on Festivity and Fantasy.* Cambridge, Harvard University Press, 1969.

Cullen, Gorden. *Townscape.* New York, Reinhold Book Corporation, 1968.

Dattner, Richard. *Design for Play.* Cambridge, The MIT Press, 1969.

Dulles, F. R. *A History of Recreation.* New York, Irvington Publishers, 1965.

Dunn, Diana. *Open space and recreation opportunity in America's inner cities.* Washington, D.C., U.S. Department of Housing and Urban Development, 1974.

Fabors, J.; Milde, G.; and Weinmayr, V.M. *Frederick Law Olmsted, Sr.* Amherst, University of Massachusetts, 1968.

Fein, Albert. *Frederick Law Olmsted and the American Environmental Tradition.* New York, George Braziller, 1972.

French, Jere Stuart. *Urban Green – City parks of the western world.* Dubuque, Iowa, Kendall/Hunt Publishing Company, 1973.

Friedberg, Paul M. *Handcrafted Playgrounds.* New York, Random House, 1975.

Fries, S. *The Urban Idea in Colonial America.* Philadelphia, Temple University Press, 1977.

Fruin, John J. *Pedestrian Planning and Design.* New York, Metropolitan Association of Urban Designers and Environmental Planners, 1971.

Gardiner, Richard A. *Design for Safe Neighborhoods.* Washington, D.C., National Institute of Law Enforcement and Criminal Justice. U.S. Department of Justice, 1978.

Garland, Madge. *The Small Garden in the City.* New York, George Braziller, 1974.

Halprin, Lawrence. *Cities.* Cambridge, The MIT Press, 1972.

Halprin, Lawrence. *The RSVP Cycles* (Creative Processes in the Human Environment). New York, George Braziller, 1977.

Heckscher, August, with Phyllis Robinson. *Open Spaces: The Life of American Cities.* New York, Harper and Row Publishers, 1977.

Hester, Randolph T., Jr. *Neighborhood Space.* New York, Halsted Press, 1975.

Huizinga, Johann. *Homo Ludens: A Study of the Play Element in Culture.* Boston, Beacon Press, 1955.

Jacobs, Jane. *The Death and Life of Great American Cities.* New York, Random House, 1961.

Jorgensen, Jay. *Landscape Design for the Disabled.* McLean, Virginia, American Society of Landscape Architects Foundation, 1975.

Lees, Carlton B. *Gardens, Plants and Man.* Englewood Hills, New Jersey, Prentice-Hall, 1970.

Lynch, Kevin. "The Openness of Open Space," *Open Space for Human Needs.* Washington, D.C., Marcou, O'Leary and Associates, 1968.

Lynch, Kevin. *The Image of the City.* Cambridge, The MIT Press, 1960.

Malt, Harold Lewis. *Furnishing the City.* New York, McGraw-Hill, 1970.

Mann, Roy. *Rivers in the City.* New York, Praeger, 1973.

McHarg, Ian L. *Design with Nature.* New York, Doubleday & Company, Natural History Press, 1971.

McLaughlin, Charles Capen. *The Papers of Frederick Law Olmsted,* Volume I. Baltimore, Johns Hopkins University Press, 1977.

Melville, Ian S. "The Role of the Public Piazza." *Planning Outlook,* Volume 3, No. 4, pp. 63-82, 1956.

Moore, Charles. *Daniel H. Burnham.* New York, DaCapo Press, 1968.

Moholy-Nagy, Sibyl. *Matrix of Man.* New York, Praeger, 1968.

Mumford, Lewis. *The Culture of Cities.* New York, Harcourt, Brace and Company, 1938.

Newman, Oscar. *Defensible Space.* New York, Macmillan Publishing Company, 1972.

Novak, Michael. *The Joy of Sports* (Part 2: "The Seven Seals"). New York, Basic Books, 1978.

The Parks Council. *A Little About Lots.* New York City, May, 1969.

Pushkarev, Boris S., and Zupan, Jeffrey M. *Urban Space for Pedestrians.* Cambridge, The MIT Press, 1975.

Rasmussen, S. *Towns & Buildings.* Cambridge, The MIT Press, 1969.

Reed, Henry Hope, and Duckworth, Sophie. *Central Park – A History and a Guide.* New York, Clarkson N. Potter, 1967.

Reuss, Henry. *To save a city.* Washington, D.C., Subcommittee on the City, Committee on Banking, Finance and Urban Affairs, U.S. House of Representatives, 1977.

Reps, John W. *The Making of Urban America: A History of City Planning in the United States.* Princeton, Princeton University Press, 1963.

Roper, Laura Wood. *FLO: A Biography of Frederick Law Olmsted.* Baltimore, Johns Hopkins University Press, 1973.

Rudofsky, Bernard. *Streets for People.* New York, Doubleday & Company, 1964.

Safdie, Moshe. *Beyond Habitat.* Cambridge, The MIT Press, 1970.

Seymour, Whitney North, Jr. , ed. *Small Urban Spaces: The Philosophy, Design, Sociology, and Politics of Vest-pocket Parks.* New York, New York University Press, 1969.

Simon, Donald. "A Prospect for Parks." *Public Interest,* Summer, 1976.

Sitte, Camillo. *City Planning According to Artistic Principles,* translated by G.R. Collins and C.C. Collins. New York, Random House, 1965.

Smith, Alice U. *Patios, Terraces, Decks, and Roof Gardens.* New York, Hawthorn Books, 1969.

Smith, C. Ray. *The American Endless Weekend.* Washington, D.C., American Institute of Architects, 1973.

Specter, David Kenneth. *Urban Spaces.* Greenwich, Connecticut, New York Graphic Society, 1974.

Spreiregen, Paul. *Urban Design: The Architecture of Towns and Cities.* New York, McGraw-Hill, 1965.

Strong, Anne Louise. *Open space for urban America.* Washington, D.C., Urban Renewal Administration, U.S. Department of Housing and Urban Development, 1965.

Sutton, S.B. *Civilizing American Cities: A Selection of Frederick Law Olmsted's Writings on City Landscapes.* Cambridge, The MIT Press, 1971.

Tilly, Stephen, and Carr, Stephen, "Streets for People." *Progressive Architecture,* December, 1976.

Thomas, David L. "Critical Reflections on Planning or Piazzas by Accident or Design?" *Town Planning Institute Journal,* Volume 41, April, 1955.

Thrupp, Sylvia L. "The City as the Idea of Social Order" in Burchard & Handlin's *The Historian & the City.* Cambridge, The MIT Press, 1968.

Tunnard, Christopher. *A World with a View.* New Haven, Yale University Press, 1978.

Tunnard, Christopher. *The City of Man.* New York, Charles Scribner's Sons, 1970.

Ward, Colin, ed. *Vandalism.* London, Architectural Press, 1973.

Waugh, Frank Albert, "Park vs. Grove." *Garden and Forest,* No. 373, 1889.

Whyte, William H. *The Last Landscape.* Garden City, Doubleday & Company, 1968.

U.S. Department of Housing and Urban Development. *Barrier-Free Site Design.* Washington, D.C., July 1977.

U.S. Department of the Interior. *National Urban Recreation Study,* Executive Report. Washington, D.C., U.S. Government Printing Office, 1978.

U.S. Department of the Interior. *Urban Waterfronts, Findings and Recommendations.* Volume I, Executive Summary; Volume 2, Case Studies of 17 Urban Waterfront projects, Washington, D.C.. 1979.

Zucker, Paul. *Town and Square: From the Agora to the Village Green.* New York, Columbia University Press, 1959.

Acknowledgements

Saul Steinberg. Wallpaper design "Paris," 1946, pencil, pen, and ink drawing

IMMOVABLE OBJECTS: URBAN OPEN SPACES is a celebration of outdoor public places organized by the Cooper-Hewitt Museum as part of an ongoing study of the urban environment. It includes not only this publication, but a series of lectures, walking expeditions, film showings, outdoor performances, street festivals, a postcard tour of Outdoor Art, a neighborhood improvement study, a video production on Community Gardens, and ten on-site exhibitions: Parks, Plazas, Playgrounds, Recreation Areas, The Street, Public Furniture and Graphics, Pedestrian Malls, Waterfronts, Open Spaces in New Towns, and Conceptual Open Spaces.

This vast undertaking was made possible through the generosity of the Arthur Ross Foundation, New York Council for the Humanities, and the J.M. Kaplan Fund. Complementary exhibitions were sponsored by the U.S. Department of the Interior's National Park Service and Heritage Conservation and Recreation Service, by the U.S. Department of Transportation's Federal Highway Administration, and by New York State's Urban Development Corporation. Additional support was provided by the U.S. Department of Housing and Urban Development

The Museum gratefully acknowledges the contributions of the above, as well as those of the writers, illustrators, photographers, lenders, and other participants in the project.

URBAN OPEN SPACES was conceived by Lisa Taylor, editor of this publication. The project was coordinated by Lucy Fellowes, who also supervised the research. Pamela Theodoredis assisted with the coordination, particularly of the catalogue. The Museum's exhibitions were organized by Lucy Fellowes, Dorothy Twining Globus, Richard Oliver, and Lisa Taylor. The installations were designed by Heidi Humphrey and Robin Parkinson.

The catalogue was designed by Heidi Humphrey, and the text was edited by C. Ray Smith. Peter Arnold, Elaine Evans Dee, David McFadden, Christian Rohlfing, and Sylvia McKean helped with the proofreading; the latter also wrote the picture captions. Caltone Lithographers, Inc., H-Y Photo Service, and Film Art Computer Typography were responsible respectively for printing, photo production, and typesetting.

Peter Scherer and Ann Stewart were the general research assistants. The former also worked on the installation and the latter on photography and the coordination of a film series. The photographic research was conducted by Ilana Dreyer and Renée Beauchamp, with assistance from Irene Dicks, Margaret Luchars, and Sheila Smith. Susan Yelavich coordinated "Museum Mile" activities and organized the accompanying programs, along with Mary Kerr and Jennifer Jarvis. Barbara Foss, Rosalie Genevro, Robert McGlynn, Lee Stedman, and Mimi and Lloyd Taft were helpful in a number of important ways.

The complementary exhibitions were organized by Ada Ciniglio, Jean Henderer, Letitia C. Langord, Judith Symonds, and Anthony Walmsley. Their installations were designed by Susan Cadwallader, Judy Farmer, and Nori Hall; the models were made by students in the Department of Landscape Architecture and Regional Planning at the University of Pennsylvania. The video program on Community Gardens was produced by the office of Telecommunications, Smithsonian Institution. The "Museum Mile" study was conducted by the Project for Public Spaces.

In addition, courtesies were extended by the New York City Departments of Parks and Recreation, Cultural Affairs, Ports and Terminals, Sanitation, Police, and Traffic; City of New York Transportation Administration; Mayor's Offices for Development and Special Events; Urban Design Group; City Planning and Landmarks Preservation Commissions; Council on the Environment; Institute for Environmental Action; New York Horticultural Society; Trust for Public Land; Parks Council; South Street Seaport Museum; the Henry Street Settlement; The Mt. Sinai Medical Center; the institutions on Museum Mile; Asphalt Green; the Arsenal Gallery; Federal Hall National Memorial; Downtown Brooklyn Development Association; Fulton Mall Improvement Association; Greater Jamaica Chamber of Commerce; 165th Street Mall Improvement Association; Rockefeller Center, Inc.; McGraw-Hill, Inc.; Chase Manhattan Bank; and the cities of Mexico City and Helsinki.

Special thanks to Arthur Ross for his encouragement and help, August Heckscher for his advice, Bernard Rudofsky and Lawrence Halprin for their inspiration, and Mayor Edward I. Koch for his endorsement and proclamation of the season of celebration that launches this project.